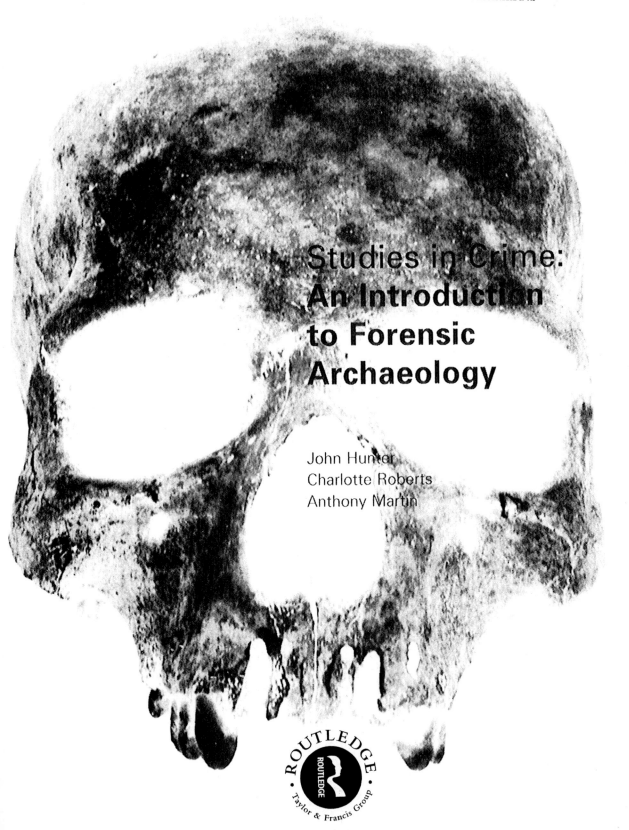

Studies in Crime:
An Introduction
to Forensic
Archaeology

John Hunter
Charlotte Roberts
Anthony Martin

ROUTLEDGE
ROUTLEDGE
Taylor & Francis Group

First published 1996 by B. T. Batsford Ltd

Reprinted 1997, 1999, 2002 (twice)
by Routledge
11 New Fetter Lane, London EC4P 4EE
29 West 35th Street, New York, NY 10001

Transferred to Digital Printing 2003

Routledge is an imprint of the Taylor & Francis Group

British Library Cataloguing in Publication Data
A catalogue record for this book is available from the British Library

Library of Congress Cataloguing in Publication Data
A catalogue record for this book is available from the Library of
Congress

ISBN 0–415–16612–8

Printed and bound in Great Britain by
TJI Digital, Padstow, Cornwall

Contents

Acknowledgements

The authors and contributors would like to express their gratitude to the following for their support, encouragement, advice, guidance or general assistance in the writing, production and illustrating of this book: Arnold Aspinall, Berthe Kjølbe-Biddle, Graeme Bickerdyke, Jean Brown, Paul Cheetham, Chris Chippendale, John Crummett, Sharon Dale, Malcolm Fletcher, Eric Roberts, Ansel Dunham, John Gater, Mike Green, Dave Lucy, Tim Grogan, Gerry Handcock, Raymond Petre, Sue Phillips, Tony Ridley, Brian Rankin, Mick Swindells, James Turnbull, Patrick Quinney and Miranda Schofield. Thanks are also due to the many indiividuals and organisations, acknowledged separately in the illustration captions, who kindly allowed us to reproduce their photographs or line drawings.

Chapter one

A background to forensic archaeology

J. R. Hunter

1.1 Archaeology, anthropology and forensic science

Archaeology is beset by a perceptual problem. If pressed, most members of the public will profess interest or even enthusiasm in its practice, but few will have any accurate idea of what archaeology really involves or the nature of the scientific principles which underlie its study. To some extent this irony is understandable: the basic raw materials of archaeology are often uninspiring; archaeological trenches, like those of the gas and water utilities, provide an immediate attraction but thereafter contain little in the way of spectator interest. Visitors to working archaeological sites are often to be disappointed if they expect instant visions into the past - walls, buildings, roads or caches of objects abandoned by earlier societies and in some extraordinary way fossilized in time. Instead they see layers of drab earth or soil, perhaps interspersed with spreads of stones; vague differences in colour will indicate where walls or posts once stood, where roads ran, where pits were dug, or the place where fires had burned and food prepared, hundreds or even thousands of years earlier. Each layer of earth will be removed, examined and recorded systematically: its nature and formation will be analysed; its contents - artefacts, seeds, pollen, and animal bones - sent to specialists; and its position in a sequence of other layers identified for dating. Excavation is in many respects routine, unexciting and clinical; not so much a breathtaking discovery as a slow accumulation of data. With these data the archaeologist produces his or her own interpretation of the past, not just the physical reconstruction of what has been excavated, but a perception of the environment, the

economy and the social attitudes of the people who existed within it. Other excavations in other places provide complementary data, and in this way visions of the past are slowly created in the same way that a wall is built, brick by brick.

The nature of the whole exercise has much in common with detection processes used in certain types of criminal investigation; in fact media phrases such as 'time detectives' are deliberately used to apply a known market interest in crime and crime solution to things of a historical and archaeological nature. The word 'clue' is often used in the same way, not for popularizing how archaeologists work, but for placing archaeological method in a context that people can understand. A book explaining archaeology to children even has the title *How to be a Detective* (Turner, 1991).

Reconstructing the past takes time, and disseminating the results in a way which is informative, interesting and uses the basic evidence in a way which is comprehensible takes skill. Archaeologists have spent almost as much time debating how to do it as in doing it (see Hills, 1993; Parker Pearson, 1993). But as a result archaeological literature has become more popularized and less stuffy, museums have shed their musty Victorian images, and exhibitions and reconstructions have become more sympathetic to the expectations of a public accustomed to theme parks, videos and visitor centres. Whether the perception the public is given is the 'correct' one continues to be argued in archaeological circles.

Buried remains, by their very nature of being hidden and unknown, also tend to generate a contrasting aura of public interest, no less curious, but less scientific in approach and differing in objectives from those of the archaeologist. To many people, things derived from the ground possess a strange aura of the past, of unknown times, peoples and beliefs - a perception fed by mass media which have long identified a huge popular market with an appetite for the unknown, the glamorous and the valuable. The same media have also generated images of the archaeologist as an individual, variously as the bearded, bumbling professor, the romantic figure, or the adventurer personified by Indiana Jones. There may be elements of truth in each, but the caricature is (sadly) unreal as much as the obsession with objects is wholly contrived. In these perceptions buried objects are seen as somehow containing an element of mystery because the circumstances which caused them to be made, used and ultimately deposited in the ground are, and will continue to be, unknown. It suits human nature within a predictable, science-based society that this uncertainty should persist. Unfortunately, it is a further irony that the very nature of archaeological work is to understand and to explain; and hence this stands in direct conflict with what many people believe archaeology to be about.

It is also ironic that during the last 30 years, and particularly in the last decade, the way in which archaeology has broadened as a discipline and developed as a field science is remarkable (Hunter and Ralston, 1993). The result is that the perceived gap between what archaeologists actually do and what it is thought they do seems to become increasingly wide. While in the late 1950s and early 1960s archaeology was very much a seasonal activity carried out on a purely research basis by a relatively small number of academics, it rapidly expanded in response to a threat posed by modern development, particularly in ancient towns. By the 1980s, archaeological units and groups had become established in most parts of the country, nearly every county possessed an archaeologist within its planning department, and the discipline achieved a level of professional acceptance within the allied construction and planning professions. This has since been extended to the tourist and leisure industry and, most recently, into private practice as the by-product of new guidelines stemming from central planning directives (DOE, 1990). Somewhere in the order of over two thousand archaeologists now work in Britain, mostly within the planning and development arenas. There are a number of profes-

sional networks, for example based on museum, district, or county associations; there is also a professional institute (The Institute of Field Archaeologists) which, among other things, advises on working practices.

The work of an archaeologist has many different facets, not only excavation but also survey, study of finds, environmental analysis, recording of standing buildings, education and a host of other areas both scientific and non-scientific which have a direct application in other fields and other professions. One of archaeology's strengths is its breadth, but one of its problems lies in integrating the many different strands of the study. Nor does it have any sharply defined starting or finishing points: a student in archaeology will cover topics ranging from anthropology to nuclear physics; some archaeologists spend all their working days in the field; some spend their time in the laboratory, while others write reports, plot aerial photographs, compile inventories of sites and monuments or draw up specifications for necessary archaeological work ahead of redevelopment.

Of the many fields into which archaeology's tentacles extend, and with which the relationship is probably least well defined, is anthropology (see also chapter 6). In the UK the discipline of anthropology is used quite separately from archaeology; it covers the study of mankind within the cultural parameters of behaviourism, ethnography and even folklore (*social* anthropology). Alternatively it can be used in an evolutionary metrical sense in which physiognomy (the study of facial characteristics) plays an important part (*physical* anthropology). In the United States anthropology is firmly rooted within the rigours of physical anthropology but has developed a much wider application to past human society, including aspects of archaeology itself. It was inevitable that its application in issues of race, gender, age and identity should eventually be recognized in a society increasingly faced with homicides, scattered or buried skeletal remains, air disasters and explosion, not to mention military conflict. Thus in the United States anthropology was able to operate within a *forensic* context - that is within the context of a legal arena -to the extent that *forensic anthropology* successfully emerged as an accepted discipline (see 1.3 below); under its wing *forensic archaeology* crept its way into respectability, partly due to the impossibility of finding a boundary between the two. In a major review of forensic anthropology one of its chief proponents, Clyde Snow, documents at length how physical anthropology emerged from the closet, how its potential was slowly realised - that its proponents needed to 'expand the concept of forensic anthropology beyond its traditional and largely self-imposed boundaries of skeletal identification' (Snow, 1982, p. 97). This book applies similar arguments to the discipline of archaeology.

Forensic anthropology, although undefined as such, is traceable back to the nineteenth century. In the United States a distinguished Professor of Anatomy, Thomas Dwight, was the first to identify the legal implications of skeletal identification (1878, reprinted 1978). A major legal precedent had already been set in the case of the Parkman murder of 1849, later used as a model for the interdisciplinary identification of unknown remains. The case is well amplified: it summarily consists of an instance of academic and financial dispute at Harvard University which culminated in the discovery of the dismembered remains of one of the protagonists, some attempt having been made to destroy those parts which might make identification possible (Snow, 1982, p. 102-4).

Forensic science itself goes back much further; Bono (1981, p. 162) cites the career of Ambrose Pare, a Belgian authority on wound ballistics as well as chemistry, who presented the first scientific case on record in a law court. Scientific opinion subsequently began to emerge as a natural consequence of scientific and technological discovery; Lawton (1980, p. 237) cites a precedent in the late eighteenth century, the case in point being whether the building of an embankment had caused the silting of a harbour - a factor which enabled a famous engineer of the day to enter the witness box in order to give his expert opinion. In the mid-nineteenth century William Palmer, a Midlands doctor and the so-called 'Rugeley Poisoner', was caught by new advances in forensic science. These were not based on factors of physical anthropology but on the general development of science with which anthropology was becoming entwined, in this case toxicology. Palmer was accused of a number of murders and is even said to have attended a post mortem of one of his own victims to try and save his own skin. Efforts to jog the pathologist's elbow, steal the forensic samples, and bribe the cart driver to crash all failed. Analytical chemistry, or its precursor, identified strychnine; and Palmer was hanged (Knight, 1987, p. 63). Meanwhile, in contemporary Europe anthropometrical theory was widely upheld, the Italian Cesare Lombroso and a French anthropologist Alphonse Bertillon being among its proponents. The latter developed a number of indices and measurements of the body which became accepted as

diagnostic of criminal tendencies, and created a bizarre vision of conviction being carried out by 'burly policemen armed with calipers' (Snow, 1982, p. 98).

George Dorsey, a Chicago anthropologist, is widely held as being one of the earliest true forensic experts (Stewart, 1978). His most notorious case was of a well-to-do local sausage manufacturer, Adolf Luetgert, who was arrested in 1897 for the murder of his wife Louisa who had mysteriously disappeared. Fragments of bones were recovered in the factory from a vat used for sausage production and were identified by Dorsey as the remains of Louisa Luetgert. The case received national coverage and was closely followed in Chicago itself where, as Snow observed, 'the **per capita** consumption of bratwurst reached an all time low' (1982, p. 100). A defence argument that the remains were of animal bone elevated the case even higher into forensic history by demonstrating that scientific opinion could differ.

The British had to wait somewhat longer for cases of national importance in which the skills of the physical anthropologist were applied, in fact until 1937 when the Lancaster doctor of French-Indian extraction, Dr Buck Ruxton, killed and dismembered his wife and a nursemaid, dumping the mutilated pieces over a bridge at Moffatt on the road to Edinburgh (Glaister and Brash, 1937). The case provided an early model for the identification of remains using evidence from both the house in Lancaster and the decomposed remains. Another forensic milestone occurred in 1953 when John Christie brutally murdered at least six women, one of whom was his wife, depositing their carcasses variously within the house and garden of 10, Rillington Place, London. Death was by both strangulation and by gassing, some of the bodies being papered behind walls and others being buried in the garden. The method of recovery by the Scotland Yard officers of the day probably lacked much in the way of archaeological sensitivity, but was sufficient to recover the remains from what has to be an unusually open burial site, and to make at least one identification on the basis of dental characteristics (Knight, 1987, p. 60). The investigation contained much archaeological relevance, although it is arguable as to whether archaeological methodology could have improved upon the outcome, but it could have come up with no less.

The uses of physical anthropology in cases of this type centre around a set of five basic questions which the discipline is uniquely empowered to answer. The same questions, perhaps with different emphasis or wording, appear in almost all anthropological manuals, courses and publications where the context is forensic:

1. Are the remains human?
2. How many individuals are represented?
3. What is the interval of time since death?
4. Can the individual(s) be identified?
5. What was the cause and manner of death?

While these questions are central to the practice of physical anthropologists, they are also close to areas which are frequently considered from an archaeological perspective in the study of buried remains. The third, for example, has a high degree of archaeological relevance: in evaluating the elapsed time since death, there is often a strong archaeological input from a contextual standpoint (see chapter 3), including the state and character of associated materials (and indeed in the proving of contextual association) - elements which are also relevant in the fifth question. In this respect the role of the archaeologist may be recognized, but may also be underplayed: 'archaeologists and palaeopathologists can assist if there is doubt about how long ago the person died' (Knight, 1987, p. 60). Archaeological principles are based on relative rather than absolute criteria and are therefore *always* relevant in the question of buried remains, irrespective of the age of the burial. There can be as much archaeological evidence gained from excavating a victim the day after the murder as in excavating the body ten years or even a thousand years later (see chapter 3). Other relevant buried factors and evidence may lie in association with the victim, and a number of these are discussed in later chapters, including the specialized field of entomology (Erzinclioglu, 1983) in which some researchers undertook controlled experiments using human cadavers (Rodriguez and Bass, 1983; also Mann, Bass and Meadows, 1990). Other examples, more clearly aligned with archaeological principles, have included branch growth and the development of root rings (Vanezis, Grant Sims and Grant, 1978; Willey and Heilman, 1988) as well as those cases which recognize the importance of burial factors in rates of decay (Knight, 1968; Knight and Lauder, 1969; Angel, 1985; Henderson, 1987). Extreme examples are cited, for example, during a British summer when circumstances conspired to reduce a body to 'separate bones embedded in maggot infested slime within the extremely short period of three weeks' (Knight, 1968, p. 94). There is now a relatively substan-

tial literature on decay phenomena covering *inter alia* associated death scene materials (Morse, 1983), climatic factors (Galloway *et al.*, 1989), effects of scavenging and scatter (for example, Haglund, Reay and Swindler, 1989) and a number of case studies (for example, Bass, 1984). Such are the variables in this area of study that one early authority was moved to comment that the only sure way of establishing the time of death was to be there when it actually happened (cited in Knight 1968, p. 96).

1.2 Commonality and overlap

As archaeology developed in its own right, archaeologists borrowed or fed from other disciplines in order to sustain its growth and to explore the relevance of other, older disciplines. They applied the rigours of environmental and earth sciences to interpret past economies and ecologies, and utilized developments in instrumental survey techniques to be able to plan ancient landscapes. Sociological theory and statistical method were borrowed in order to understand how earlier populations behaved, and why, and scientific dating and methods of physical analysis were commandeered to discover more about early technology and its development. But in relatively recent years the boot has been moved to the other foot - archaeology began to develop techniques of its own which could be seen to have relevance in other subject areas, often with direct application. Some of these techniques, such as remote prospecting, analytical chemistry and certain developments in physical anthropology can be termed 'scientific', while others derive from practical field archaeology. Mostly the application is by straightforward transference of archaeological methodology or idea but there are also occasions, as here, where it becomes possible to identify an area of middle ground between archaeology and another, ostensibly different, area of study. Forensic archaeology, a tract of commonality between archaeology and criminal investigation, might be argued to be one such area of middle ground. It is not an entirely new subject of enquiry in the United Kingdom: there is already an admirable platform on which to build in the form of a pioneering work *Death, Decay and Reconstruction* (Boddington, Garland and Janaway, 1987) which has allowed the framework of forensic archaeology to become extended (Martin, 1991) and the implications explored further (Davis, 1992; Hunter 1994). It is also a context which has enabled this author to provide operational archaeological support at scenes of crime and to make regular presentations on forensic archaeology within detective training courses throughout the United Kingdom.

There is a theme common to the work of archaeologists and the work of investigating police officers; both endeavour to understand the nature, sequence, and underlying reasons for certain events in past time. The final goals may differ, but the philosophy is much the same. Both groups use evidence, and both present evidence in order to make their cases. There is an inevitable difference in timescale; investigating officers will normally be dealing with events which occurred in recent time and which were of short duration, while archaeologists may be working in units of thousands of years. In buried environments this difference of timescale becomes irrelevant because the nature of the evidence and the way it can be maximized is identical in both cases. One of the aims of this book is to show how methods of finding, recording, recovering and understanding buried evidence have been developed by archaeologists, and how these methods can be utilized for forensic purpose by the police. For this to work effectively the archaeologist must understand the protocol and processes of criminal investigation, and the policeman the nature of archaeological theory, although both are easily thwarted by practical difficulties and by the complexities of the judicial process (see chapter 2). In the United States, where this type of co-operation has already occurred, practical 'crime-scene archaeology' has proved to have a number of positive advantages (for example, Rathbun and Buikstra, 1984; Morse and Dailey, 1985; Haglund, Reichert and Reay, 1990), especially with respect to the issue of evaluating the elapsed interval since death. On a more academic level theoreticians have begun to consider the implications for the discipline itself - 'from a purely anthropological standpoint, forensic archaeology provides a modern testing ground for archaeologists. It allows assumptions made about a burial site to be verified if the crime is solved' (Iscan, 1988, p. 219).

In the United Kingdom the instances of crime scene or disaster in which archaeological field skills can be utilized, while infrequent, are by no means rare, as witness the number of murder enquiries which result in physical spadework for the recovery of evidence, or where items are collected by fingertip search over a wide area. The use of fingertip searching suffers from the same problems of 'visibility' encountered by archaeologists also involved in the collection of surface material. Two incidents in particular are often cited as those which evoked particular archaeological interest at the time, not just with the comfortable benefit of hindsight: the Nilsen murders in north London which came to light in 1983; and the so-called Moors Murders of 1965 and the renewed search of 1987. Both generated press comment; the latter did much to stimulate the development of forensic archaeology and was probably the earliest major scene to apply archaeological methodology in the UK. The first case received notoriety because of the gruesome nature of the incident in which several victims (probably fifteen in number) were dismembered and their partial remains interred in gardens in Muswell Hill and elsewhere. The investigation of that garden, which was accompanied by much television and newspaper hype, was a strong but unwitting argument in favour of the use of archaeological techniques. Press Association photographs which appeared in both *The Times* and *The Guardian* on 14 February 1983 showed the garden of 195 Melrose Avenue, Willesden suitably gridded out for excavation (plate 1.1). On the evidence of *The Times* reporter, a broad but vague archaeological methodology seems to have been adopted:

'Tools including spades, sieves and rakes, were lent by the London Borough of Brent, and the search team of seven officers arrived on Friday morning. They had been working during the hours of daylight on ground which had been sectioned off into blocks by white tape.... The police do not believe they have to dig deep. As the soil is turned over it is poured into a sieve and searched carefully by hand. Anything unusual is put to one side and collected by an officer who has responsibility for keeping a log and annotating exhibits'.

But by 16 February it was clear that Professor David Bowen, the Home Office Pathologist, was having a horrendously difficult task in trying to correlate the various skeletal remains. A large quantity of bones had been found but only six possible victims could be named. At this point any archaeological methodology appears to have been wholly abandoned: white screens were erected according to *The Guardian* 'to allow deeper digging to continue unobserved' and police cadets were brought in to assist in the search. By the end of that day, according to *The Times*, the cadets had found 'a six-inch piece of thigh bone, four more teeth, a cheque book and parts of a pen'.

Plate 1.1 Police investigating a garden in Melrose Avenue, North London in 1983 in the search for the dismembered victims of Dennis Nilsen. Copyright Press Association.

A well-known archaeologist wrote to *The Times* on 17 February criticizing the garden investigation as being 'incredibly crude', and lamenting the lack of basic archaeological method. The rest of the letter is worth quoting in full:

'As an archaeologist who has fairly frequently to deal with coroner's officers when human remains are discovered, I have often been surprised by the cavalier way in which these remains are treated; the bones that are found are usually thrown in a bag or box and taken to the pathologist.

Most of these remains are 'ancient' (i.e. Roman, medieval, etc.) and it is only the historian who loses out on the destruction of the evidence when the bones are not examined *in situ*. In the present case where human remains are being sought in a back garden, the areas should be properly excavated using modern archaeological techniques (including leaving *in situ* any bones found until properly recorded).

Loose bones found by crude sieving will tell the pathologist virtually nothing. Articulated groups of bones found in the feature (a pit, grave etc.) in which they were buried will tell one a great deal more.

Were the police to call in some professional archaeologists to advise them it would probably be quicker, cost less, and produce more evidence.'

The letter was to the point, perhaps too obviously, and evoked little public response. But the same event did result in a constructive relationship between archaeological researchers at Sheffield and the police in researching a new method for ageing human bone (Sampson and Branigan, 1987). However, the author of the letter was correct in pointing out that a greater level of evidence and understanding could have been generated with a different methodology and by using the experience of those who carry out systematic excavation routinely. But in a sense he was also wrong; in pressing the need for archaeological methodology, he also believed that the two types of evidence, archaeological and forensic, were equitable. On that particular occasion, and using the techniques of the day, the evidence was sufficient for the purpose required (namely a conviction and the identification of at least some of the victims). But on other occasions under different circumstances, and with a greater refinement of what does or does not constitute appropriate evidence, this may not be the case.

The Moors Murders require little in the way of an introduction; they involved the abuse, torture and ultimate murder of at least five children in the Manchester area of northern England. Four of the bodies were buried on Saddleworth Moor, an expanse of moorland on the Lancashire/Yorkshire border. Some of the victims were recovered at the time of the initial enquiries in 1965, but others were the subject of later search and investigation culminating in 1988 (see chapter 5). As at Muswell Hill, the situation was of classic archaeological proportion which, in a purely archaeological context, would have elicited a response of systematic fieldwalking, mapping, aerial reconnaissance and trial excavation in selected locations. Some of these avenues were sucessfully pursued in the 1987 search following archaeological advice, notably by David Hill of Manchester University and Bruno Frölich of the Smithsonian Institution, Washington D.C. (see chapter 5) but by then much damage had already unwittingly occurred; in the intervening twenty years parts of the moor had been subjected to search and digging, to which innumerable media archives bear witness (plate 1.2). Most of this was unsystematic and unrecorded, with the effect of creating ground disturbance and to some extent negating those landscape characteristics which may have been of most use.

The 1965 search took place in one of the most unfavourable types of landscape to interpret. Bleak peat moors undulate naturally and contain vegetational scarring which make anomalies harder to identify; they are also relatively easy to dig into because a reasonable depth can be obtained without encountering bedrock. Worse still, the topography tends to erode and change according to climate. But other factors also occurred; given the strength of public interest, media hype and the pressure placed on the achievement of results, a huge show of manpower was involved which did even more to reduce the odds of discovery. In many respects the 1965 moors murders operation represented the first field search to take place on such a large scale. The methods used were those thought to be appropriate at the time, the basis being that the larger the exercise

the greater the degree of manpower and resources required. In archaeological terms neither of these is true.

If nothing else, field archaeology is common sense -a matter of logic deduction based on observation. Archaeological reasoning, although not its methodology, was applied during the recovery of human remains from Bedfordshire as early as 1978 in a case which combined a range of field initiatives (Vanezis, Grant Sims and Grant, 1978). The case was of a victim buried in a confined garden area where it was noted that a number of associated factors including tree growth, other burial material and vegetation, might all have a role to play in the investigation. The remains were recovered using small stainless steel garden trowels: 'cheaper painted items are known to contaminate scenes. All of the top soil was examined for any obvious pieces of evidence and was then placed in plastic bags.' (ibid, p. 210). The skeleton itself was impossible to lift intact in view of the limited space but it exhibited classic evidence of differential decay - the more deeply buried parts (in this case the back) decay at a slower rate than some other parts. A working guide which takes greater depth as offering slower decay was here usefully applied. The limbs were wholly skeletal but the brain 'was in a semi-fluid state and had an offensive odour. Being enclosed in the cranium, it was in a lesser state of decomposition' (ibid, p. 216).

In this case observation was also made of the absence of pupae cases on the remains, indicating burial within a short time of death: 'a body which is buried prior to the onset of putrefaction will decompose at a much slower rate than one that is already partially decomposed' (ibid, p. 216). The case also provides a precedent for using root injury, by comparing ring growth between non-wounded roots and those roots argued to have been wounded at the time of burial. The resulting likely date-range within a three year band was also supported by a similar type of evidence - a root which had grown into, and then out of the victim's clothing, displayed a particular number of rings thus giving a *terminus ante quem* (time before which an event must have occurred) for the burial itself (ibid, p. 218). This was possible by careful recording and recovery of textile fragments - a process which also enabled incisions in the clothing to be correlated with wounds on the ribs and sternum. Above all else the case emphasizes the importance of teamwork, perhaps more strictly, the importance of different types of specialists working within the recovery team.

Plate 1.2 A search commences for bodies on Saddleworth Moor in the early 1960s. Archaeological advice was later to be taken up in the re-investigation during the late 1980s. Copyright Manchester Evening News.

Burials

No two crimes are the same, but in most instances involving buried remains the investigating officer, or the scene of crime unit on hand, will be placed in a situation which is encountered only rarely. The recovery of human remains is undertaken routinely by archaeologists, with the same rigour as forensic work, although without the gravity that applies to the latter. Human remains are common and primary elements of archaeological work; archaeology is, after all, concerned with the understanding of past societies to which ritual and belief are often the main pointers. Human remains usually survive while much of the rest of the contemporary environment does not; gravefields provide a substantial part of the available evidence where 'for archaeologists, rather than forensic scientists who are concerned with the drama of individual loss of life, the day to day treatment of death is of outstanding importance' (Boddington, Garland and Janaway, 1987, p. 4).

Archaeologists have developed a massive collective experience in the recovery of human remains of

this type. Even students or relatively inexperienced archaeologists will have been taught how to uncover, excavate and record a human skeleton in order to maximize the information which may help in ascertaining its date, the manner of its deposition or the nature of any associated objects or surviving elements of clothing - all before it is removed from the ground (McKinley and Roberts, 1993). They will be taught how to gather this evidence within a few hours and to record it so that any shortcomings or special problems can be returned to. Most experienced archaeologists will have excavated numerous human remains within their working lifetime, under different conditions and in different soil environments (plate 1.3). Most investigating officers will supervise the recovery of buried human remains only rarely; they may lack the knowledge that these skills exist at all and that certain types of evidence can be lost. The situation is unlikely to have been as extreme as an American criticism which saw surface skeletons being 'collected with a garden rake and buried bodies with a backhoe' (Morse *et al.*, 1984, p. 53), but similar

Plate 1.3 The archaeological excavation of human remains from an Iron Age/Romano-British cemetery in West Yorkshire in 1983. By courtesy of West Yorkshire Archaeology Service.

Plate 1.4 Police investigating a house and garden in Gloucester in 1994 which resulted in a number of bodies being found. The apparent method of their recovery caused some consternation among archaeologists. Copyright Yorkshire Post Newspapers.

anxieties exist and are not entirely unfounded (plate 1.4). Once archaeological skeletons are removed from the ground their examination is undertaken by a further set of archaeological specialists in order to assess their age, gender, stature, likely diet, cause of death, and a host of other factors of physical anthropology which help build up a picture of past society. This element of the investigation, at least in part, also reflects a constant forensic process (Stirland, 1987; see also chapters 6 and 7). The archaeologist is also perhaps now equally aware of the health hazards in excavating and handling human materials; remarkably little is known of microbial survival under various buried environments, irrespective of the date of burial. In the few instances where potential hazards were thought to exist, for example in the removal and examination of some 1000 individuals (many still bearing soft tissue) from a crypt at Christ Church, Spitalfields, London, suitable precautions were taken

but no pathogens observed (Reeve and Adams, 1993, pp. 17-19; see also chapter 4). In more recent contexts, particularly with respect to Acquired Immune Difficiency Syndrome (AIDS), hazards are likely to be more predictable.

The adoption of these archaeological processes into forensic contexts moves the application more ominously into areas of legal restraint and admissibility. These are not the same rigours as scientific 'good practice' but have a more complex basis: 'Professional responsibilities arise from four distinct sources: law enforcement (what am I expected to do?), the adversary system (how must I do it?), science (what can I do?), and from within the individual (what should I do?)', (Lucas 1989, p. 720). These are all elements to be reconciled; all are identified in discussions of scene of crime/disaster techniques in the American literature (for example, Morse, Duncan and Stoutamire, 1983; Fisher, Svensson and Wendel, 1987; Ubelaker, 1989). The expansion of the human osteologists' and odontologists' role into these areas has been considered in some detail (Galloway *et al.*, 1990), into a range of murder, scatter and disaster scenarios much of which would seem to lie well beyond the scope of traditional anthropological or archaeological intervention (although the excavation of charnel houses or plague pits carries equivalent problems). But the application of techniques is consistent: documentation of recovery processes (including surveying); recording and photography; the identification and preservation of evidence, footprints together with ecofactual as well as artefactual materials; and the packing, marking and numbering of finds. Hardly surprising is the use of the anthropologist as 'finds processor' (*ibid*, p. 42). But while many of the processes may be 'archaeological' the over-riding context is legal, not scientific. Appropriate authority has to be received before removal or disturbance; access routes have to be defined; and the handling of material *via* a defined and logged chain of custody is critical. Without these safeguards the admissibility of the evidence might otherwise run the risk of being jeopardized. This is no longer 'straight' archaeology; the practice is archaeological but the methodology is forensic.

Location

Although the recovery and recording of criminal burials marks an obvious point for archaeological input, there are other areas of commonality, notably location, where the application is equally relevant. The need to identify buried sites has long been fundamental to the archaeol-

ogist's professional routine, becoming more pronounced as local authority planning controls for building
and landscape development required information on the
location and importance of archaeological sites (Baker,
1993). The resulting database, usually known as the
sites and monuments record (the SMR), acts as the
basis for all planning decisions likely to affect the historic environment. Much of the archaeological work that
took place in the 1970s and early 1980s was directed
towards the creation of this database; it required topographical landscape analysis, the interpretation of aerial
photographs, geophysical surveying and, perhaps most
significantly, the use of systematic field walking in
order to identify diagnostic indications of buried
remains on the ground surface. Both aerial photographic work and geophysical surveying have a special
contribution to make in this study (see chapter 5); both
are now far from being straightforward applications of
military prototypes, and both have been dedicated
towards issues of common concern to both archaeology and forensic investigation. Field walking, a
fundamental experience to most archaeologists, has no
lesser role to play. It involves the recognition of landscape anomalies such as vegetational differences,
undulation and crop marks, all of which can point
towards changes in a local sub-surface environment
(Brown, 1987). To neglect this area of skill in instances
of landscape search is to lose the benefit of much collective expertise and field background - experience
which is unlikely to have been gained by either the
investigating officer, his staff or the scenes of crime
team. Perhaps more ominously (see chapter 5), the use
of intensive line searching -the traditional police
response to landscape cover -may have an adverse
effect, possibly even destroying those very anomalies
on which the archaeologist relies.

Recording

Had this book been written some ten years ago, excavation and location would have probably provided the
totality of the field overlap between archaeology and
criminal investigation. However, a third, more recent
development in archaeological methodology has since
become applicable, namely the use of recording techniques based on the computerization of multiple-point
surveying involving the logging and itemizing of large
numbers of objects in three dimensions. Archaeology,
or for that matter any activity which involves digging
into the ground, is destructive and unrepeatable, in that
the very process of recovery involves disturbing and

removing all the evidence. Archaeological recording
processes are normally used to ensure that all layers of
earth and objects are recorded in a manner which
enables the site to be reconstructed afterwards, either
by superimposed scale plans or on a computer screen.
This has long been possible on a relatively small scale,
but with data logging techniques and the application of
electronic distance measurers (EDMs) greater scale is
possible, for example with thousands of points, either
below or above ground. Further discussion of these
techniques occurs below (chapter 3), but the type of
application for which the systems are relevant can be
outlined here. At one extreme is a localized search
involving scattered or dispersed human remains in
which relatively small numbers of objects are recovered; at another extreme, on a larger scale, are air
disasters, fires, or explosions, in fact any incident which
requires multiple-point evidence to be recorded from a
wide area, logged within a database framework for plotting and spatial analysis, and removed rapidly from the
scene.

The landscape

The common sense of field archaeology has a number
of other advantages - there can be few professions in
which an integrated understanding of cartography, geology and landscape change is so fundamental. In
enquiries involving search or investigations over a wide
area, or even in narrowing down a wide area for concentrated or priority search activity (see chapter 5), the
factors involved are often second nature to experienced
field archaeologists. The skills are by no means
uniquely theirs, but a background in landscape analysis
and topography brings to bear a rapid appreciation of
what may or may not have been possible in a given
area, what geological factors may be relevant as well as
the nature of vegetation and soil cover. This same background can be used to gain access to geological maps,
suitable aerial photographs, Ordnance Survey maps of
the appropriate scale and other relevant topographical
data, *and* provide the experience to interpret them
within a search context. The exercise is essentially a
'desk-top' study; it requires one person working as a
necessary preliminary to any work commencing in the
field. Why, for example, search an area of landscape
where the bedrock geology is too hard for burial and
the soil cover too thin? Why give equal priority to
unploughed as to ploughed field edges, or to copses of
deciduous as opposed to coniferous trees? The cost
savings can be staggering.

The laboratory

Location of buried remains, excavation and multiple-point recording are the main elements of fieldwork where the disciplines merge, but in the laboratory there are additional, equally important areas of cross-reference (see chapter 9). The relationship here is more with forensic science and might be seen as ancillary to police work as such, but the relevance is undeniable. Archaeology, or perhaps more strictly archaeological science, is concerned with the analysis and understanding of materials and technologies of earlier societies, and has achieved considerable success (Tite, 1991). Part of the enquiry process has been dedicated to the solution of outstanding questions on the development of primitive technologies, the exploitation of raw materials, dates of use, and provenance. Various physical and chemical methods have been applied and a range of instrumental techniques adapted to these specialized areas. Energy too has been devoted to the refinement of these techniques in order to make them more accurate and more effective. Nor is the overlap restricted to physical sciences; areas of environmental archaeology - the study and identification of pollen and other botanical remains, insects and organic deposits - also follow parallel routes.

Much scientific effort has been directed towards provenance studies for which accurate quantitative analysis is a prerequisite. By 'fingerprinting' the finished artefact or the materials used in its manufacture, and then relating these to natural sources (for example, by tracing pottery to its natural clay source or to its kiln), the archaeologist is able to show not only where the objects may have originated, but how widely they were traded, how they were used and the nature of the economic markets and networks involved. It is the first of these - the characterization and sourcing of the materials - which has the closest association with aspects of forensic science where materials found in one place can be traced to another. In many instances the two disciplines are identical with the same reliance on trace or major compositional elements derived from identical analytical facilities. Often the materials are the same, for example glass, metals or geological fragments; even soils undergo common similarity tests (Antoci and Petraco, 1993), but the two parties are otherwise entirely separate and appear to work within separate literatures despite being part of the same scientific community. Archaeologists publish their scientific work in dedicated journals such as *Archaeometry* or *Journal of Archaeological Science*,

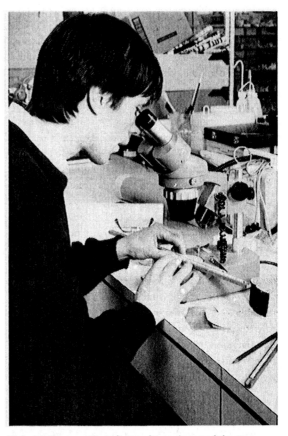

Plate 1.5 **The counting of annual tree rings and the measurement of their widths in the Bradford laboratory. Tree ring counting is used in the study of dating and in palaeoclimatology; it has important analogies in dating forensic burials from severed roots and branches. Copyright Jean Williamson/Mick Sharp.**

or as appendices in excavation reports; the main vehicles for forensic science literature are *Journal of Forensic Sciences*, *Journal of the Forensic Science Society* (now **Science and Justice**) and *Forensic Science International*. This division is understandable: forensic science is essentially routine, whereas archaeological science is more involved in research. But there is a more fundamental difference: the archaeologist uses the data in a conjectural way, either to create models or inferences in a manner which the forensic scientist could not. The latter is concerned with the production of facts in order to present scientific opinion. Common to both, however, is the integrity of the analytical data and the levels of confidence derived from them.

An area of scientific enquiry of specific interest to archaeologists is that of dating, whether absolute or relative. This is an issue less relevant in forensic science where events under investigation are normally of short duration and unexceptionally modern.

Archaeology is a time-based discipline; many of its most important innovations have concerned the development of new methods for dating materials or the refinement of existing methods (plate 1.5). Ostensibly, forensic science and archaeology contain little overlap in this quarter, but there are two important areas of common ground: one in the relative dating of burial deposits or victims; and the other in the absolute dating of human remains. For the former, stratigraphical and contextual factors (chapter 3), including severed roots and branches, are devices which underlie all archaeological studies and have a direct bearing on the sequencing of burial. For the latter, there is a particular problem (partly aided by the former) in that no known or developed scientific dating method is sufficiently refined to give an accurate or even unambiguous date of death from skeletal meterial. Given the police requirement of knowing whether a burial is sufficiently old not to need further enquiry (usually more than 100 years but, depending on circumstances, often somewhat less) this is a severe flaw in the investigative process. Chapter 8 below details the progress of archaeological method in this direction and considers not only the value of existing dating methods but also the likelihood of improved techniques in the future. This is an area of rich archaeological science involvement and potential.

1.3 Forensic archaeology in the United States

The rise and development of forensic anthropology in the United States is well documented in a number of key papers published over the last twenty years. Snow (1982) and Iscan (1988) in particular detail the origins of the Physical Anthropology section of the American Academy of Forensic Sciences (AAFS) since its founding in 1971, Snow more properly providing guidelines for professional practice, while Iscan's text is more strictly concerned with the evolution of the discipline. The two are effectively complementary and together provide any student of the subject with an enviable breadth of reference material.

While the relevance and early usefulness of physical anthropology in criminal cases has already been outlined, it was the unfortunate experiences of the Second World War and Korean War that brought an accelerated need for victim identification, and hence the skills of anthropological techniques. Snow also identifies a marked increase in FBI activity in this field at around the same time (1982, p. 105) which may have had some weight behind the change of office of Coroner (a non-medical appointment) to that of Medical Examiner (a medically-trained appointment) throughout the United States during the 1960s. Many physical anthropologists started their professional lives as advisors to Medical Examiners but nearly all their work was geared to the needs of medico-legal officials, little being directed towards law enforcement personnel where the need was perhaps even greater (Iscan, 1988, p. 204). This was the period of anthropological textbooks: Krogman's *The Human Skeleton in Forensic Medicine* which appeared in 1962 (subsequently re-edited by Krogman and Iscan in 1986); Stewart's *Essentials of Forensic Anthropology* (1979); and the point at which (around 1964) Snow identified the term 'forensic anthropology' appearing in a more accepted way within scientific literature (1982, p. 107). There also appears to be an understandable correlation between this outflow and a shift of the forensic anthropologist from an advisory to an authoritative role (Iscan, 1988, p. 205); this was no doubt aided by well publicized application in the Chicago DC-10 disaster of 1979, not to mention forays into the identity of less anonymous human remains, including those of both Josef Mengele and Mozart.

From then on the strength of anthropology's contribution is undoubted. Iscan's synthesis of research trends and areas of associated concern (1988, p. 206f.) also demonstrates its breadth which is seen as covering three important areas: identification of *group biology* (including gender, stature and racial affinity); identification of *personal biology* (including handedness, stress markers, elemental analysis, DNA and facial reconstruction); and *positive identification* based on dental comparison, congenital anomalies and skull photograph superimposition. Such might be the routine nature of basic testing and measurement that in some areas United States pathologists are provided with a methodology for sexing and providing racial information on 'a clear cut case' while waiting for more detailed anthropological consultation (Angel, 1985).

Professional competence, or more correctly its recognition, derives from Diplomacy of the American Board of Forensic Anthropology (ABFA) whose remit covers the maintainance of professional standards, an examination system, certification of competence, and the circulation of courts with lists of Diplomates. The Forensic Sciences Foundation (FSF) which sets professional standards for practitioners within ABFA certifies physical anthropologists as Diplomates; the requirements for certification include publications, practical work, and (since 1978) examinations (Iscan, 1988, p. 204). While supporting the need for formal qualifications and experience Snow also identifies the practical requirements for working in the field with other specialists: a knowledge of crime scene investigation; a familarity with odontology; and an understanding of, *inter alia*, such diverse areas as radiological anatomy, photography, recording and courtroom presentation (1982, p. 115). But top of the list is the need to maintain archaeological awareness, not simply in evaluating the relationship of a contextual environment of the scene to the stage of skeletonization and weathering of remains for death estimation, but also in accepting that 'systematic recovery of the material from burial and surface sites is best accomplished by suitably modified methods long employed by archaeologists to solve similar problems' (*ibid*, 117; see also Boyd, 1979).

The relevance of archaeology in forensic contexts has now been widely recognized in the United States for many years. There its growth not only represents an awareness of available skills for the investigation of buried environments, but also the generally greater range of scenes that a homicide rate of some 24,000 cases per year might bring. Current Home Office figures show that in England and Wales offences initially recorded as homicide are approaching 700 annually, although a number of these have court decisions pending and the figure may be reduced slightly. The relevant United States literature, therefore, has a better established base, not to mention a larger existing pool of significant case studies upon which to draw. Although the application of archaeological techniques and skills is common to both the United Kingdom and the United States, that is probably as far as the similarity can be taken; differences in police structure, scene of crime organization and legal processes and statutes make further analogy impracticable.

Whilst much of the relevant American literature has a physical anthropological bias (for example, *American Journal of Physical Anthropology*), there is also a clear trend towards an awareness of field recovery in which the increased application of field techniques is seen as desirable (for example, Sigler-Eisenberg, 1985). A pioneering work in this field, the *Handbook of Forensic Archaeology and Archaeology*

(Morse, Duncan and Stoutamire, 1983), effectively covers the whole remit of field studies for non-specialist personnel. Now outmoded rather than outdated, and inevitably deficient in technological advances, it still stands as the only comprehensive field guide available, although other writers have since produced texts on more detailed specialist topics (Killam, 1990; France *et al.*, 1992). Sigler-Eisenberg also identifies the need to correct the perceptual difficulties that tend to surround the work of an archaeologist, to show that there is more to archaeology 'than just digging a neat square hole'. She argues that during the recovery of a buried victim the archaeologist is most likely to observe the importance and relationship of associated materials (1985, p. 651). There can be shortcomings too, and these are relevant wherever forensic investigation and archaeology meet or mix, particularly since archaeologists are normally untrained in police, scene and forensic structure and organization. Even at scene level a 'standard' archaeological procedure may be totally at odds with the recovery of a different type of forensic evidence using different means.

This book is in no way intended to suggest that the development of forensic archaeology is one-way traffic - archaeologists have an equal obligation to understand, and work within, a much wider system of operations and methodologies. A set of guidelines drawn up for this purpose by Sigler-Eisenberg shows that these difficulties have already been encountered in the United States (1985, pp. 653-4). The points are crucial; they stem from experience unavailable in this country, and are worth summarizing:

* The work of the archaeologist is complementary to that of others working on a case. Archaeologists should be aware of the limits of their expertise.

* The work can often be unpleasant; not all archaeologists may find it suited to their interests and capabilities.

* Field evidence may be presented in a courtroom. Archaeologists should prepare their evidence accordingly.

* Few authorities are aware of the potential value of archaeological input. Information dissemination and 'educational' work is often essential.

* Methods of reporting archaeological data, particu-

larly visually, should be thought out carefully with a view to courtroom presentation of evidence.

With this type of requirement there was a clear need for both archaeologists and anthropologists to undergo formal training in awareness of the functioning of crime scenes and investigations; there was an equal need for investigating officers and other members of the group to be given some basic introduction to physical anthropology and archaeological methodology. The philosophy was ostensibly simple: ' an archaeologist should be a member of that team whenever the investigation involves a buried body. The most practical solution would be to have the law enforcement agency employ an archaeologist as a consultant during the short and infrequent periods his services would be needed. As an alternative, the crime scene investigator or his assistant could be trained in the use of archaeological techniques' (Morse, Crusoe and Smith, 1976, p.325).

On this basis a course in forensic anthropology was implemented at Florida State University (Morse, Stoutamire and Duncan, 1976) in conjunction with the local Department of Law Enforcement in order to provide mutual awareness of the issues involved. Part of the programme involved modified field techniques, excavation methodology and recovery. Deliberately created buried environments were used to test awareness of footprint survival and the differential preservation of a range of different associated materials. Students were assessed on their ability to locate, excavate, find, recover and identify the items which had been deposited. The exercise also had a useful experimental value in that the filled graves provided a controlled environment in known soil conditions for assessment of blood stain survival, corrosion of different bullet types and the relative preservation of materials such as paper. Exercises of this type often result in practical recommendations, in this case the experimentation generated a logistical model for burial recovery: 'since large numbers of people hinder accurate investigation, we estimate that the optimum number of individuals needed to excavate a single grave would be four; two working in the grave, one supervisor taking notes and photographs and the fourth in charge of dirt screening' (Morse, Stoutamire and Duncan, 1976, pp. 746f.).

The course, whose places were filled with a mixture of anthropologists, police officers and scene of crime specialists, remains unique despite the number of different personnel working in the field and the breadth of specialisms now involved. A survey undertaken in 1981 across the whole of the United States identified the existence of a laudible range of relevant workshops, seminars and lectures in the general area of forensic anthropology/archaeology, including those involving legal issues (Brooks, 1981). But there were no recognized degree programmes nor even programmes which combined physical anthropology and criminal justice.

The relevance and development of forensic archaeology appears to have had even less impact outside the Unites States, despite the obvious advantages offered. It is perhaps ironic that its application has so far been identified not in the nominally enlightened EC member states but in the less likely location of Argentina. There, in the so-called dirty war of the late 1970s thousands of civilians, including children, 'disappeared', presumably at the hands of government forces. The discovery of mass graves led, in 1984, to the introduction of an American forensic anthropologist, Dr Clyde Snow, to supervise the excavation and exhumation of the victims. His presence as an experienced fieldworker was in every respect an acknowledgement of archaeology's role within the prevailing circumstances. It was an acknowledgement that the controlled recovery of numerous skeletal remains undertaken in a manner which provided the greatest potential for victim identification could be best carried out by persons with archaeological training. Snow's team - the *Equipo Argentino de Anthropologia Forense* - consisted of anthropologists, doctors and archaeologists, together embracing all the skills necessary to recover, record, correlate and, where possible, identify the respective individuals. The exercise was one concerned with human rights rather than criminal investigation but the methodology, and the need to maximize the evidence, are identical. Exercises of similar sensitivity, including the excavation and subsequent removal of the murdered Russian Tsar and his family, have since taken place elsewhere .

References

Angel, J. I. (1985), The forensic anthropologist's examination, *Pathologist*, 39 (5).

Antoci, P. R. & Petraco, N. (1993), A technique for comparing soil colours in the forensic laboratory, *J. Forensic Sci.*, 38 (2): 437-441.

Baker, D. (1993), Local authority opportunities, in J. R. Hunter & I. B. M Ralston (eds), *Archaeological Resource*

Management in the UK: An Introduction, Stroud: 100-114.

Bass, W. M. (1984), Time interval since death, in T. A. Rathbun & J. E Buikstra (eds), *Human identification: Case Studies in Forensic Anthropology*, Springfield: 136-147.

Bono, J. P. (1981), The forensic scientist in the judicial system, *J. Police Sci. and Admin.*, 9 (2): 160-166.

Boddington, A., Garland, A. N. & Janaway, R. C. (eds), (1987), *Death, Decay and Reconstruction: Approaches to Archaeology and Forensic Science*, Manchester.

Boyd, R. M. (1979), Buried body cases, *FBI Law Enforcement Bulletin*, Federal Bureau of Investigation, US Department of Justice, February 1979: 1-7.

Brooks, S. T. (1981), Teaching of forensic anthropology in the United States, *J. Forensic Sci.*, 26 (4): 627-631.

Brown, A. (1987), *Fieldwork for Archaeologists and Local Historians*, London.

Davis, J. (1992), Forensic archaeology, *Archaeology Review from Cambridge*, 11 (1): 151-156.

Department of the Environment, (1990), *Planning Policy Guidance Note 16: Archaeology and Planning*, London.

Dwight, T. (1878), *The Identification of the Human Skeleton: a Medico-legal Study*, Boston. Reprinted 1978.

Erzinclioglu, Y. Z. (1983), The application of entomology to forensic medicine, *Medical Science Law*, 23 (1): 57-63.

Fisher, B. A. J., Svensson, A. & Wendel, O. (1987), *Techniques of Crime Scene Investigation*, New York.

France, D. L., Griffin, T. J., Swanburg, J. G., Lindemann, J. W., Davenport, G. C., Trammell, V., Armbrust, C. T., Kondratieff B., Nelson, A., Castellano, K. & Hopkins, D. (1992), A multi-disciplinary approach to the detection of clandestine graves, *J. Forensic Sci.*, 37 (6): 1435-1750.

Galloway, A., Birkby, W. H., Jones, A. M., Henry, T. E. & Parks, B. O. (1989). Decay rates of human remains in an arid environment, *J. Forensic Sci.*, 34 (3): 607-616.

Galloway, A., Birkby, W. H., Kahana, T. & Fulginiti, L. (1990), Physical anthropology and the law: legal responsibilities of forensic anthropologists, *Yearbook of Phys. Anthrop.*, 33: 39-57.

Glaister, J. & Brash, J. C. (1937), *Medicolegal Aspects of the Ruxton Case*, Edinburgh.

Haglund, W. D., Reay, D. T. & Swindler, D. R. (1989), Canid scavenging/disarticulation sequence of human remains in the Pacific Northwest, *J. Forensic Sci.*, 34 (3): 587-606.

Haglund, W. D., Reichert, D. G. & Reay, D. T. (1990), Recovery of decomposed and skeletal human remains in the Green River murder investigation: implications for medical examiner/coroner and police, *Am. J. Forensic Medicine and Pathology*, 11 (1): 35-43.

Henderson, J. (1987), Factors determining the state of preservation of human remains, in A. Boddington, A. N. Garland & Janaway, R. C. (eds) *Death, Decay and Reconstruction: Approaches to Archaeology and Forensic Science*, Manchester:43-54.

Hills, C. (1993), The Dissemination of Information, in J. R. Hunter & I. B. M. Ralston, (eds), *Archaeological Resource Management in the UK: An Introduction*, Stroud: 215-224.

Hunter, J. R. (1994), Forensic archaeology in Britain, *Antiquity*, 68: 758-769.

Hunter, J. R. & Ralston, I. B. M. (eds), (1993), *Archaeological Resource Management in the UK: An Introduction*, Stroud.

Iscan, M. Y. (1988), Rise of forensic anthropology, *Yearbook of Phys Anthrop.*, 31: 203-230.

Killam, E. W. (1990), *The Detection of Human Remains*, Springfield, Illinois.

Knight, B. (1968), Estimation of time since death: a survey of practical methods, *J. Forensic. Sci. Soc.*, 8: 91-96.

Knight, B. (1987), Murder in the laboratory, *New Scientist*, Dec/Jan 1987: 59-63.

Knight, B & Lauder, I. (1969), Methods of dating skeletal remains, *Human Biology*, 41 (3): 322-341.

Krogman, W. M. & Iscan, M. Y. (1986), *The Human Skeleton in Forensic Medicine*, Springfield, Illinois.

Lawton, Lord Justice, (1980), The limitations of expert scientific evidence, *J. Forensic Sci. Soc.*, 20: 237-242.

Lucas, D. M. (1989), The ethical responsibilities of the forensic scientist: exploring the limits, *J. Forensic Sci.*, 34: 719-729.

Mann, R. W., Bass. W. M. & Meadows, L. (1990), Time since death and decomposition of the human body: variables and observations in case and experimental field studies, *J. Forensic Sci.*, 35: 103-111.

Martin A. L. (1991), *The Application of Archaeological Methods and Techniques to the Location, Recovery and Analysis of Buried Human Remains from Forensic Contexts*, Unpublished MA Dissertation, University of Bradford.

McKinley, J. I. & Roberts, C. A. (1993), *Excavation and Post-Excavation Treatment of Cremated and Inhumed Human Remains*, Institute of Field Archaeologists, Technical Paper No 12, Birmingham.

Morse, D. (1983), Studies on the deterioration of associated death scene materials, in D. Morse, J. Duncan & J. Stoutamire, (eds), *Handbook of Forensic Archaeology and Anthropology*, Tallahassee, Florida, Appendix A.

Morse, D., Crusoe, D. & Smith, H. G. (1976), Forensic archaeology, *J. Forensic Sci.*, 21 (2): 323-332.

Morse, D., Stoutamire, J. & Duncan, J. (1976), A unique course in anthropology, *Amer. J. Phys. Anthrop.*, 45 (3): 743-748.

Morse, D. & Dailey, R. C. (1985), The degree of deterioration of associated death scene material, *J. Forensic Sci.*, 30 (1): 119-127.

Morse, D., Dailey, R. C., Stoutamire, J. & Duncan, J. (1984). Forensic Archaeology, in T. A. Rathbun & J. Buikstra, (eds), *Human Indentification: Case Studies in Forensic Anthropology*, Springfield, Illinois: 53-63.

Morse, D., Duncan, J. & Stoutamire, J. (eds), (1983), *Handbook of Forensic Archaeology and Anthropology*, Tallahassee, Florida.

Parker Pearson, M. (1993), Visitors welcome, in J. R. Hunter & I. B. M Ralston, (eds), *Archaeological Resource Management in the UK: An Introduction*, Stroud: 225-231.

Rathbun, T. A. & Buikstra, J. E. (eds), (1984), *Human identification: Case Studies in Forensic Anthropology*, Springfield, Illinois.

Reeve, J. & Adams, M. (1993), *The Spitalfields Project. Volume 1 - The Archaeology*, CBA Research Report 85.

Rodriguez, W. C. & Bass, W. M. (1983), Insect activity and its relationship to decay rates of human cadavers in East Tennessee, *J. Forensic Sci.*, 28 (2): 423-432.

Sampson, C. & Branigan, K. (1987), A new method of estimating age at death from fragmentary and weathered bone, in A. Boddington, A. N. Garland & R.C. Janaway, (eds), *Death, Decay and Reconstruction: Approaches to Archaeology and Forensic Science*, Manchester: 101-108.

Sigler-Eisenberg, B. B. (1985), Forensic research: expanding the concept of applied archaeology, *American Antiquity*, 50 (3): 650-655.

Snow, C. C. (1982), Forensic anthropology, *Ann. Rev. Anthrop.*, 11: 97-131.

Stewart, T. D. (1978), George A. Dorsey's role in the Luetgert case : a significant episode in the history of forensic anthropology, *J. Forensic Sci.*, 23 (4): 786-791.

Stewart, T. D. (1979), *Essentials of Forensic Anthropology*, Springfield, Illinois.

Stirland, A. (1987), The contribution that human skeletal biology may make to forensic science, in A. Boddington, A. N. Garland & R. C. Janaway, (eds), *Death, Decay and Reconstruction: Approaches to Archaeology and Forensic Science*, Manchester: 217-223.

Tite, M. S. (1991), Archaeological science - past achievements and future prospects, *Archaeometry*, 33 (2): 139-151.

Turner, V. (1991), *How to be a Detective*, Shetland Times, Lerwick.

Ubelaker, D. (1989), *Human Skeletal Remains. Excavation, Analysis and Interpretation*, Washington.

Vanezis, P., Grant Sims, B. & Grant, J. H. (1978), Medical and scientific investigations of an exhumation in unhallowed ground, *Med. Sci. Law*, 18 (3): 209-221.

Willey, P. & Heilman, A. (1988), Estimating time since death using plant roots and stems, *J. Forensic Sci.*, 32: 1264-1271.

Chapter two

The police and judicial structure in Britain

J. R. Hunter and
G. C. Knupfer

2.1 Police structure and organisation

The origins of the modern British police service can be found in the Metropolitan Police Force Act of 1829, which was introduced by the then Home Secretary, Robert Peel. As its title would suggest, the Act created a police service for the metropolitan area, under the overall control of the Home Secretary, but commanded by two justices who were later to become known as commissioners.

The success of the Metropolitan Police Force ensured the adoption of an organized system of policing. The criminal fraternity, in its endeavours to avoid arrest and conviction, had begun to move out into the relatively unprotected boroughs, in search of easier pickings. This situation led to the passing of the Municipal Corporations Act of 1835, which required all boroughs to establish police forces. The County Police Act of 1839 empowered, but did not compel, county authorities to follow suit in establishing police forces, a situation which remained until the passing of the County and Borough Police Act of 1856, which demanded the establishment of police forces in all areas.

Whilst some amalgamations followed the passing of the 1856 Act and the subsequent 1946 Police Act, the Service as we see it today came about as a result of the major reorganization of police areas in the late 1960s and early 1970s. This rationalization of the police service was conducted under the provisions of the 1964 Police Act, which granted the Home Secretary powers to promote efficiency in individual forces and to require the amalgamation of police areas.

The present structure of the Service can be found in the *Police and Constabulary Almanac*, a commercially produced publication which is updated annually and is available upon written application to the publisher. The *Almanac* contains details of all United Kingdom police forces, their senior officers and a breakdown of the various departments and units within each organisation. It also provides information on relevant Home Office departments, other emergency services, courts, prisons, professional societies and the Forensic Science Service.

England and Wales effectively constitute a single area of administration with a total of 43 individual police forces formed largely on a county basis. This includes the Metropolitan Police Force which covers all of London apart from the City, and some areas of the home counties, embracing a population of some 7.5 million and covering almost 800 square miles; it is larger (some 28,250 officers) and differs administratively from other police forces. A further 8 forces cover Scotland. Formerly, Scotland had no fewer than 33 forces until the enforcement of the Police Act; this situation evolved from the arrangement of Scottish constables prior to the Act of Union in 1707 and to some extent is also the cause of differences in criminal law (see below, this chapter). Northern Ireland has its own force, the Royal Ulster Constabulary. There are, in addition, other police forces but with reduced or specialized statutory powers, for example within the armed services, the atomic energy industry and transport systems (including airports, ports and docks). Less well known forces include those concerned with Royal Parks and the Royal Botanic Gardens.

Each of the main police forces is governed by a police authority. Prior to the Police and Magistrates' Courts Bill receiving Royal Assent in July 1994, authorities consisted of two-thirds elected local councillors and one-third appointed local magistrates. Now, authorities generally consist of seventeen members: nine councillors, three magistrates and five independent members selected from a panel from a short-list prepared by the Home Secretary. Each force is accountable both to the Home Secretary and its police authority for both public expenditure and its actions. Force budgets are paid jointly by central and local government, 51% and 49% respectively. However, under the provisions of this Act, the Home Secretary can give extra grants for either capital expenditure or to safeguard national security.

Under the provisions of the Police Act 1964, a police authority is required to maintain a suitable and effective police force within its locality. Exceptionally, in the case of the Metropolitan Police, the role of the police authority is taken by the Home Secretary. This anomaly is historical and stems from the time when Scotland Yard was the designated centre for crime detection on the basis of its central metropolitan location. By comparison, provincial policing was then altogether more rudimentary; it was less able to cope with the occasional serious crime, notably murder, and was obliged to call in detectives from Scotland Yard - an event which became the backbone of many early murder novels. Since then, however, provincial forces have become autonomous and equally self-sufficient in most areas of expertise, although the Home Secretary continues to exercise influence over provincial forces by virtue of approval of senior appointments and by the appointment of inspectors of constabulary who are required to review the workings of all forces.

The Police and Magistrates' Courts Act amends the 1964 Police Act. It is a wide-ranging piece of legislation covering a variety of topics, many aimed at improving the effectiveness and efficiency of the police service. The Home Secretary can, for example, now merge forces (except the City of London) without the need for a public enquiry, providing the interested parties are consulted first. Other sections provide new, less formal, discipline procedures and a new appeals tribunal. There is also provision for fixed term contracts to be introduced for officers of and above the rank of superintendent.

In 1992, the Home Secretary initiated an enquiry into police pay and conditions. The enquiry was chaired by Sir Patrick Sheehy. The report, which was published in July 1993, made some 272 recommendations, the most significant, as far as this study is concerned, being those relating to the rank structure.

Essentially the Sheehy team concluded that the existing structure was top heavy and required flattening. To that end it was suggested that the ranks of chief inspector, chief superintendent and deputy chief constable should be abolished and the roles of the remaining ranks reassessed and, where appropriate, expanded to fill the void. It would appear that Parliament did not reach the same conclusion as Sir Patrick. Whilst the Police and Magistrates' Court Act, 1994 abolishes the rank of deputy chief constable and chief superintendent, the rank of chief inspector is retained. Exactly how this thinning out of the supervisory ranks is to be accomplished is, as yet, unclear. Virtually every force has a deputy chief constable and a relatively large number of chief superintendents remaining in post. If forces are to rely on natural wastage to reduce numbers, it is clearly going to take some years to achieve the desired result. In future, one assistant chief constable in each force will be designated to deputise for the chief constable in his absence, and the superintendent's salary scale has been expanded to fill the void left by the departing chief superintendents.

Provincial police forces are presently headed by a chief constable, a deputy chief constable and one or more assistant chief constables, depending on the size of the force, each with specific administrative functions. The Metropolitan Police is headed by a commissioner and seven assistant commissioners, one of whom is designated deputy commissioner. Whilst chief constables jealously guard their independence, the commissioner is often viewed as a spokesman on police affairs generally. All officers of the rank of assistant chief constable and above (commander and above in the Metropolitan Police) are invited to join the Association of Chief Police Officers (ACPO) on appointment. ACPO provides a further co-ordinating link for policy review and dialogue between individual forces.

The essential structure of policing has always been regarded as tripartite, the three integrated elements being represented by the chief constable, the Home Office and the police authority. This somewhat delicate balance may, however, have been disturbed by the Police and Magistrates' Courts Act which enables the Home Secretary to set objectives for the policing of the areas of all police authorities, and to direct these authorities to establish levels of performance (performance targets) to be aimed at in seeking to achieve these objectives. In addition, police authorities must, at the beginning of each financial year, issue a 'local policing plan' setting out the proposed arrangements for the policing of the area during that year. For his part, the chief constable 'shall have regard' to the local policing plan issued by the police authority.

The Home Secretary is also responsible for the provision of a number of central services which are available to the individual forces. These include: the Police Staff College, Bramshill, Hampshire; the Central Planning and Training Unit, Harrogate and the six District Police Training Centres; the National Identification Bureau, New Scotland Yard; the Police National Computer Organization, London; the Home Office Crime Prevention Centre, Stafford and the Police Scientific Development Branch, St Albans. A recent addition to the list of central services is the National Criminal Intelligence Service (NCIS). This organization is commanded by a senior police officer holding the title of director general. He is based at NCIS Headquarters, London and, in addition to his responsibilities in respect of the five regional NCIS offices, he has control of the United Kingdom's International Criminal Police Organisation (Interpol) Office, which is also based in London.

All police officers holding central service appointments are drawn from local forces on secondment, generally lasting two to three years. This is also the case with Regional Crime Squad (RCS) officers. Whilst not strictly a central service the RCS is headed by a national co-ordinator, based in the London Headquarters. This officer has command of six regional offices situated throughout the country, staffed by officers drawn from forces within each respective region. The Regional Crime Squad was formed in the 1960s and its existence reflects the need for force boundaries to be crossed in matters of professionally organized or extensive mobile crime. It is, to some extent, an acknowledgement of the limitations of a regionally autonomous policing system. There are also working practices in other instances of geographical overlap; forces can, and frequently do, work jointly on cases of homicide, serious and series crime, often making valuable use of the Home Office Large Major Enquiry System (HOLMES) major incident computer system.

With the growth of central services and the Home Secretary's stated desire to reduce the number of police forces, observers could be forgiven for drawing the conclusion that these developments are all steps along the inexorable road to a national police force. In fact this proposition is fiercely rejected by many senior police officers and politicians alike, who would prefer to see the present non-political force kept largely separate from direct government control. Whilst economics, effectiveness and efficiency militate towards centralisation, there is little political will for the formation of a national service at the moment.

Within each police force there is a clearly defined chain of command and division of responsibilities from chief constables, their deputies and assistants to chief superintendents and superintendents to chief inspectors and inspectors to sergeants and to constables. The infrastructure of three of the largest forces (Greater Manchester, West Midlands and the Metropolitan) is shown below and can be used to gain some idea of the number of officers per rank as a percentage of the total force complement.

Rank	G.M.P.	W.Mid.	Met.	Total (per rank)	%
Constable	5342	5337	21208	31887	75.6
Sergeant	1061	1052	4610	6723	15.9
Inspector	420	380	1451	2251	5.3
Ch. Insp.	116	100	475	691	1.6
Supt.	78	75	224	377	0.9
Ch. Supt.	23	21	120	164	0.39
ACC/Cdr.	5	5	30	40	0.09
DCC/DAC.	1	1	11	13	0.03
CC/Coms/AC	1	1	6	8	0.02
Total (per force)	**7047**	**6972**	**28135**	**42154**	

Source: (G.M.P.) Greater Manchester Police, Chief Constable's Annual Report 1993; (W.Mid.) West Midlands Police, Chief Constable's Annual Report 1993; (Met.) Metropolitan Police, Report of the Commissioner of Police of the Metropolis 1993/4.

Nationally some 60% of officers are uniformed and approximately a further 15% belong to the Criminal Investigation Department (CID); the remainder belong to other operational or administrative branches.

The senior command of a typical provincial force of approximately 7,000 strength might be composed as follows:

Chief Constable
Deputy Chief Constable - Discipline and Public Relations
Assistant Chief Constable - Personnel and Training
Assistant Chief Constable - Discipline
Assistant Chief Constable - Management and/or Inspectorate
Assistant Chief Constable - Operations

Assistant Chief Constable - Crime
Administrator (or ACC)   - Finance and Estate

These responsibilities would also reflect pertinent regional matters. The Metropolitan Force, for example, would also have responsibility for Royal and diplomatic protection.

Whilst some forces are still divided into operational divisions under the control of a chief superintendent, there has been a steady move to flatten the command structure by replacing divisions with Basic Command Units (BCUs) under the control of a superintendent. BCUs may be smaller than the traditional division and many powers, including some budgetary control, have been devolved to the superintendent. In the traditional divisional model, a chief superintendent would have had a superintendent as a deputy, plus two or more superintendents in charge of sub-divisions. CID matters would possibly have fallen to a detective superintendent, again under the overall command of the divisional chief superintendent.

Sub-divisions or BCUs may have a chief inspector as second-in-command and possibly a detective chief inspector or detective inspector with sub-divisional CID responsibilities. A further tier can often be found below sub-division/BCU level - the section - often based on the smaller police station and headed by a station sergeant. Generally a patrol or shift inspector will have operational control of a sub-division at any one time, day or night. In order to provide this type of twenty-four hour cover a typical sub-division/BCU may have a four or five shift rota, each shift having one inspector and perhaps three or four sergeants supervising fifteen or more constables. The sergeant/constable relationship, which is traditionally seen as the foundation stone of the police organisation, stems from the early nineteenth century (Mervyn Jones, 1980, p. 29).

There has been a general expansion of numbers of officers over the last two decades, with a slight levelling off during recent years. Figures show an establishment of some 79,000 in 1964 increasing to 121,000 by 1982 (Stead, 1985, ch 8) and to 127,000 in 1992 (H. M. Inspectorate). There has also been an increased degree of civilianization, extending from clerical and catering work to technical maintenance and, most recently, to scenes of crime departments and technical services which have specialist CID status (see below).

All police forces are publicly accountable and each chief constable produces an annual report. This public document details the nature of the force complement, activities and statistics pertaining to crime and other matters. Under the provisions of the Police and Magistrates' Court Act, police authorities will have to issue a report relating to the policing of their area for the year. In addition, police forces are inspected annually by a member of the Home Office Inspectorate. Her Majesty's Chief Inspector of Constabulary commands a team of six inspectors of constabulary (HMIs), each with largely regional responsibilities. One HMI, for example, is based in Worcester and is responsible for carrying out inspections on Derbyshire, Leicestershire, Northamptonshire, Staffordshire, Warwickshire, West Mercia and the West Midlands forces.

To some extent the crime statistics published in constabulary annual reports allow the usefulness of archaeology and associated technical skills to be placed in a realistic forensic perspective. For example, according to past West Yorkshire Police annual reports, the number of homicides has varied annually between 26 and 43 over recent years (between 600 and 700 nationally, see Chapter 1) and has accounted for less than 0.2% of visits made by the scenes of crime department. This can be compared with assaults (9% of visits) and burglary (over 60% of visits). None of the homicide figures consulted indicate the methods, if any, of disposal of the body, nor do Home Office records provide this information on a national basis. However, in the year 1991, Greater Manchester Police, one of the larger provincial forces, dealt with only one buried homicide victim, and one further case of a victim concealed in water (total homicides for year: 49). In 1992 the same force again dealt with only one buried homicide victim (total homicides for year: 47). There have been no similar incidents in the years 1993 and 1994. Homicide statistics are based solely on offences reported (or discovered) and offences detected (i.e. charged).

Upon entering the service, recruits commence a two year probationary period. The initial training programme spans that period, commencing with four weeks in-force training, followed by a ten-week residential course at a District Training Centre (see above). Upon return to their home force, recruits attend the Force Training School to receive instruction in local practice and procedure. The training process continues with formal continuation courses at District and Force Training Schools and informal or 'on the job' training provided by the officers' tutor constable, sergeant and inspector. At the conclusion of the two year probationary period, constables who have achieved the necessary standard will be 'confirmed' in the post.

In addition to providing probationer and 'in service' training to their own staff, some force training schools offer specialist courses, regionally and nationally, to other forces. Detective constables, for example, on appointment to the CID will attend a six week foundation course. Several forces offer CID training and, with the exception of this foundation course which is now a national syllabus, course content is usually agreed between the training schools concerned. Some examples of courses falling into this category are: firearms, dog handling, fraud investigation, general management, gaming, research skills and public order.

CID training follows a set pattern. Following the foundation course, CID officers not aspiring to promotion may attend a three week refresher course at some point later in their career. Officers promoted to the rank of detective sergeant, however, will attend the intermediate CID course which is of six weeks duration. Senior CID officers, detective superintendents, chief inspectors and possibly some Inspectors, may attend a three week CID Senior Management Course. Some schools have now developed links with local business schools and universities and converted this into a modular course incorporating residential sessions and remote learning packages. Candidates who complete the course successfully will be awarded a Certificate in Business Management. One other course available to senior detectives is the Serious and Series Crime Course offered nationally by the Police Staff College, Bramshill. As its title implies, this course deals with the management and investigation of major crime enquiries.

The content of all courses is specifically geared to the students' needs and each syllabus is regularly reviewed to take into account new developments, updates and trends. Under the present rank structure a murder investigation is likely to be led by a detective superintendent or, in some cases, a detective chief inspector. As decision makers, these officers possess the greatest operational influence, thus topics incorporating new ideas and techniques featuring in courses which they attend are likely to have most immediate field implementation. However, topics housed within courses for decision-makers of the future, namely detective sergeants and inspectors, potentially guarantee a longer term, but more enduring educational investment.

National senior level police training is carried

out almost exclusively at the Police Staff College, Bramshill. In addition to graduate entry training, the College provides a series of command courses for officers of identified potential. What used to be known as the Junior, Intermediate and Senior Command Courses are now known as the Leadership Development Programme, the Advanced Leadership Development Programme and the Strategic Leadership Development Programme respectively. It is anticipated that these titles will be changed yet again in the near future as links with universities and schools of management are forged and modular training programmes developed. Other specialist courses for senior officers are also offered by the College, as is an Overseas Command Course for senior police officers from abroad.

2.2 The police scientific support organisation

Whilst many force Criminal Investigation Departments contain a number of specialist units targeted at specific areas of criminal investigation, for example the Drug Squad, Commercial Fraud Squad or Stolen Vehicle Squad, other units provide operational support, notably the Scenes of Crime Department whose primary function is to visit and examine crime scenes to locate, preserve, record and recover evidence which could identify the offender(s) and prove the case. The scenes of crime officer (SOCO) will also provide advice on the need and availability of other specialist facilities and services. In recent years, most force Scenes of Crime Departments have been merged into a larger Scientific Support Department, which typically would incorporate the Fingerprint Bureau, the Fingerprint Development Laboratory and the Photographic Department. The new Scientific Support Departments are headed by scientific support managers, many being qualified and experienced forensic scientists in their own right. Virtually all fingerprint officers, technicians and photographers are civilian 'support staff' posts and there is now a concerted effort within the Service for the majority of scenes of crime posts to follow a similar pattern.

With the notable exception of the Metropolitan Police (which trains its own staff), virtually all scenes of crime training is now provided by the National Training Centre for Scientific Support to Crime Investigation. The training school is run by Durham Constabulary and is based at Harperley Hall, Crook, Co. Durham. A number of courses are offered including the initial nine week Scenes of Crime Course, a two week development course and a two week refresher course. The school also provides all national fingerprint training (except for the Metropolitan Police).

A recent development for scenes of crime officers now undergoing initial training is the option to study for a Diploma in Crime Scene Examination, awarded by Durham University in conjunction with the National Training Centre. To achieve the diploma, students must have successfully completed the initial and development courses within their first two years and produce a lengthy project or case study for evaluation. Whether studying for the diploma or not, scenes of crime officers are continually assessed throughout their first two years of service.

In addition to the general scenes of crime and fingerprint training courses, the Durham Training Centre offers specialist courses for police surgeons and scenes of crime supervisors and managers, the latter being generally known as the Crime Scene Managers' course. This course trains students in the skills required to manage the scientific support input to a major incident scene. (Again, a similar course is run by the Metropolitan Police for its staff).

Whilst a scenes of crime officer will almost certainly be left to his/her own devices to examine the scene of a burglary or similar offence, at a murder or other major incident scene, he/she will probably work under the direction of a crime scene manager who, in turn, will be working under the authority of the senior investigating officer (the head of the investigation team). The scientific support role, in cases of this nature, is to examine, preserve, record and recover evidence, to ensure the integrity of exhibits and to address all continuity and cross-contamination issues. In addition, the scenes of crime officer or crime scene manager will be required to advise the senior investigating officer as to the desirability of other experts being called to the scene, for example, a forensic scientist. As a general rule, where evidence found at a scene requires some 'interpretation' (blood splashing or bullet trajectory perhaps) a 'specialist' will normally be required to attend.

Since all exhibits requiring scientific examination now attract a charge from the forensic laboratory concerned, careful consideration is given to the number and type of exhibits submitted for laboratory examination, and the potential outcome. When visiting a crime scene, the scenes of crime officer will generally complete a Scene Report detailing his/her actions (fig. 2.1).

It would be by no means unusual for that officer to be required to attend court at a later date to give evidence as to what had been found and what action had been taken at a particular scene, so care and attention to detail are essential. The composition of a scientific support team at a major incident will vary to suit the nature of the situation, but a typical homicide team might consist of a crime scene manager, two or more scenes of crime officers, a photographer, a video operator, a pathologist (a police surgeon may have attended at an earlier stage to pronounce life extinct), one or more forensic scientists and an exhibits officer. Other police officers at the scene or in the general proximity may include the senior investigating officer and/or a deputy, detectives making house to house or other enquiries, and a small uniform presence to protect cordons or deal with traffic problems. Any searches of open land, perhaps for a murder weapon or missing clothing, will generally be undertaken by a Task Force or similar group, trained in the role.

The exhibits officer plays a recording role in this process and holds responsibility for retaining the integrity of the exhibits by overseeing the proper packaging, labelling and logging of all recovered items and samples, their ultimate dispatch to the forensic science laboratory, and their presentation in court. It is the responsibility of the exhibits officer to create a numerical property register (now often held on computer in more complex cases) which contains details of all items recovered, from where and by whom, together with appropriate information regarding their condition, any work carried out on the items, details of storage and details of any material consumed in laboratory work (for example during drug analysis). Each piece of evidence is also required to be marked by both number and signature in order that it can be identified in court. This is a fundamental aspect in maintaining the chain of evidence and is most closely paralleled by the work of the finds specialist on an archaeological site (see chapter 3).

In cases of homicide, protocol is critical for the presentation and integrity of evidence (plate 2.1). Entry to the scene will be restricted solely to those with a role to play. The recovery of the body will only take place once the scene has been photographed, video recorded and the body carefully examined *in situ* by the pathologist, forensic scientist (if in attendance) and the scenes of crime officer. Exhibit recovery will commence at this stage. The senior investigating officer or his deputy will almost certainly be on hand whilst this

SCENE OF CRIME EXAMINATION

DIV. NUMBER			

INCIDENT _____ DATE _____ 19 _____

LOCUS _____

VEHICLE _____

S.O.C.O. _____ COMMENCED _____ COMPLETED _____

APPROACH		ENTRY/EXIT			MEANS		VEHICLE	
FRONT		FRONT		GF WINDOW		INSECURE		INSECURE	
REAR		REAR		UPPER WINDOW		DUP. KEY		DUP. KEY	
ADJ. PROP		SIDE		WALL		BODILY PRES		BROKE GLASS	
OPEN GROUND		DOOR		ROOF		BROKE GLASS		DOOR FORCED	
UNKNOWN		PATIO		OTHER		INSTRUMENT		IGN. FORCED	
				EXIT AS ENTRY		BOGUS			
						VEHICLE USED			

ROOM (WINDOW ENTRY)		LINKED OFFENCES	

RECOVERED PROPERTY EXAMINED		GENERAL PHOTOS	

FINGERPRINT EXAMINATION   POSITIVE [   ]   NEGATIVE [   ]

	PHOTO	LIFT	ENT.	SEIZED	RECEIPT	ELIMS TAKEN	REQSTD	POSTAL

FOOTWEAR		OTHER MARKS/ IMPRESSIONS		OTHER EXHIBITS		REMARKS
TRAINER		GLOVES		FIBRES		
SMOOTH		LEATHER/PVC		LIFT		
OTHER		FABRIC		GLASS		
		RUBBER		PAINT		
		OTHER		DEBRIS		
PHOTO		TOOLMARK		SWAB		
CAST		TYREMARK				
LIFT		PHOTO		OTHER		
CODING		CAST				

SKETCH

SUSPECTED	

Fig 2.1 A typical scene of crime examination form for detailing types of evidence recovered and important factors relating to the scene itself.

Iscan, M. Y. (1988), Rise of Forensic Anthropology, *Yearbook of Phys. Anthrop.*, 31: 203-230.

Knight, B. (1987), Murder in the laboratory, *New Scientist*, 25, Dec/Jan: 59-63.

Knight, B. (1991), *Forensic Pathology*, London.

Lawton, Lord Justice. (1980), The limitations of expert scientific evidence, *J. Forensic Sci. Soc.*, 20: 237-242.

Locard, E. (1928), Dust and its analysis: an aid to criminal investigation, *Police J.*, 1: 177-192.

Longworth, I. (1993), Portable antiquities, in J. R. Hunter & I. B. M. Ralston, (eds), *Archaeological Resource Management in the UK: An Introduction*, Stroud: 56-64.

McConville, M. & Baldwin, J. (1981), *Courts, Prosecution and Conviction*, Oxford.

Mervyn Jones. M. (1980), *Organisational Aspects of Police Behaviour*, Farnborough.

Mildred, R. H. (1982), *The Expert Witness*, London.

Neufeld, P. J. & Colman, N. (1990), When science takes the witness stand, *Scientific American*, 262 (5): 18-25.

Parker Pearson, M. (1993), Visitors welcome, in J. R. Hunter & I. B. M. Ralston, (eds), *Archaeological Resource Management in the UK: An Introduction*, Stroud: 225-231.

Priston, A. (1985), A forensic scientist's guide to the English legal system. Parts 1, 2 and 3, *J. Forensic Sci. Soc.*, 25 (4): 269-280, 25 (5): 329-342, 25 (6):415-424

Simpson, K. (1980), *Forty Years of Murder*, London.

Skyrme, T. (1983), *The Changing Image of the Magistracy* (2nd edition), London.

Sloam, K. A. (1984), The investigator and the specialist - a problem in communication? in A. R. Brownlie, (ed), *Crime Investigation: Art or Science?* John Donald, Edinburgh: 29-32.

Snow, C. C. (1982), Forensic anthropology, *Ann Rev Anthrop*, 11: 97-131.

Stead, P. J. (1985), *The Police of Britain*, Oxford.

Tanton, R. L. (1979), Jury preconceptions and their effect on expert scientific testimony, *J. Forensic Sci.*, 24 (3): 681-691.

Chapter three

Recovering buried remains

J. R. Hunter
with contributions by
S. Dockrill

3.1 Stratigraphy

There is a general misconception that anything (or any-body) buried under the ground surface somehow vanishes into a disordered and amorphous mass of earth and stones. This is a misconception which belies the fundamental principles of geology and archaeology both of which are based on the laws of stratigraphy - the existence of an ordered state of *strata* or layers which underlie the ground surface. In the natural environment soil scientists (pedologists) identify the development of these strata as a formation process; its results are visible by excavating a small pit in a pasture or moorland where neither agriculture nor building has taken place. The side of the pit (known as the *section*) will normally exhibit at least three superimposed layers defined by pedologists as the A, B and C horizons. The formation process starts with the C horizon, the lowest natural geological bedrock composed, for example, of chalk, sandstone or clay. With exposure to air and climate and with the accumulation of organic matter, particles and windblown soils, this C horizon will begin to develop a growth medium on its surface. The speed and thickness of this growth depends on numerous variables, for example, rainfall, general climatic factors, animal and insect activity, and the physical characteristics of the C horizon itself. This new layer is known as the A horizon, commonly referred to as topsoil. Its development is accompanied by that of an interface layer located between the A and C horizons. Referred to (unsurprisingly) as the B horizon, this tends to merge with the other two layers at the top and the bottom respectively. All three are otherwise distinctive in terms of both colour and texture, although their relative thicknesses and depths can vary according to geology and environment. This profile is essential for soil stability; it will remain unchanged throughout time other than by the impact of external intrusion. For example, when a burial takes place its effect is to cause local disturbance to these natural strata. This disturbance is irreversible; its anomalous nature in relation to the surrounding, undisturbed ground is the basis of many of the detection methods that can be used (see chapter 5).

In most circumstances, however, this natural stratigraphy will have been supplemented or eroded, in rural areas by ploughing and general agricultural use, and in less rural areas by building development, roads, and habitation activities. Human occupation tends to produce its own kind of stratigraphy caused by builders' trenches, spreads of hardcore and sand, redeposition of earth and materials for levelling, and layers of rubble or burning. These can be quite slight, particularly in earlier times when they might typically be formed by spreads of charcoal, pits for rubbish, thin layers of black occupation soils, buried turf horizons and small discoloured patches where posts or stakes for building had been set. Layers can also be created by the decay of organic materials, including cadavers, and much research has been directed towards the whole issue of formation processes (see chapter 4). However, as a rule of thumb, the greater the density and antiquity of an urban population in a given place, the greater the depth of these various man-made deposits. This is partly because of the accumulation of debris and building materials, but also a result of settlements having become successively superimposed by the levelling of earlier buildings. Similar effects occur in roadways where the same route may have been used consis-

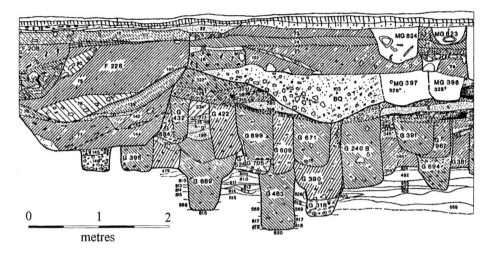

Fig 3.1 Part of a complex stratigraphy in a section through an archaeological cemetery. By courtesy of Berthe Kjølbe Biddle.

tently over many centuries; this can be seen best in utility trenches dug into modern road surfaces where the trench section will show the layering of (mostly recent) resurfacing. In fact, in many former Roman towns which still survive as major urban centres (for example, York, Lincoln and the City of London) the accumulated deposits are several metres deep. Individual layers within these deposits are usually identifiable by their colour and their physical component (for example, mixed ratios of sand, soils and rubble, density of inclusions, texture etc), although colour tends to be used as a primary distinguishing characteristic. Many layers are similar, few are the same; archaeologists use soil science criteria in order to identify and describe each one. Understanding stratigraphy and the significance of formations is a complex issue and the focus of much discussion (for example, Barber, 1993; Harris, 1989; Harris, Brown and Brown, 1993; Steane, 1992).

Another important task, having defined the individual layers, is to determine the sequence of their formation. Where layers are superimposed in simple sequences this causes little anguish, but in complex urban stratigraphies where layers are cutting and intersecting, where pits have been recut or wall trenches robbed of their foundation stones (a remarkably common action in earlier times), the task is somewhat harder. The very nature of archaeology is destructive to the arrangement of these layers, hence their relationships are always recorded in section; the illustration from an archaeological cemetery site (fig. 3.1) which shows a series of inter-cutting graves illustrates the potential complexity of these relationships and the effort required to record them. In effect, layers make a

statement about formation processes at that site: they identify a sequence between the individual layers and hence the relative chronology of those layers.

The date of buried deposits has no absolute relationship with depth. This is another general misconception, namely that the deeper something is found in the ground, the older it must be. The age of a layer (or burial) can only be seen as *relative* to other layers which pre- or post-date it in a sequence. Some relatively modern layers can be found deep in the ground, for example if a recent ground surface has been levelled or built over; some ancient layers can lie close to the surface if, for example, the place has been subsequently unused for centuries or if the layers which lay above it have been eroded or removed by building work. A useful analogy is the comparison between Anglo-Saxon settlements at York and at Southampton: at York the deposits tend to lie at least two metres below the modern ground surface as a result of later settlement deposits; but at Southampton contemporary Anglo-Saxon deposits lie a matter of centimetres below the ground because the site of the town shifted elsewhere in the vicinity. Nor is there any relationship between thickness of layer and the duration of time represented. Some layers become formed over decades, others only take a matter of minutes. There is, therefore, no linear relationship between time and depth. In each piece of ground the stratigraphy has its own statement to make regarding sequence and chronology. Within this stratigraphy the grave can be seen as a simple layer. Like all other layers it is identifiable by colour, texture and physical characteristics, and also like all other layers, it has an identifiable position within a local buried chronology.

Each layer has to be treated as a separate unit because it represents a specific action (for example, a layer of burning) or the duration of a sequence of actions (for example, the slow formation of an occupation layer). Many are part of more complex strata, for example individual layers which make up a set of deposits in a pit. However, each layer treated as a separate unit of formation, can be visualised as representing a period of time within the much longer duration of the total. Archaeological excavation involves the individual removal of these layers - a process which necessarily takes place in the reverse order of their deposition from the ground surface downwards. A useful analogy lies with scattering individual playing cards from a pack on to a small table top. The only way to pick them up again and restore them to anything like their original order is to take the top one first and then each successive card according to its overlap on other cards. Sometimes two cards will sit without touching on the card below; sometimes cards will have landed on their own without subsequent cards landing on top. But the cards can be returned to what was *probably* their original order although there will be points in the sequence where there are a number of possible options. Archaeologists interpret excavation sections in much the same way. Like the spread of playing cards, once the layers have been excavated the evidence has been removed and there is no second chance to try it again. Archaeology is a destructive process and this is why recording is so important.

Most layers contain material of one form or another that has become encapsulated within the layer during the period of its formation. Typically this consists of fragments of pottery, bone and general midden. Some of the material will be approximately the same date as the layer (contemporary); some will be earlier (residual); but none of it can be later than the formation of the layer. Because each layer is seen to offer this discrete time value it is essential not only that they are treated separately, but also that any material that they contain is also kept separate. While the layer itself can be given a relative position in the chronology of a section, it is only the material within, such as coins or other datable items, which can give it an absolute chronology. Giving the layer an *absolute* (i.e. fixed) date within a particular range can only be done if there are some datable objects, for example coins or material which can be dated by scientific means, in the same layer or in adjacent layers. Even then, the formation of a layer can often only be given a *terminus ante quem* (the time before which it must have been formed), or a *terminus post quem* (the time after which it must have been formed). These are important constraints in attempting to date forensic situations.

3.2 Graves

When a grave is dug into the ground the existing arrangement of strata, either natural, manmade or a combination of both is disturbed, and the grave itself takes up a place in the stratigraphic matrix. The very process of its creation is likely to have involved digging through some layers which are earlier and, in time, it may become superimposed by layers which are later. It may itself even become cut into: in many early graveyards, for example, individual burials are cut and recut by subsequent graves. The archaeologist then has the unenviable task of trying to determine the original burial sequence. But in all cases, the grave can be seen within a self-contained environment.

In section a burial will be defined by a burial *cut*, that is the line of definition between the ultimate fill of the grave and the layers through which the burial has been dug (fig. 3.2). In most cases this line of cut will be uneven and reflect different angles of spading or problems encountered with buried obstacles such as large stones or roots. Nevertheless, because of differences in colour and texture between the grave fill and the layers through which it has been cut, the definition will be quite sharp. Although minor blurring of the cut may occur over time, a high degree of definition may survive not just for a few years, but for thousands of years, in fact, until another intrusive action occurs and destroys it. Recovery of the body by non-archaeological means, by failure to identify the layer, will provide precisely that type of destruction.

The burial itself can be viewed as a specific event. As such, the material which belongs to the layer (i.e. the *evidence*) lies within, and only within the grave itself. Recovery of the victim and therefore the recovery of evidence which pertains to the victim and to the action of burial is entirely concerned with excavation of the grave fill, nothing more. In order to maximise the available evidence, excavation has to remove the totality of the grave fill, in order to recover items of evidence which may have dropped or been pushed against the grave wall, or items which, through gravity and decomposition, may have fallen to the grave bottom, such as

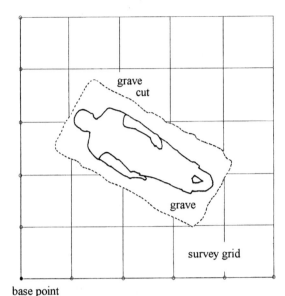

Fig 3.2 Schematized human burial in three dimensions, showing undisturbed layers, grave infill and simple framework for planning. After Boyd, 1979, with changes.

metallic objects, zips, buttons, contents of pockets etc.

Maximizing the evidence is one thing, but contaminating it is another. If, for example, the grave cut is *not* adhered to during the recovery process then there is every probability that material from surrounding layers (i.e. layers earlier than the burial) will be artificially introduced as evidence. This can easily occur if recovery takes place in poor light or very wet conditions either of which can make it difficult for the grave cut to be followed. Also, if the concept of stratigraphy is wholly

ignored and the victim recovered by digging down irrespective of the grave cut, then the potential for introducing unrelated material is heavily increased. If layers had formed over the burial site, this method could generate objects both earlier and later than the date of the burial. In such cases a situation could arise in which material evidence might be 'selected' as being most appropriate. This selection of evidence is unacceptable in other forensic contexts, in archaeology generally and, in view of the emerging role of archaeology in forensic matters, it is now unlikely to be acceptable to a court. If a burial is excavated archaeologically, the archaeologist will be able to **prove** that material is, or is not, associated with the burial. A less constructive view is perhaps to point out that if a burial is not excavated archaeologically, then an archaeologist can be called by defence counsel to demonstrate that it is **not possible to prove** association of objects as evidence. The implications of this are far-reaching not only in terms of the date of the burial, but also in questions of identity and even in the cause and manner of death. In fact the set of five questions which burials pose (see chapter 1) can be reiterated here:

1. Are the remains human?
2. How many individuals are represented?
3. What is the elapsed time since death?
4. Can the individual(s) be identified?
5. What was the cause and manner of death?

Successful resolution of all these questions is increased by using archaeological methodology. In fact, all but the first can be disputed on technical grounds if archaeological methodology is *not* used.

In most practical circumstances human remains, usually skeletonized, are found by accident, often in the process of building work, drainage, or general mechanical digging. There has been an understandable tendency for the remains to be collected from the site and submitted for examination in order to establish approximate date of death. Working practice has tended to use an interval of at least 70-100 years as a guide to whether further enquiries are necessary, crimes older than that being adjudged to be beyond any realistic chance of solution. Calculation of the interval since death within this period, and indeed the margin around 70-100 years, offers a number of difficulties to which pathologists have adapted various techniques (see chapter 8). Their task could be assisted immeasurably if the remains were to be left *in situ* and the context of the burial assessed according to archaeological principles; that is, in terms of the position of the grave in relation to other layers and the presence of associated material within the same context. In many instances, particularly in urban areas, there will be local records regarding dates of building developments, pipe and services construction, surfacing, or even agricultural use. Often landfilling, ditch recutting and drainage activities are recorded, some in local authority records, some only in memory. All leave visible stratigraphic traces in the ground, and many of them can be firmly dated. Leaving the human remains in the ground therefore will preserve the integrity of the grave in relation to a potentially useful buried environment. In one instance human remains were recovered during building work in Buckinghamshire. These were deliberately left *in situ* by the investigating officer until archaeological advice could be summoned. The archaeologist was able to define the outline of the grave and showed that it had been dug partly into the backfill of a trench carrying a major sewer. Later building work over the site had served to seal the burial with hardcore for levelling for a surface associated with the foundation of a new swimming pool. Both the sewage pipe and the swimming pool could be given construction dates; as a result the date of the burial could be narrowed down to within a few years.

In another case in Leeds a mechanical excavator had unearthed human skeletal remains from the side of a bank during building operations. Inspection of the fragmented bone suggested that more than one individual was represented. Clearance of the surface debris and cleaning of the section made by the machine indicated that additional bone material lay within a context defined by lines of loose brick walling with a mortared base between which the thin stain of decayed (coffin) wood could be made out. The development had strayed into a closed late 19th century burial ground. By conducting the investigation *in situ* it was possible to **prove** that the human remains had been enclosed in coffins within a burial vault. This would not have been the case had the remains been removed from the scene.

This question of interval since death is perhaps the most important question to resolve. We can consider two hypothetical instances. First, for example, the case of a victim buried in a rural environment. The body has become wholly skeletonized and there is no associated evidence to enable identification or to determine interval since death. Recovery of the victim ignores the edges of the grave and involves the collection, for sieving, of all loose soil around the body. This involves parts of the layers through which the grave was cut and includes a coin or similar dated item from the earlier part of the century which had become dropped or lost in the vicinity during the formation of the surface layers. In agricultural areas farms traditionally threw their rubbish into the muckspreader for general dissemination in the fields and much material becomes spread locally this way within otherwise unaffected layers. The naive outcome of this scenario is for the coin to be immediately associated with the body and the crime dated accordingly. Pathological investigation of the surviving skeleton is unlikely to depart significantly from this view, unless the remains are quite recent. The same scenario might envisage other material, such as a knife, being introduced erroneously by similar means. Equally, in ignoring the grave walls, the recovery might also ignore identifiable material or even a murder weapon in the base of the grave.

In another imaginary situation a mechanical excavator (JCB type) is used to search for buried human remains in a general location designated by a convicted informer. The method is systematic in that digging is carried out from one end of the site to the other, but it otherwise ignores any concept of stratigraphy and context. Earth is gathered in the machine bucket and dumped in a heap for raking through by task force officers. Included within this spoil are a number of bones which are identified in the laboratory by the pathologist as being human. Back on the site localized spoil is subsequently sieved and other bones recovered, but the chances of a **total** skeletal recovery is minimal (there are normally 206 individual bones in the adult human skeleton, more in younger individuals). With them are gathered all manner of material ranging from coca-cola cans to fragments of medieval pottery, objects which may be associated with the victim as well as more modern objects which are not associated with the victim. There is no way of telling which are which. Nor is there any remaining buried context which might help determine the interval since death. The number of individuals represented and factors of identification both depend on the quantity and type of remains recovered. The probable outcome will be to machine strip and sieve the entire area 'to make sure' that nothing has been missed and to 'select' material which is considered likely to have been associated with the victim. Not only is this massively costly, it is also an abuse of the evidence.

3.3 States of decay

Human remains recovered from archaeological burials and cemeteries normally consist only of hard tissue, although the extent of preservation can be influenced by a number of factors (Henderson, 1987; Mann, Bass and Meadows, 1990). Occasionally soft tissue and hair can survive according to the burial environment, although this is partial and is restricted to specific parts of the body where there has been contact with other materials (see chapter 4). Excavation takes the form of the careful removal of the grave fill and the gradual uncovering of the remains *in situ* in order to preserve the posture of the body and the relationship to the body of any other material within the grave fill. In many pagan (i.e. pre-Christian) burials the posture may be significant for cultural or dating purposes, for example crouched burials, or there may be associated grave goods which will present important demographic, social or ritual information. In most circumstances the excavation of a skeleton can be carried out well within a working day, depending on conditions and degree of difficulty. Once uncovered, the skeleton will be photographed, drawn to scale and lifted for further study before the part of the grave below the body is removed and the grave finally cleaned of all its fill. The integrity of the grave cut, the body, the grave fill and all the material recovered from within the grave fill is essential for evidence purposes.

There are, however, instances when the degree of human decomposition is such that different types of approach may be necessary. This can depend on depth of burial, climate, factors of clothing which may induce differential decay, or the local soil conditions. These features are discussed in detail in chapter 4 but are introduced here in as far as they are relevant to the actual recovery process. In extreme circumstances even a body which is centuries old may have undergone minimal decay. Well-known examples include the so-called bog-men of Denmark (and more recent examples from Cheshire, England) where the tanning properties of peat and the anaerobic conditions (i.e. the absence of oxygen) have provided almost total preservation of the soft tissue. A similar state of preservation was found with the more recent Moors Murders victims some of whom were also buried in peat environments. Other conditions include permafrost or ice, for example the body of a man several thousand years old found preserved in ice in the Alps in 1992, or anaerobic conditions which are created artificially, for

example by the use of plastic bags. Anaerobic states can be achieved in lead coffins leading to almost intact survival of the soft tissue. In all these extreme conditions human remains have been preserved in a state of equilibrium with their respective environments; this has prevented biological or chemical decay processes from taking hold. However, on exposure to air during recovery, these processes can occur immediately and dramatically to the extent that evidence can be lost unless due care is taken. Normal working practice is to preserve the original environment as much as is feasible and to remove the body and its surrounding cover to where it can be investigated under more controlled conditions. This action may appear to be at odds with the practice of archaeological recovery but, if conducted carefully, can still be carried out paying full regard to the buried context. Contrasting extremes of survival can also occur, namely in those buried environments where soil conditions are such as to degrade even the hard tissue into a state which is barely recognisable as bone. This can occur in highly acid soils where, on excavation, the body manifests itself as merely a stain in the base of the grave (shadow burial) or as a hard discoloured crust formed by chemical replacement of the hard tissue, illustrated best by the so-called sand men of Sutton Hoo (Bethell and Carver, 1987), (see Plate 4.8). In these circumstances there is little chance of *recovery* as such, rather the process is one of definition and recording. In both cases an inexpert excavator may fail to identify the remains at all, particularly if light and climate are unfavourable. Survival extremes such as these are predictable by advance soil testing and will necessitate a greater degree of preparation, care in excavation and recording procedures (see below). These extremes also have implications for initially detecting the location of buried remains (see chapter 5).

3.4 Recording and excavating

Archaeological excavation is carried out by the removal of individual layers, and by the careful investigation of the contents of respective layers. This is the basic principle on which modern archaeology operates (for example, Barker, 1983; Renfrew and Bahn, 1991), although various schools of opinion, and indeed the circumstances of recovery, may provide a degree of variation on this essentially inflexible theme. In theory, the archaeological excavation of a grave presents an ostensibly simple operation in that the grave fill is represented by a single layer in which the body can be envisaged as a simple artefact. In practice, however, burial excavation presents a more complex picture: the fill may contain a number of discrete layers which have a bearing on the method and duration of deposition (fig. 3.2); the body itself may have decomposed (in all or in part) and generated additional layers; other associated items may also be buried; the grave wall may illustrate markings diagnostic of the digging implement used; and there may even be shoe impressions left in the grave base. Nor is it easy to conduct the proper excavation of a deep burial without destroying part of the grave wall. A modern burial also brings with it an associated ground surface and upstanding remains such as walls; all these are contemporary with the burial and require a dimension of study in which most archaeologists are wholly inexperienced. Problems such as these are well documented in the United States literature and are taken into account in the manuals now available (for example, Skinner and Lazenby, 1983; Stoutamire, 1983; -which also carries a useful field recovery *pro forma*; Boyd 1979), and in papers carrying valuable case study experience (for example, Morse, Crusoe and Smith, 1976; Brooks and Brooks, 1984; Morse *et al.*, 1984). The general principles are also expounded in works more strictly concerned with forensic anthropology (for example, Bass and Birkby, 1978; Krogman and Iscan, 1986; Wolf, 1986). All stress archaeological methodology as being a considerable improvement on less enlightened attitudes towards forensic excavation in which, to quote a well-cited lament, surface skeletons were 'collected with a garden rake and buried bodies with a backhoe' (Morse *et al.*, 1984, p. 53).

At this point it seems prudent to outline general recovery procedures. Although each scene is different, the general methodology of approach is similar, perhaps most effectively listed according to Skinner and Lazenby (1983, p. 13):

> Appraising constraints on recovery
> Evaluating the search and recovery areas
> Establishing spatial controls
> Excavating to expose the remains
> Excavating to remove the remains
> Cataloguing, packing and transport

The first two of these are essential stages of pre-planning and are customarily carried out at briefing meetings headed by the investigating officer. These meetings will establish procedures to be adopted, per-

sonnel and equipment to be used and factors which may constrain the investigation (for example, safety, climate, time etc.). At the scene decisions will be taken as to which individuals will be involved and as to the manner of approach; these decisions will be made after due consultation with the specialists present and with respect to the interests they represent. An access route will be designated, perimeters set up and the scene will be copiously photographed before any investigation commences.

Once these preliminaries have been completed it will be necessary to determine the position of the grave within its immediate environment. This enables spatial relationships to be established, for example with trees, walls, large objects, pathways or areas of disturbance, by means of a base line set between two fixed points (e.g. fig. 3.2). This can be set up using two thin metal rods hammered into the ground, typically 10 or 20 m apart, from which the grid can be laid out, usually in 1 x 1m squares, using nylon string and 30 m tapes; the total cover of the grid will be determined by local factors and by any spread of evidence. The two fixed points allow the grid to be re-established if necessary and offer a check against measurements. Furthermore, if a grid is neither possible nor necessary, the base line can be used to plot surface features (or even the grave outline) by triangulation -that is by taking direct measurements from each end of the base line to the point in question and then plotting out the distances to scale using a ruler and a compass on graph paper. The establishment of a grid is more desirable in that it can be used not only for any surface planning which may become necessary, but also as a useful tool for ensuring systematic and comprehensive search and for parallel metal detector scanning (Stoutamire, 1983, p. 33). Initially the grave will probably represent the focus of the grid but, depending on what is discovered during a surface search, for example a concentration of items, areas of surface marking, or scattered surface human remains, the extent and direction of the grid may need to be amended. On most archaeological sites where the extent of the buried deposits are unknown and where extension may be required in any direction, similar gridding applies; this is usually set out according to a co-ordinate system (similar to an Ordnance Survey grid) which allows individual points to be plotted both inside and outside the grid at whatever level of accuracy is considered appropriate. On complex surface sites the use of electronic instrumentation may negate the need for a manual grid of this nature (see below). In addition, because the excavation of the grave will introduce a depth factor, there is need for a datum - a constant mark to use as a measure of height. This can normally be incised on a suitably convenient tree or solid feature and given an absolute value in due course when time allows.

It has been suggested that there are two main types of burial discovery: those where the burial place has been located by a suspect or informant or by careful search; and those made by chance discovery during building or drainage operations (Wolf, 1986, p. 7). In the former the evidence is undisturbed and can be approached in a manner which will maximize all the evidence; in the latter the burial has already been damaged and the recovery may take the form of a salvage operation. Both, however, necessitate the same degree of preparation and care in excavation - 'the methods used will determine the ease and reliability with which the case is resolved' (Skinner and Lazenby, 1983, p. 11). Excavation is a specialist skill and is best left to archaeologists working as a co-ordinated part of a scene team with whom there is constant dialogue as the work progresses. The composition of appropriate tool kits for this work is well documented (for example, Stoutamire, 1983, pp. 22-4; Wolf, 1986, appendix. A) -all emphasize the need for small implements, typically a small flat-bladed pointing trowel, a small metal plasterer's 'leaf' and brushes. Most archaeologists have well-worn trowel blades around 4cm in length; these can be extremely effective and allow a skilled person to 'feel' changes in the soil environment. The plasterer's 'leaf' comes in both pointed and rectangular forms; their thin flat blades are essential for the finer work involved in removing soil from bones. Some dental tools can be equally effective. Brushes are also useful but can smear soil unless used carefully. The scene may also require soil to be sieved ('screened' in the United States literature) which can be carried out normally if the soil is dry, or by breaking down with water if the soil is wet. The latter is more effective but can also dissolve or disintegrate materials. It is, however, the only way to break down deposits such as clay. The size of sieve mesh depends on a number of factors, but most gardening meshes are usually too coarse - a mesh of around 5mm will provide an effective, if slow recovery method.

The investigation will also be concerned with the *absence* of material. Are some of the small bones of the foot or hand absent because they were not in the grave in the first place, or because of poor recovery? The latter eventuality has to be seen to be discounted.

Archaeology has a famous mystery (verging on an embarassment) precisely of this type with a royal burial of the seventh century AD found at Sutton Hoo in East Anglia (Bethell and Carver, 1987). The grave, excavated in 1939, was one of the most richly furnished ever found in Britain but appeared to contain no human remains either interred or cremated. More recent investigation of the spoil heap has since identified centres of high phosphate value in the acidic soils. These are possibly of human origin but it is no longer feasible to say where in the grave they belong, or what they may represent.

Archaeological and crime scene recording

Archaeology is a destructive process. The recovery of buried remains is not replicable in the same way that a laboratory experiment can be repeated or a formula tested. Once the recovery has been made the local buried environment has been destroyed and with it any evidence that may lie in association. As a result archaeology is necessarily concerned with systematic recording; this is a fundamental part of the discipline and is continually emphasised (Stoutamire, 1983, p. 26; Skinner and Lazenby, 1983, p.17). As at crime scenes, nothing is moved or removed without first noting its position and marking it for later identification. We have already discussed the concept of identifying archaeological layers as discrete units of sequence. On archaeological sites the recording of these layers also extends to a description of their physical characteristics, such as texture, consistency, inclusion type and inclusion density etc., in order that a definition can be made for future interpretation. Samples might also be taken for further study. On most archaeological sites the amount of necessary recorded information is considerable and requires computer handling for hundreds of layers and thousands of associated finds. Material is being recovered throughout the excavation and systems have to be devised in order to process, clean, conserve, record and pack material as the excavation continues.

Layers are normally numbered uniquely as individual contexts; finds material recovered from within them is also given that same context number in order that it can be related to that layer both throughout the recording process and afterwards when the site is being interpreted. The same applies in forensic excavations (Bass and Birkby, 1978). However, in archaeology there is normally an additional numerical sequence which covers finds material alone. The two numerical sets can be distinguished either by a prefix letter or, more commonly, by writing the numbers inside a rectangle or a triangle respectively. For example, a recovered object might be packed in a small polythene bag on which would be written the site code which distinguishes the site from any other, the layer number (inside a rectangle) and the find number (inside a triangle). The last two can be cross-referenced by means of a written or computer-based index. Usually the finds material can be additionally indexed by material type (for example, glass, iron, bone etc) and sets or lists of similar objects can be called up for study purposes. In each case however the usefulness of the object is only as good as the integrity of the layer from which it belongs. If there is some doubt about the definition, extent or the way in which the layer was excavated, or indeed from which layer the object was recovered, the object might be regarded as *unstratified*. Only *stratified* objects can be used as evidence by archaeologists. Hence any material ousted from the ground without a defined context by the use of a mechanical digger or by spading would be unstratified. Technically, therefore, it may not be admissible as forensic testimony.

At scenes of crime there is a high degree of similarity between the recording method used by the exhibits officer and that used by archaeologists; both need to be able to identify and retrieve specific items, and both need to be able to demonstrate the integrity of the material in their possession. The exhibits officer is only concerned with objects, not layers, and therefore the recording requires no larger system of cross-reference. However, because different specialists or experts may be involved in the recovery of evidence and may produce objects at places away from the scene (for example, forensic or pathology laboratories), it becomes impossible to generate a single sequence of numbers. Instead, sets of sequences are produced; these can normally be defined by prefixing each sequence by the initials of the individual concerned. These sequences are then recorded in a record book together with a discription of each item. Retrieval *via* the record book is therefore potentially cumbersome when large numbers of objects are involved, but the system facilitates the use of exhibits in court where objects are presented by each expert. In scenes where forensic archaeology is being employed and where layer numbers are also involved, it is desirable to ensure that the numerical finds sequence used by the archaeology team is the same as the one used by the exhibits officer to record the archaeological objects. Double sets of numbers for the same material present a recipe for later confusion.

Like archaeological sites, there is no explicitly defined procedure for recording a scene of crime; no two scenes or sites are the same and each requires the material to be handled in a manner which is most appropriate. On relatively straightforward or small scenes the exhibits officer may be able to operate a single numerical sequence in co-operation with the scene of crime officers, but it will be open to him/her to devise whatever system is most suitable. It is, however, critical to ensure the integrity of the evidence - the 'chain of custody'. In archaeological situations the material is bagged, labelled and stored using the layer and finds numbers on the bags as identification. At scenes of crime the material will also be bagged, but the bags will be sealed and attached with a label which identifies the scene and the contents *and* bears the signature of the individual who recovered it. If the object is used as an exhibit in court, that individual will be required to identify both object and signature from the witness box. The exhibits officer's job extends to ensuring that all these objects are kept secure, that no cross-contamination of exhibits occurs, that they are suitably relabelled if they are removed or opened for inspection, and that they can be made available for presentation in court according to the wishes of either counsel.

Neither archaeological sites nor scenes of crime restrict themselves to the written record. Photography plays a large part in both processes with video becoming an essential element in more serious crime scenes. However, there is often a difference in the underlying reason for recording: in scenes of crime the function is to provide a scene archive and information for use in court; on archaeological sites the need for archive and information purposes is equally great, but there is also a need to demonstrate *sequence*. Archaeology is often concerned with identifying change by recording features systematically as successive layers are removed from a site, for example to show changes in the development of building foundations over periods of time. This is most effectively carried out by taking photographs (both black and white and colour) from roughly the same location and height - a process not normally routine on most crime scenes where there is little in the way of sequential change to record. However, in the event of excavating a grave at a scene of crime it is important to ensure that a set of photographs is taken at specific points during excavation from a consistent location, usually from the feet end of the grave. This is unlikely to be done unless requested by the archaeologist who should be able to identify appropriate points which demonstrate stratigraphic change or significant features during the recovery process. These photographs will constitute a fundamental part of the archaeologist's evidence. Archaeologists tend to be more familar with soil changes and features than either investigating officers, police photographers or juries and it therefore becomes important to point out to those at the scene exactly what is significant and why it is being photographed. After the scene an official set of photographs will be compiled. Each photograph will be numbered and these can be cross-referenced in the archaeologist's statement and report.

On archaeological sites a further recording method is also employed - that of the planning of all layers and features. This is conventionally carried out at a scale of 1:20 but with section drawings at 1:10. In archaeology planning is more important than photography because it has a fixed base, is orthographic and is able to cover more detail than a photograph is ever likely to capture. Planning is normally based on the site grid usually with specially designed planning frames each measuring 1 x 1m worked systematically across the site surface. The planners will record edges of layers, pits, walls, and even every stone visible on exposed surfaces. As excavation progresses, successions of superimposed plans allow the site to be reconstructed. The process is painfully slow but it is the only way of ensuring that the record made is *total*. Inevitably, however, the process contains a subjective element in determining the precise edges of layers and changes in soil. This is particularly pertinent in the evaluation of the excavation sections; all archaeologists would agree that in complex sections there may be a number of possible interpretations of the order of the formation of the layer sequences and of their meaning. There is no such thing as a 'right' interpretation but, provided that the recording has been carried out properly, at least the plans can be returned to for future consideration. The site in the meantime has been destroyed.

In forensic work it is important that, where appropriate, this element of subjectivity and interpretation is made clear at the scene. If it becomes necessary for sections to be drawn or layers to be defined it is essential that both evidence for the definition and the reasoning behind the interpretation is given to the investigating officer or another person in authority. Stratigraphy can be used to prove or disprove the relative timing of events and it is therefore essential that stratigraphic decisions are both understood and witnessed at the scene. In Scotland additional witnessing

may be necessary to satisfy Scottish law. Site planning also extends to human remains (plate 3.1). In archaeological cemeteries skeletal remains are planned bone by bone, a method which is still arguably the most accurate recording procedure and for which various techniques have been developed (for example, Carver, 1987). If this method is adopted at a crime scene it will again be essential for the investigating officer to check and approve the plan before the remains are lifted.

Planning, however, is only two-dimensional. The recording of excavations (or burials) involves a third dimension, depth. Although to some extent this can be carried out by the use of vertical sections to which the plans can be related, it does not satisfactorily resolve the need to record either the parts of layers which do not feature in sections, nor the spatial relationships of material within individual layers. For the first of these problems, archaeologists can use basic levelling instrumentation and take readings at regular intervals across each individual layer before it is excavated. These level readings can be made absolute by being tied into Ordnance Survey levels which can be identified locally. For the second problem, individual objects can be recorded in three-dimensions, again using a level reading and by being plotted within the site grid during the planning process. This gives the object a fixed point in three dimensions. Such systems can be laborious but modern surveying equipment (see below) is now capable of carrying out this type of spatial recording rapidly and with a minimum of interference to the site. In graves there is often associated material: in archaeological contexts the presence and positions of grave goods play an important part in the understanding of the nature of the burial and of the individual concerned; in forensic contexts the position of any material (for example, weapon, clothing or associated evidence) may have a bearing on the manner or cause of death, or on the way in which the grave was backfilled (fig. 3.2). In both cases the spatial recording of any material may ultimately prove to have been unnecessary or irrelevant, but unless the process has been carried out its usefulness will never be known.

Excavation

In the excavation of burial fills the excavator is usually faced with the removal of a seemingly single, but mixed layer. In view of its unknown or potential depth, excavation can be carried out in even 'spits' -i.e. by the systematic removal of horizontal bands of the fill each a few centimetres deep. This effectively treats the whole

Plate 3.1 Planning an archaeological skeleton in situ.
By courtesy of the Department of Archaeological Sciences, University of Bradford.

layer as a series of arbitrary horizontal layers each of which can be allocated a separate recording number, and from each of which the spoil can be treated as a separate layer and samples taken. This is a precautionary method in case the fill becomes more complex and, in the unfortunate event of error, it at least allows different depths of the burial to be treated separately, for example for sieving. The method is exampled in the excavation of a well of unknown depth with a suspected body at the base where the sequence of spits could be used to indicate different trends in the rubbish infill (Levine, Cambell and Rhine, 1984). By using spits, objects or material targeted for three-dimensional recording can be identified and subsequently lifted once they have been photographed and recorded, and the next spit can be taken off. For recording purposes the position of an item can be marked using a small white garden-type plastic marker bearing the same number as that allocated to the item. Items left in the ground during excavation become vulnerable; often it is preferable to mark the spot, lift the object and conclude the spit before undertaking the recording. Each situation is different, but the main danger derives from an excess of

people and feet. Until the victim is encountered the process is best conducted by one person however time-consuming it may appear. As in all archaeology, there is only one chance to get it right.

Clandestine graves are unlikely to be evenly dug, particularly if executed in a hurry, and the edges are unlikely to have a regular profile. They may, however, bear traces of implement marks or severed roots which may enable dating to be carried out (Vanezis, Grant Sims and Grant, 1978; Willey and Heilman, 1988); Stoutamire suggests leaving a narrow edge of fill against the grave wall for more detailed consideration after the removal of each spit (1983, p. 39). If the depth of the burial increases beyond the point at which it becomes impossible to excavate properly it may be necessary to sacrifice one long side of the grave (*ibid.* fig. 2.6). This can be taken down in stages as the excavation progresses in order to create a type of level working platform. Its height should always be slightly greater than the excavated surface, and it can only be made lower after the grave wall has been recorded at each stage. Before undertaking this, it is worth considering the viability of producing a profile *across* the grave when the burial has been emptied. This can be a useful recording element, but will not be possible if one of the grave walls has been removed. The problem can be overcome by identifying a line of profile before excavation commences and taking measurements before each stage that the platform is lowered or, less conveniently, by leaving a narrow upstanding baulk for measurement when the excavation is concluded.

There are numerous manuals on skeletal recovery (for example, Skinner and Lazenby, 1983; Ubelaker, 1989; Bass, 1987); the detailed methodology will be familar to archaeologists and is covered here only in outline. Suffice it to emphasise that the anxieties shown by many forensic anthropologists in the United States where police are directly responsible for the recovery of remains are less acute in the United Kingdom; here the work is carried out by forensic pathologists better versed in factors of identification, age and postmortem interval (see chapter 6). Various guidelines have been proposed for the lifting of skeletal remains, both in the numbering of the individual bones (Stoutamire, 1983, p. 44) and in the order of their recovery (Krogman and Iscan, 1986, p. 21), but every burial has to be viewed individually and may pose idiosyncratic problems. These may emerge as a result of soft-tissue preservation, body orientation, the degree of articulation, the degree of bone fragmentation or the age of the individual (Skinner and Lazenby, 1986, p. 28). Each burial has to be treated on its own merits but the adopted procedure is, wherever possible, to expose the remains in their totality, record and sample as appropriate and then recover.

Once excavation has begun to expose the victim the onus of expertise will shift heavily to the forensic pathologist and forensic scientist; all those involved will now need to ensure that their evidential needs are satisfied without jeopardising those of the other two. This will involve sampling both in and around the body, photography, further removal of fill and measurement before the remains are lifted. Much of the sampling may apply to the establishment of elapsed time since death and be dependent on specialist entomological evidence (Erzinclioglu, 1983; Rodriguez and Bass, 1983; Krogman and Iscan, 1986, pp. 21-32; Lord and Rodriguez, 1989); this evidence is familar ground to both the forensic scientist and the pathologist and is discussed further in chapter 4. The lifting process itself may produce problems in cases of differential decomposition and may present potential damage to the grave walls, or to the grave floor. Once the victim has been removed from the scene, excavation of the fill can be completed in the vul-

nerable area of the grave floor where controlled experimentation has shown the potential survival of footprints, pollen and implement marks according to conditions (Morse, Stoutamire and Duncan, 1976, p. 746). Only when the grave fill has been completey emptied and the grave sides revealed can it be argued that all the potential evidence has been taken. Although, on stratigraphic grounds, the grave floor marks the point at which the evidence stops it is always conceivable that the floor may have been penetrated in a visually unrecognisable manner, for example by bullets fired through the victim or by the permeation of toxic fluids. Consequently, the grave should be left undisturbed until after the postmortem examination of the victim in case further work is necessary. A useful precaution, however, is to take soil samples systematically from in and around the grave at recorded points as a matter of routine throughout the excavation process. This is normal practice for scene of crime teams if toxins are suspected, although the sampling strategy should also take into account the appropriate stratigraphic data.

Multiple-point recording

The need to collect numerous items of evidence and to record accurately their positions is a problem common to both archaeological sites and scenes of crime. In both instances there is usually a need for these positions to be related to a background plan of the area in order to enable a reconstruction to be made after the individual items have been removed and logged. Several methods have been attempted, the most successful being photogrammetry and three dimensional recording using conventional surveying instrumentation. Photogrammetry has a preference for open spaces and is particularly useful for the rapid logging of larger objects; however, it lacks the depth dimension and cannot be viewed in the field as the data are being collected. Conventional surveying, by contrast, has benefitted from a number of technological developments; these have seen the surveyor's 'simple' theodolite evolve from a straightforward mechanical tool for the precise measurement of angles to sophisticated electronic devices also capable of measuring distances. With the addition of small field computers these instruments are able to satisfy most of the needs of archaeological recording and were recommended in field manuals as early as 1980 (Joukowsky, 1980, pp. 87-89). Known as Electronic Distance Measurers (EDMs), these systems are able to record and display the spatial distribution of thousands of objects with both accuracy and speed (plate 3.2).

Plate 3.2. An electronic distance measurer (EDM) in use for the recording of scattered items. Here a pole holding the reflector prism is positioned on each item to be recorded in turn while the instrument (out of picture) logs the data.

An EDM consists of a theodolite type of instrument in which the telescope not only provides the line of sight to the target but also acts as an optical transmitter and receiver for a modulated infrared beam used to calculate the distance. This infrared beam is directed to a prism held at the point to be measured and is then reflected by the prism back to the EDM. The time taken for the travel of the beam is then calculated by the instrument and this then allows the determination of the distance between the instrument and the target prism (Bettess, 1992, p. 113). Most modern EDM's have a range of a kilometre with a single prism and two kilometres with a bank of seven prisms. The measurement of the slope distance together with the horizontal and vertical angles is used to calculate the three dimensional (X,Y,Z) position of an object relative to known points. In many instances this calculation is carried out by software on an external computer although a number of EDM systems have the ability to produce and display co-ordinates as a function of the instrument.

The system has great versatility: it can operate within a landscape where there is a need to map items accurately over several kilometres (for example, an air disaster, spread of evidence, location of vehicles, distribution of archaeological sites, etc.); or at a site or scene where accuracy is required to millimetres in the plotting of objects either buried or on the surface (for example, individual shot pellets, blood stains, objects, etc.).

The system has a limited intervention effect on other workers, which dispenses with the interfering need of tapes being strung across a scene or a site. This offers a distinct advantage in a scene of crime investigation where the traditional 'fingertip' search line has to be halted to allow the logging of evidence and its position has to be measured using tapes. It is now possible to record the position of items with as little interference as an individual following the search line with a staff and reflective prism and a means of data logging, either manual or computerised.

Most modern EDM systems are of the *Total Station* variant and have an electronic output which enables the machine to be linked to either a data logger or computer acting as a data logger. This enables a scene reference number or description of the individual item to be entered and recorded together with the raw survey data. Many archaeological sites now find it useful to create a separate database system using a hand-held computer to log the category of the object together with descriptive details with an index number acting as a relational link between the two databases. This presents a number of useful possibilities, for example the spatial distribution of artefacts can be selected from the database into a file for plotting on a programme such as Auto-Cad.

Other methods now involve the capture of data, the calculation of co-ordinates and the display of the data in map form in the field. The computer used for this application has been the portable pen computer developed by *Grid* which uses a 'touch screen' survey-cad software programme called 'Penmap' (Strata Software, Bradford). The computer is ideally suited to this form of CAD operation, with the programme both controlling the setting and the firing of the EDM. This software and computer configuration is also capable of displaying digital Ordinance Survey maps allowing the surveyed data to be added as layer overlays. All of the operations are controlled by a bar-menu system activated by a stylus pen. The stylus can also be used to enter text to a simple referencing database or text upon the screen. An important element of the software is its ability to change scale and to zoom in and out of detail. The files are designed to be converted to Auto-Cad DXF format for post-survey work and final presentation.

The computer software requires the surveying instrument to be set on a known point at the scene and zeroed on a further known point, for example the two ends of the base line from which the grid is generated (other methods are also possible if fixed points are unavailable). It is then possible to survey individual points whilst simultaneously logging descriptive details on a simple database. The item can immediately be removed from the scene. Alternatively the computer can be used to draw vectors (lines) so, for example, the outline of a grave could be accurately recorded upon the map overlay. In many ways the staff carrying the prism acts as a giant pencil for an electronic drawing board. Providing that the two known survey points are preserved, the instrument can be relocated for further work if additional material comes to light or if other local features require logging as the investigation proceeds.

3.5 Case studies

The Murder of Hashmat Ali and Sharifan Bibi

The first case study involves the disappearance and presumed murder of two individuals in the West Yorkshire area. The case embraces several cultural and social factors and involved enquiries both in England and in Pakistan. In short the individuals, a man and a young woman, were co-habiting to the apparent disapproval of the girl's family who made a number of unsuccessful efforts to break up the relationship. The couple went missing in 1988 although their house showed no signs of an intended departure - fresh food was still in the refrigerator and the man's wages were unclaimed. His car was eventually found at Heathrow Airport some months later. Police enquiries in Pakistan regarding another incident provided an opportunity to visit the village of the girl's family where information was received to suggest that the couple had been murdered in England, probably by the girl's brothers, and their bodies buried in a pit.

As a result of this information police enquiries were stepped up and a number of houses identified which were known to have been in the ownership of the girl's extended family. All had stone-flagged cellar floors and all were searched by a body dog and examined for any signs of disturbance. In one cellar the flagged floor had been concreted over. Enquiries also revealed that the cellar of the same house had been singled out by visitors to the house (which by then was under different ownership) because of a bad smell. This was confirmed by the builder who concreted the floor who also noted that some of the flags had been lifted and replaced. As a result of this information the concrete skim was removed from the floor; not only did this reveal broken relaid flags in a small back room to the cellar, but it also accentuated the already unpleasant smell in the room. Archaeological assistance was brought in, the relaid flags lifted, and a filled pit identified below the floor. This was duly excavated according to archaeological methodology and the findings presented to court when two of the girl's brothers were eventually tried for the couple's murder in 1991. The pit was found to be approximately 1.5m deep and a similar, schematised section is reproduced in fig 3.3.

Any pit dug into the ground involves at least three processes: firstly, the initial digging of the pit; secondly the use to which the pit is put, once made; and thirdly the backfilling when the pit's use is concluded. Excavation and interpretation of the pit's use is based on only the third of these. The illustration indicates that, once the flags had been lifted, the pit had been dug through two layers, an upper layer of cinder, soil and some rubble which provided the levelling for the flagged floor, and a lower layer of yellow clay. This was natural (i.e. undisturbed) clay which had been unaffected by the construction of the house or for that

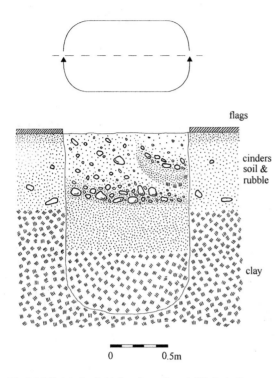

flags

cinders
soil &
rubble

clay

0   0.5m

Fig 3.3 Schematized section through an infilled pit discovered in the cellar of a terraced house in West Yorkshire.

matter by any other event since its geological formation. Natural clay is very stiff, compact and distinctive from disturbed or redeposited clay. Consequently one would expect to find the backfilling to consist of a jumbled mixture of these two layers, not a clear separation of deposits as the section shows. Moreover, the backfilling appears to consist of different types of material from those which were dug out of the ground in the first place. Clay only appears in the fill at the bottom part of the pit; some excavated clay has clearly been removed from the site. The other layers, particularly the rubble at the top has been brought from a different place in order to conclude the backfilling. In short, there is a substantial difference between what was taken out of the ground and what was eventually used to fill in the hole.

Excavation was carried out down through these backfilled layers taking care to ensure that the edges of the original cut were followed and that no contaminating material was introduced. The discovery of a small number of items within the backfill was therefore able to provide some dating evidence; these included a soap wrapper and an ice-cream wrapper both of which had batch numbers which could be dated by the respective manufacturers. These could be used to help date the

backfilling of the pit (not its original digging); they gave a *terminus post quem* (time after which) for this third part of the process and provided incontrovertible evidence for the backfilling having taken place during the ownership by the accused's family. When excavation reached the surface of the lowest part of the fill (the clay), there was some doubt as to whether the bottom had been reached or not, but the subtle difference between the dense natural clay walls of the pit and the slightly less dense, wetter fill enabled an edge to be defined and the clay fill removed. This had been sealing several items of material including a pick-axe handle, items of clothing and a number of broken bricks in a wet malodorous liquid. The clay was broken down by water sieving and yielded a number of further items including a human finger nail. In all over 300 items were recovered.

In view of its fill and contents, the pit can be best interpreted as being used in a combined concealment and storage capacity. After its original digging, any items which may have provided evidence were dumped in the bottom together with residual liquid from the washing down of the cellar floor consequent to dismemberment of the remains and the use of disinfectant. This was then sealed by a covering of compressed clay, although the non-porous nature of the clay ensured that the liquid was retained until police excavation and provided the characteristic unpleasant smell in the cellar. The bricks in the bottom of the pit derived from one of the cellar walls which had been knocked through in order to dispose of excess spoil from the pit in a narrow cavity between adjacent terrace houses. This had then been plastered over. It seems that the pit was then used for storage, probably for about eleven months, during which time the dismembered remains were kept in bags with the flags relaid on top. These were then removed and disposed of, probably on the night of November 5th 1990, and the pit backfilled with earth and rubble brought in specially for the purpose. There appears to have been minor disturbance or difficulty near the surface which might be accounted for in several ways.

The section was presented in court as part of the prosecution evidence. The girl's two brothers were convicted of murder and are now both serving life sentences.

The Stephen Jennings Murder

The second case study, also from West Yorkshire, involves the disappearance of a three-year old boy from a small Pennine town in 1962. The case began as that of a missing person, the boy being reported missing by his father after apparently visiting a friend's house. The boy's family was well-known to both the social services and the police and although suspicion was directed towards the boy's father at the time, no charges were made, nor was the boy discovered in the intensive search that followed.

His disappearance coincided with one of the worst winters known in the area; temperatures were at a record low, snow fall was heavy and there were real fears for the boy's safety. This situation, which occurred shortly before Christmas, generated massive public interest and concern. Search parties were organized, reservoirs drained and the local landscape scoured for traces of his whereabouts. Even parts of the rail network were brought to a standstill in the eventuality that he may have fallen from a bridge into a goods truck. The searching proved fruitless and suspicion eventually turned towards the area of Saddleworth Moor where his disappearance found a contemporary parallel in the children murdered by Myra Hindley and Ian Brady.

It was not until 1988 some 26 years later that the body of a child, later identified as that of the same boy, was discovered less than half a mile from his home (since redeveloped) by a man walking his dog. The animal showed interest in what his owner thought was a doll's head lying against the foot of a tumbled drystone wall and hedge adjacent to a footpath which divided a field and woodland. The area was heavily overgrown with hawthorn and brambles, and the wall had partially collapsed and become tangled into thick undergrowth (plate 3.3). This discovery caused considerable interest amongst the local police officers, some of whom had worked on the original case. The enquiry was reopened and the 'grave' was subsequently excavated by archaeologists according to conventional archaeological methodology (Hunter, 1990). This involved an initial clearance of the undergrowth, organic materials and rubble that had accumulated against the wall base, followed by the systematic removal and recording of lower layers. After clearance of the surface debris it was clear that the burial was superficial: a pair of sandals (all that had survived of the clothing) and the skeletonized lower limbs were immediately evident within a thick black soil layer, but the area of the body between the knees and the skull was concealed under a tumble of awkwardly located stones and wall collapse. The wall had slumped forward across the area of the body; its removal revealed a single line of stones

Plate 3.3 Location of the 'grave' of Stephen Jennings now marked by a collapsed drystone wall and overgrown hawthorn hedge. Copyright Yorkshire Post Newspapers.

which had clearly been located prior to the collapse of the wall rather than as part of that collapse, and which were aligned neatly across the middle part of the remains. Their removal revealed the total position of the skeleton with knees flexed and vertebrae parallel to the side of the wall. The skeleton was almost entirely complete and was lifted after appropriate photography and recording and taken for forensic examination.

The archaeological interpretation was straightforward and provided little opportunity for interpretation. There had been no grave as such: the body had been laid on the ground surface, not dug into the ground; and the shallow, thick black layer which surrounded it was the result of decomposition products and naturally accumulated organic material. The stones which lay across the body were separate from, and prior to the collapse of the wall, and were seen as a deliberate attempt to cover the remains. This sequence implied that the body had been laid against the foot of the wall, covered with stones and abandoned; that later the wall had slumped over the remains providing a par-

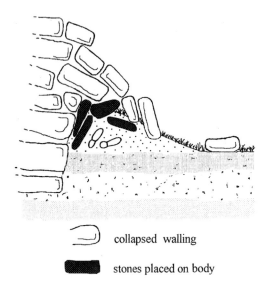

⬭ collapsed walling

▬ stones placed on body

Fig 3.4. Schematized illustration of the archaeological contexts and sequence involved in the recovery of Stephen Jennings.

tial seal (fig. 3.4). Furthermore, the recovery of all but a small number of the bones suggested that the body might originally have been wrapped. Research in the United States (chapter 5) has shown the degree of scatter of skeletal material which might be expected after only a few months if a body has been left on the ground surface. Here, after an interval of what transpired to have been 26 years, the surface remains were virtually intact - a situation which could be best explained by being wrapped or enclosed in some way.

The skeleton was identified, on the basis of the sandals and certain skeletal factors, as being that of Stephen Jennings. In the meantime his father had been traced to a location in the West Midlands and was brought north for questioning. He eventually admitted causing the boy's death having assaulted him in the house as a result of soiling the bed. He had wrapped the body in a sack, carried it away from the house and placed it against the foot of a field wall before covering it with stones and returning home to report the boy missing. The confession and the archaeological interpretation were identical.

The boy's father admitted manslaughter but was eventually convicted of murder and is now serving a life sentence. The case is the first instance in which archaeological evidence was used in a Crown Court in the United Kingdom.

References

Barber, J. (ed), (1993) *Interpreting Stratigraphy*, Edinburgh.

Barker, P. (1983), *Techniques of Archaeological Excavation* (2nd edition), London.

Bass, W.M. (1987), *Human Osteology: A Laboratory and Field Manual* (3rd edition), Columbia.

Bass, W.M. & Birkby, W.H. (1978), Exhumation: the method could make the difference, *F.B.I. Law Enforcement Bulletin*, July 1978: 6-11.

Bethell, P. H. & Carver, M. O. H. (1987), Detection and enhancement of decayed inhumations at Sutton Hoo, in A. Boddington, A. N. Garland & Janaway, R. C. (eds), *Death, Decay and Reconstruction: Approaches to Archaeology and Forensic Science*, Manchester: pp. 10-21.

Bettess, F. (1992), *Surveying for Archaeologists* (2nd edition), Durham..

Boyd, R.M. (1979), Buried body cases, *FBI Law Enforcement Bulletin*, Federal Bureau of Investigation, February 1979: 1 - 7.

Brooks, S.T. & Brooks, R. H. (1984), Problems of burial exhumation, historical and forensic aspects, in T. A. Rathbun and J. E. Buikstra, (eds), *Human Identification: Case Studies in Forensic Anthropology*, Springfield, Illinois: 64-86.

Carver, M.O.H. (1987), Graphic recording at Sutton Hoo, *The Field Archaeologist*, 7: 102f.

Erzinclioglu, Y.Z. (1983), The application of entomology to forensic medicine, *Med. Sci. Law.*, 23 (1):57-63.

Harris, E. C. (1989), *Principles of Archaeological Stratigraphy*, London.

Harris, E. C., Brown, M. R. & Brown, G. J. (eds). (1993), *Practices of Archaeological Stratigraphy*, London.

Henderson, J. (1987), Factors determining the state of preservation of human remains, in A. Boddington, A. N. Garland, & Janaway, R. C. (eds), *Death, Decay and Reconstruction: Approaches to Archaeology and Forensic Science*, Manchester: 43-54.

Hunter, W. (1990), Digging for victory, *Police Review*, 23: 2306-2307.

Joukowsky, M. (1980), *A Complete Manual of Field Archaeology: Tools and Techniques of Fieldwork for Archaeologists*, New Jersey.

Krogman, W. M. & Iscan, M. Y. (1986). *The Human Skeleton in Forensic Medicine*, Springfield, Illinois.

Levine, L. J., Cambell, H. R. & Rhine, J. S. (1984), Perpendicular forensic archaeology, in T. A. Rathbun & J. E. Buikstra, (eds), *Human Identification: Case Studies in Forensic Anthropology*, Springfield, Illinois: 87-95.

Lord, W. D. & Rodriguez, W. C. (1989), Forensic entomology: the use of insects in the investigation of homicide and untimely death, *The Prosecutor*, Winter 1989,: 41-48.

Mann, R. W., Bass, W. M. & Meadows, L. (1990), Time since death and decomposition of the human body: variables and observations in case and experimental field studies, *J Forensic Sci*, 35 (1): 103-111.

Morse, D., Stoutamire, J. & Duncan, J. (1976), A unique course in anthropology, *American Journal of Physical Anthropology*, 45 (3): 743-748.

Morse, D., Dailey, R.C., Stoutamire, J & Duncan, J. (1984), Forensic Archaeology, in T. A. Rathbun & Buikstra, J. (eds), *Human Identification: Case Studies in Forensic Anthropology*, Springfield, Illinois: 53-63.

Morse, D., Crusoe, D. & Smith, H.G. (1976), Forensic Archaeology, *J Forensic Sci,* 21 (2): 323-332.

Renfrew, C. & Bahn, P. (1991), *Archaeology: Theories, Methods and Practice*. London.

Rodriguez, W. C. & Bass, W. M. (1983), Insect activity and its relationship to decay rates of human cadavers in East Tennessee, *J Forensic Sci*, 28 (2): 423-432.

Skinner, M. & Lazenby, R. A. (1983), *Found! Human Remains*, British Columbia.

Steane, K. (ed), (1992), *Interpretations of Stratigraphy: A review of the Art*, Lincoln.

Stoutamire, J. (1983), Excavation and recovery, in D. Morse, J. Duncan & J. Stoutamire, (eds), *Handbook of Forensic Archaeology and Anthropology*, Tallahassee, Florida: 20-47.

Ubelaker, D. H. (1989), *Human Skeletal Remains: Excavation, Analysis, Interpretation*, Washington D.C.

Vanezis, P., Grant Sims, B. & Grant, J. H. (1978), Medical and scientific investigations of an exhumation in unhallowed ground, *Med Sci Law*, 18 (3): 209-221.

Willey, P. & Heilman, A. (1988), Estimating time since death using plant and root stems, *J Forensic Sci*, 32 (5): 1264-1271.

Wolf, D.J. (1986), Forensic anthropology scene investigations, in K. J. Reichs, (ed), *Forensic Osteology*, Springfield, Illinois: 3-23.

Chapter four

The decay of buried human remains and their associated materials

R. C. Janaway

4.1 The soil as a burial environment

Buried human remains, whether of archaeological or forensic timescale, are affected by the environment which surrounds them. The quality of evidence recoverable from a buried body and any associated material will depend on the degree of degradation and differential preservation in the burial during the time span between deposition and investigation. In addition to the principle factor of time, the nature of the preserved material will be determined by the interrelationship between that material and the burial environment. The burial environment can be defined as the chemical, biological and geological conditions that prevail in that particular location; these will be modified by the presence of the buried material, especially the body, and a large number of factors will be influential. Although it is possible to discuss, in general terms, conditions that will lead to the preservation or destruction of a body and its associated materials, it is unwise to make any predictive assertions about burials in a single location and in a single soil type, let alone between burials under different general conditions.

This point has been illustrated by the range of preservation of both human remains and associated materials such as textiles recovered from the excavations at Christ Church Spitalfields in London (Reeve and Adams, 1993). In this excavation over 1000 burials, dating between AD 1729 and 1852, were recovered from the intramural vaults. These were not earth burials, the bodies being contained in coffins of either wood, or multiple shell lead and wood coffins (*ibid*. pp. 78-82). The human remains exhibited degrees of preservation including extensive soft tissue through to complete skeletonization (Molleson and Cox, 1993, pp. 10-18),

while a study of the associated textiles from within the coffins illustrated the effects of body decomposition products on wool, cotton, silk and hair (Janaway, 1993, pp. 96-100).

Nature of soils and sediments

The nature of soils and sediments has been the subject of detailed study (for example, Limbrey, 1975; White, 1979; Courty, Goldberg and Macphail, 1989). Soils consist of a porous fabric that can retain water and gases; it can be divided up into four major components: mineral matter; organic matter; water and air. The relative proportions of these will vary according to individual circumstances although in most cases they will fall into the general range:

Mineral matter	40-60% by volume
Water	20-50% by volume
Air	10-25% by volume

with usually a small organic fraction (White, 1979, p. 8). The principal exception to the above are the organic sediments, notably peat. These are formed from partially decomposed plant material; they have nil or very low mineral fractions (Evans, 1978, p. 71) and form a very specialised burial environment (Painter, 1991a; Painter,1991b. Also see below).

Soil mineral particles which are originally derived from weathered rock (parent material) can be classified into primary and secondary minerals (Limbrey, 1975, p. 3), secondary minerals being formed by the re-arrangement and recombination of the primary minerals as they undergo alteration. The mineral particles in soil vary enormously in size from stones and boulders down to less than 0.2 microns in diameter (White, 1979, p. 10). Soil particle size distribution has a direct effect on factors such as drainage, temperature and soil atmosphere (*ibid*, pp.13-14), and hence preservation. There are a number of sediment classification systems based on the relative frequency of different particle size classes, for example the *Soil Survey of England and Wales* (*ibid*. p.1) classifies the soil mineral particles into six textual classes :

Clay	less than 0.002 mm diameter
Silt	0.002 - 0.06 mm diameter
Fine sand	0.06 - 0.2 mm diameter
Medium sand	0.02 - 0.06 mm diameter
Coarse sand	0.06 - 2.0 mm diameter
Stones	above 2.0 mm diameter

A description for the soil as a whole is assigned by calculating the relative percentage of silt, clay and sand. These data are then illustrated in a triangular diagram (fig. 4.1).

The sand and silt fractions are composed almost entirely of resistant residues of primary rock minerals. The primary rock minerals, derived directly from parent material, are predominately silicates which are formed from the silicate ion (SiO_4^{4-}) which forms electrically neutral crystals by the addition of positively charged ions such a Al^{3+}, Fe^{3+}, Fe^{2+}, Ca^{2+}, Mg^{2+}, K^+ and Na^+, which bond to the oxygen atoms. Secondary minerals, which are formed in the soil by the reaction of elements from the primary minerals include salts, oxides and hydroxides.

Soil organic matter derives from the debris from green plants, animal material and excreta. This includes not only material deposited on the surface but also, for example, the excreta from soil organisms which colonize dead organic matter. However, the bulk of organic material is deposited on the surface leading, in an undisturbed soil, to the typical humic rich 'A horizon' immediately under the surface (Evans, 1978, p. 74; Fitzpatrick, 1980, p. 4; White, 1979, p. 28). Organic matter is colonized by soil organisms and, in particular, those soil micro-organisms which, in aerated soils, derive energy from the oxidative decomposition of complex organic molecules (White, 1979, p. 29). During this process the elements from organic molecules are converted into simple inorganic forms - a process termed mineralization - or become incorporated into the biomass of the organisms themselves. This process will

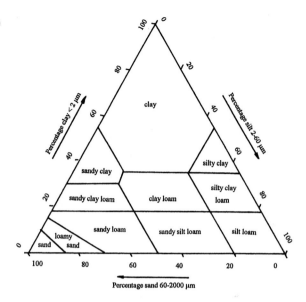

Fig 4.1 Triangular diagram of soil textural classes

normally progress until all morphologically recognizable structures are destroyed unless the soil burial environment is unfavourable to a critical set of soil micro-organisms. In terms of soil biology the same criteria apply to a buried body and associated organic materials such as textiles, wood and paper (Garland and Janaway, 1989).

The equation is made more complex by the presence of groundwater which is found within the voids between the solid soil particles or absorbed into the active surfaces of clays and humus. Where drainage is impeded or where there is a high water table, waterlogged soils have voids filled with water in its liquid state as opposed to water vapour. In fine-grained sediments such as clays and silts, where the voids are less than approximately 0.1mm in diameter, the water will be retained in the micropores due to capillary forces (Cronyn, 1990, p. 18). One of the main effects of waterlogged soils is that the small amount of oxygen which is in solution in the groundwater will be rapidly depleted by microbial activity and will only be slowly replaced by circulation. This leads to anaerobic conditions. In non-waterlogged soils gaseous diffusion allows for a more rapid replenishment of oxygen exhausted by microbial respiration, although during active decomposition this replenishment will be impeded with depth as demand outstrips supply.

The voids between soil particles will, unless filled with water, contain a mixture of gases that make up the soil atmosphere. The composition of soil atmosphere at any given location will be determined as a function of biological activity at the site and the relative ease of diffusion of gases between the site and the surface. The greater the level of activity or the more the gas flow is impeded (whether as a function of depth or soil texture), the greater the compositional differences between the soil atmosphere and the atmosphere on the surface. As a greater proportion of the soil voids become filled with water, the slower becomes the rate of diffusion of reductive gases such as carbon dioxide away from the site of organic decay, and the slower the replenishment by oxygen from the surface. As oxygen levels drop the redox potential of the soil will change (see burial conditions below) affecting corrosion reactions, and the activity of aerobic micro-organisms will be inhibited (Burges, 1967, p.12). In a well-drained soil, the atmosphere is usually composed of 10 - 20% oxygen (Russell, 1950, cited in Clark, 1967, p. 29). However, during wet periods with poorly-drained soils the oxygen content can drop to 3% or below (Clark, 1967, p. 29).

Burial conditions

The acidity or alkalinity of a deposit is determined by the activity of hydrogen ions (H^+). The acidity of a solution is described by the pH which is derived from the concentration of hydrogen ions present. Acid solutions have low pH values of less than 7 while alkaline solutions have higher pH values. The most accurate method of measuring the pH for a simple solution is by the use of a hydrogen electrode. However, the determination of soil pH is not straightforward. It is not possible simply to measure hydrogen ion activity in situ and various methods have been developed to make laboratory determinations from soil samples, although none of these accurately reproduce the conditions within the burial environment. All soil pH data should include the methods by which they were derived as this will affect the absolute pH values.

Soil pH normally ranges between pH values 3 - 9, although it occasionally lies outside these limits. Very low pH values are found in soils of drained marshes and swamps that contain pyrite or elemental sulfur, while high pH values are due to the presence of sodium carbonate (Fitzpatrick, 1980, p. 112). In soils where there are few bases present (for example, Ca^{2+}, Mg^{2+}, Na^+, K^+) the negative charged clay and humus will be surrounded by H^+ which results in a low pH. Bases are produced by the dissolution of parent material in soils which are subject to leaching. Where there is high

rainfall precipitating through a soil profile, these base ions will be transported out of the soil system (Cronyn, 1990, p. 19); where organic litter is subject to anaerobic decomposition, organic acids are produced. If these are not dissipated by the soil water system then acidic conditions prevail and microbial activity is limited. This leads to the formation of organic rich deposits such as peat bogs. Alkaline soils are formed where there are large amounts of carbonates, for example from weathered chalk or limestone, or in arid climates where evaporation exceeds precipitation (ibid. 1990, p. 20). Calcium and magnesium carbonates are common constituents in a number of soils. The important properties of carbonates are that they are relatively easily soluble in water containing dissolved carbon dioxide, and therefore can be quickly transported through the soil by the action of downward percolating rain or groundwater. Their distribution in the soil will relate partly to the presence of a carbonate source in the parent material, and partly to the soil hydrology which will determine the extent to which they will be leached out. When present in small amounts (for example, as little as 1% of the soil mass), they can raise the pH to over seven and sustain a high level of biological activity (Fitzpatrick, 1980, p. 114). Carbonates can be added to a sediment by human activity, either as lime to raise the soil pH and thus improve agricultural viability of the land or as building materials in the form of cement or mortar. Thus, typically well-drained sands and gravels will be acidic, while soils with an underlying carbonate-based solid geology will be alkaline. High-moor peat, which derives its water from rain, is acidic with a typical pH range of 3.2 - 4.5, whereas low-moor peat, which is subject to soil groundwater derived from the run off from hills that may have an alkaline geology, has a typical pH range of between 5.5 and 6.5 and may even reach 7.5 (Painter, 1991a, pp. 421-2).

Oxidation-reduction reactions (redox reactions) are those in which a molecule or ion changes its oxidation state through the transfer of electrons. The oxidative or reductive nature of a burial environment is measured as the redox potential. Where more oxidative conditions prevail, the redox potential in millivolts will be higher and elements will tend to be stable in their more oxidised form. For example, iron ions will be in the Fe^{3+} form rather than the Fe^{2+} form, while in more reducing deposits the reverse is the case. In extremely reducing conditions iron may remain in its metallic form and not ionise to yield corrosion products at all. There is a relationship between soil atmospheric oxygen and the presence of ions and compounds which either liberate or scavenge electrons; these determine the overall redox potential. When soil oxygen is plentiful its effect will dominate the redox conditions and the deposit will have oxidative properties. However, when oxygen concentrations are low, the more minor oxidising and reducing agents dominate the system. There is a theoretical relationship between pH and redox as hydrogen ions can act as electron acceptors. In theory, more alkaline conditions should be more reductive but, as pH is only one of a number of influential factors, these conditions do not always occur.

Cronyn (1990, p. 21) classifies deposits under four headings according to redox. The redox potential (EH) is quoted in millivolts:

Oxidising deposits	+700 to +400 mV
Moderately reducing deposits	+400 to +100 mV
Reducing deposits	+100 to - 100 mV
Highly reducing deposits	-100 to - 300 mV

The redox conditions of a burial environment will have a direct effect on the chemical reactivity of buried materials, for example the corrosion of metals. In general, conditions with higher redox potentials will promote the more rapid corrosion of metals (see below). In practice, however, the measurement of soil redox presents considerable difficulties and the experimental procedures are complex.

Soil organisms

Soil organisms are usually classified into three groups according to size:

Micro-organisms	- bacteria, fungi, algae and protozoa
Mesofauna	- small invertebrates (arthropods, annelid and nematode worms and mollusca)
Macrofauna	- mainly burrowing vertebrates (e.g. rabbits, moles, gophers)

In terms of their effect on buried material, soil organisms are of two basic types: those groups which are actively involved in the decomposition of organic material (for example, bacteria, fungi, arthropods etc.); and those whose burrowing activities will disturb buried

remains or open up the soil structure thereby making it more aerated (for example, moles, rabbits). Those organisms that are autotrophic - those which are active photosynthetically and do not require organic matter as a respiratory substrate - are of little direct relevance to the present discussion (for example, algae and protozoa).

Soil bacteria can be as small as 1 micron in length and 0.2 microns in breadth. They live in the water films around soil particles and in all but the smallest pores. In the presence of a suitable food-source and under favourable conditions of soil moisture, aeration etc. they can reproduce very rapidly. The numbers in one gram of soil range from one million or less to several billions (Clark, 1967, p. 16). While bacterial activity is affected by moisture, aeration, pH and temperature, under most conditions bacterial growth is limited by the availability of suitable food sources. Nutritionally the majority of soil bacteria are heterotrophs which metabolise organic compounds already synthesised by other organisms, whereas autotrophic bacteria use carbon dioxide as a carbon source and derive their energy from inorganic oxidations. Thus the activities of the heterotrophic bacteria have a major role in breaking down organic materials in the soil, whether of natural origin such as in dead plant material, faecal deposits, carrion or a buried body, or materials such as textiles, wood or paper. The autotrophic bacteria can, in certain circumstances, influence the corrosion of metals. For example, the anaerobic sulfate-reducing bacteria can facilitate metallic corrosion by producing sulfide ions. However these bacteria only function within a redox potential of -150 to + 110 mV and a pH between 5.5 - 8. These conditions tend to be characterised, for example, by dense mud deposits on waterfronts (Duncan and Ganiaris, 1987). The most common metal affected is iron, while copper-based alloys are immune because copper ions act as biocides (Cronyn, 1990, p. 169). Bacterial distribution in the soil is not uniform, and generally reflects the distribution of organic matter. In a normal undisturbed profile this will be related to depth (table 4.1).

Horizon	Depth (cm)	Organic matter (%)	Aerobic bacteria (millions/g)	Anaerobic bacteria (millions/g)
A1	0 - 6	8.04	49.2	1.0
A2	6 - 12	3.18	131.8	1.0
B1	12 - 28	2.41	158.3	10.0
B2	28 - 48	1.76	45.3	1.0
C	48 - 80	0.08	6.0	0.001

Table 4.1. Organic matter and bacterial distribution according to depth in a chernozem soil profile (cited in Clark, 1967, p. 23)

It should be noted that in this case the soil horizon with the maximum organic material - the A1 - does not have the maximum bacterial concentrations; this effect can be caused by a number of factors in the uppermost soil layer such as desiccation or excessive acidity. The general bacterial distribution in the soil will be affected by root activity as well as the presence of insect faeces or dead mesofaunal and microbial tissues (Clark, 1967, pp. 24-5). In order to flourish, bacteria require moisture, and consequently there is a reduction in microbial numbers as a soil dries out. Extremely dry conditions, while not necessarily eliminating bacteria, will severely limit their destructive capacity on organic substrates. Waterlogged soils are unfavourable to most bacteria because of the reduction in oxygen. The pH range tolerated by soil bacteria is generally between the values of 4 and 10, with optimum conditions being marginally in excess of pH 7. While some bacteria are readily limited by pH, others show a wide tolerance although, generally, soil bacteria are less tolerant of acid soils than of soil fungi which tend to dominate the same acid soils. In acidic soils with low oxygen levels, anaerobic soil bacteria will be limited by pH while aerobic fungi and bacteria will be limited by aeration; this phenomenon can partially explain the high level of preservation of acid resistant organic materials (e.g. keratin) from acidic waterlogged soils. Soil bacteria will multiply through the temperature range 10° - 40° C, with an optimum range of 25° - 35° C. (*ibid*. 1967 p. 31), although in the case of permafrost soil temperature is only a limiting factor. It is important to note that in the mixed colonization of a food-source the microbial interactions will restrict the increase of one or more species involved, in addition to any limiting environmental factors (*ibid*. 1967, p. 32). In the case of a body buried in the soil, its decay will not only be subject to the bacteria in the soil but also to the bacteria introduced with the body itself (see below).

Like bacteria, fungi are heterotrophic for carbon compounds, obtaining their food as either saprobes (obtaining food from dead organic matter) or acting as parasites on a living host. Therefore, these two groups of saprophytic micro-organisms are principal agents in the decomposition of organic materials. All fungi are filamentous or unicellular structures such as mushrooms, and are simply a number of filaments packed tightly together. Fungal filaments are known as *hyphae* and a mass of *hyphae* are known as a *mycelium* (plate 4.1). Growth in fungi occurs in the hyphal tips, food is ingested by absorption after it has been partially digested by enzymes that are secreted outside the cell wall - a process of external digestion and absorption which is particularly efficient in view of the high surface area to volume ratio (Hudson, 1972, p.1). Under favourable conditions a fungus colony may produce more than a kilometre of new mycelium in the space of twenty four hours. However, saprophytic fungi are vunerable to desiccation and require the food substrate to have a moisture content of at least 20% and prefer the relative humidity of the atmosphere to be at least 65% (Cronyn, 1990, p. 16). Fungi require oxygen for their metabolism and therefore organic materials in anaerobic environments are only subject to attack from anaerobic bacteria. For example, wood buried in damp aerobic soils will eventually be totally destroyed by aerobic fungal infestation with assistance from other agents such as insects and bacteria. In wet, anaerobic archaeological deposits soft, partially decomposed timber can be recovered, because anaerobic bacteria can only decompose some of the wood's molecular structure. In particular, waterlogged, acidic, anaerobic deposits can preserve timber for thousands of years (Coles 1984; Coles and Coles, 1989).

Meso- and macro-fauna include woodlice,

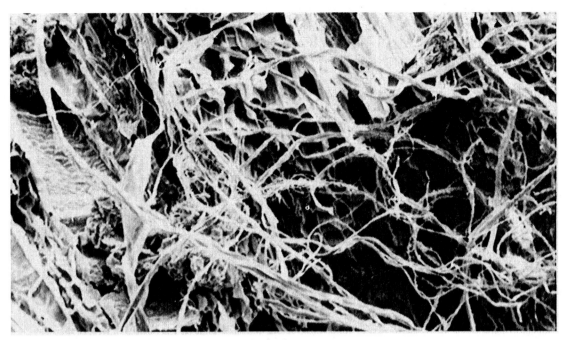

Plate 4.1 Fungal Mycelium growing on wood. Original magnification x500.

mites, insects such as beetles, centipedes and milli-
pedes. Insects may be present both in adult and larval
forms both from soil dwelling adults and from species
that exist above ground as adults. Wingless Acarina and
Collembola (mites and springtails) will feed on a range
of materials including decaying plants, fungal mycelia,
and parts of decaying earthworms. The larvae of various beetles and other insects such as certain flies are
carrion-feeders. The annelids include enchytraeid
worms and earthworms, the former being small thread-
like animals with a biomass rarely exceeding 100kg per
hectare. Earthworms are important in terms of their
consumption of litter, but while they have a key role in
humus breakdown and the formation of soils they are
less important than the insects in terms of the degradation of buried bodies and their associated materials.
Mollusca occupy a wide range of habitats and different
species live off a diverse range of foodstuffs. In addition to the familiar species which are found living in the
vegetation above the ground surface, other species will
burrow, especially when attracted by a suitable food
source. Macro-fauna includes all the larger animals living in the soil, including burrowing animals such as
moles, rats, rabbits etc. Certain carrion-feeders such as
foxes and dogs will dig to uncover buried food, and
thus be principal agents for the disturbance of a buried
body (see below).

4.2 Cadaveric decay

Problems of variability in burial environment present
major dangers in making generalizations regarding
decay to specific cases. Much of the background work
on soft tissue decay has been undertaken on modern
buried bodies in differing burial environments; the
knowledge gained from this work has then been
applied to forensic circumstances. Buried bodies are
contained in a much less predictable decay environment in which a whole host of factors will affect the
rate and nature of the interaction between the body and
associated buried materials. Factors such as the specific nature of that particular soil, with its own range of
oxygenation, water content, redox potential, ion
exchange capacity and pH variation; the nature of the
body itself - its biochemistry, fat content; the cause of
death; the time interval between death and burial;
whether the body is clothed or unclothed, or wrapped
in a polythene sheet; and the depth of the burial. In
short, it is very unwise to draw direct predictive paral-
lels between one specific case and another.
Experimental work can indicate general trends for the
specific parameters tested, although it is worth noting
that in the less complicated field of material biodeterioration it has been found difficult to produce
systematically replicable results for the burial of materials in the soil (Turner, 1972). The chemical and

biological interactions of a body with associated materials in a specific soil is impossible to model in a realistic manner. The result is that it may be possible to predict general trends within a specific soil type (provided factors of soil moisture and microbiology are largely similar) but it is unlikely that valid predictions can be made between widely different geographical regions or differing burial situations.

Changes occurring after death

Immediately after death the destructive processes of autolysis and putrefaction commence. Autolysis occurs independently from any bacterial action whilst putrefaction, the reduction and liquefaction of tissue, is a microbiologically dominated process. Soft tissue decomposition is characterised by the progressive breakdown of protein, carbohydrate and fat. The soft tissues eventually liquefy and disintegrate, leaving skeletonized remains articulated by ligaments (Janssen,1984, pp. 13-22; Polson, Gee and Knight, 1985). The chemical changes which occur in the fat, protein and carbohydrates during putrefaction are important as it is these changes which may influence the decay of both associated materials buried with the corpse and the body itself.

After somatic death, which is attested by loss of ECG (electrocardiogram) rhythms and cessation of respiration, certain tissues, cells and enzymes will continue to function although this will be influenced by factors such as the cause of death, the condition of cells and tissues and their oxygen requirements (Mant, 1984, p. 131). For example, contraction of voluntary muscles may occur if subject to appropriate mechanical or electrical stimulation for periods of up to two hours after death.

After death the body starts to cool, that is, the heat which it possessed in life is lost to the external environment. The rate of heat loss from the cadaver offers one of the more reliable methods of estimating the time since death for a period of up to twenty four hours. The rectal temperature of a healthy adult at rest is approximately 37° C with daily variations between to 0.35 - 0.52° C. The temperature varies throughout the day being at its lowest between 2.00 and 6.00am and highest between 4.00 and 6.00pm. Initial body temperature will be affected by the physiological state of the individual, for example heavy exercise will raise the temperature, as will certain causes of death which affect the thermal control centres of the brain (Mant, 1984, p.132). For example, in many cases of asphyxia-

tion a severe rise in temperature can occur. and the recorded temperature may even continue to rise after death in the case of certain severe bacterial infections and after haemorrhages into the brain stem (*ibid*. p. 132). The rate of cooling is determined by the difference in temperature between the body and its environment. Thus the temperature at the time of examination will be a result of :

1. Temperature at death
   (may vary with cause of death)
2. Temperature conditions of environment since death (may vary diurnally)
3. Physical condition of body (size, physique)
4. Interval of time between death and examination.

In temperate climates it has been suggested that for an average adult the heat loss in air will be 1.5° F per hour while in tropical climates 0.75° F per hour (Mant, 1984, p.134). The estimate of time since death will be complicated by a number of factors, not least, those environmental factors that affect the rate of heat loss, such as conduction through a cold surface, insulation of the body by clothing etc. (see also chapter 8). Thus, while the use of body cooling can be of assistance to a criminal investigation there are a number of complicating factors. For example, the time of injury may not be the same as the time of death, such as in a case of an individual who has been subjected to a severe assault and bled to death some hours afterwards. The time of death in this case is of less importance to the investigating officers than the time of assault. In practice great care must be taken in measuring the body temperature; cooling curves have been derived which can compensate for external factors.

Immediately after death the destruction of soft tissue commences; this is initially caused by autolysis which is defined as the 'postmortem fermentative processes which operate without the participation of bacteria' (Janssen, 1984): autolysis is a result of the release of intra- and extra-cellular lytic enzymes, a failure of matrix renewal and the cessation of pumps at the cell membrane (Walker *et al.*, 1988).

Once the heart has ceased to pump, the blood will drain to the lowest available parts of the body. The heavier red corpuscles will tend to settle first, thus colouring these areas of the body. This process, known as postmortem hypostasis or lividity, can be of assistance in determining the position of the body in the hours immediately following death. It occurs within an hour or so of death although its onset may be advanced by conditions where the circulation is severely inhibited, such as in narcotic poisoning. At first hypostases form patchy or mottled areas, but within twelve hours they are complete in their primary form due to coalescence of the smaller areas which become fixed by clotting (Mant, 1984, p. 136).

Except in the case of cadaveric spasm (which is where instantaneous stiffening occurs at the time of death in particular circumstances), the first effect of death in most cases is a general relaxation of muscular tone (Mant, 1984, p. 140). The lower jaw drops, the eyelids lose their tension, the muscles are soft and flabby and the joints are flexible. Within a few hours after death, and generally while the body is still cooling, the muscles of the eyelids and the jaw begin to stiffen and contract followed by similar changes in the muscles of the trunk and limbs so that the whole body becomes rigid. This condition is known as *rigor mortis*. After death the muscular tissue passes through three phases:

1. It is flaccid but contractile, still possessing cellular life
2. It becomes rigid and incapable of contraction, being dead
3. It once more relaxes but never regains its power of contractility

Subsequently the muscular tissue will become subject to decay depending on the environmental conditions such as mummification, putrefaction or adipocerous change.

Rigor mortis is caused by all of the muscles' ATP (adenosine triphosphate) being broken down and to a build up of lactic acid reaching about 0.3%, at which point the muscle goes into an irreversible state of contraction. In temperate climates this condition usually commences within two to four hours of death, reaching a peak at twelve hours and starts to disappear at twenty four hours with the cadaver becoming limp in thirty six hours. Flaccidity following *rigor mortis* is caused by the action of alkaline liquids produced by putrefaction. A number of factors cause variations in the onset of *rigor mortis*, the most important being the metabolic state of the muscles at the time of death. For example, if at the time of death the deceased was violently exercising or convulsing then the condition develops more rapidly and can be instantaneous. This is often found in hunted animals or with deaths from convulsant poisonings such as strychnine. Ambient temperature has a profound effect and in tropical climates *rigor mortis* may be complete in two hours, while cold will cause it to persist. Bodies deposited in cold water will retain rigidity for a long time, as cold water tends to retard putrefaction.

Cadaveric spasm, or the instantaneous tensing of certain muscle groups at the time of death should not be confused with very rapidly developing *rigor mortis*. As a phenomenon it has forensic importance due to the fact that it cannot be artificially induced. A person who shoots himself may be found gripping the pistol in cadaveric spasm but it is quite impossible for a pistol to be placed in someone's hand and the contraction of *rigor mortis* made to appear as cadaveric spasm. There are records of buttons or pieces of clothing of an assailant being firmly gripped by the victim. It is more likely to occur when great muscular exertion has been made prior to death in emotionally tense individuals and when sudden death is a predisposing factor.

Putrefaction

More widespread decomposition is soon caused by putrefaction brought about largely by the action of bacterial enzymes, mostly anaerobic organisms from the bowel. The process of putrefaction, having commenced immediately after death, is visible under normal conditions from forty-eight to seventy-two hours afterwards and is a result of both bacterial and enzymic degradation (Polson, Gee and Knight, 1985) : micro-organisms from the intestine migrate into the local tissues, and gain access through the lymphatics, blood and lymph to the body tissue generally. Aerobic organisms deplete the tissues of oxygen and, although their numbers decrease as the available oxygen is diminished, they create conditions which are more suitable for the more destructive anaerobic organisms that ultimately come from the intestinal canal (*ibid*); thus the bacterial flora change from aerobic groups, as exemplified by the coliform *Staphylococcus proteus* varieties, to the anaerobic, in which the *Clostridia* predominate (Evans 1963, p. 4f). In later stages micro-organisms may be derived from the soil; here soil history is an important factor and will influence the size and nature of the population of dormant micro-organisms. Most fungi that are found on decomposing remains are aerobic and consequently their growth is restricted to the surface of the cadaver and little deep penetration of the tissues takes place.

The initial signs of putrefaction are green or

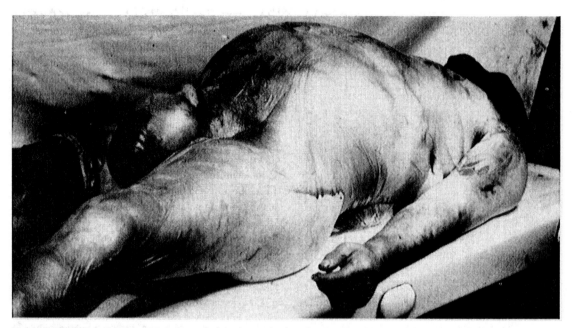

Plate 4.2 Distension of abdominal cavity and general putrefactive changes. By courtesy of the Medico-Legal Centre, University of Sheffield.

greenish-red discolouration of the skin of the anterior abdominal wall due to the formation of sulf-haemoglobin. This spreads to the whole of the abdominal wall, chest, thighs and eventually to the skin of the entire body, the process usually taking about seven days.

The process is accompanied by changes to the body fats. Neutral fat is hydrolyzed to some extent by intrinsic tissue lipases. This proceeds slowly and the activity of this enzyme system soon diminishes. Analyses of postmortem fat exhibit the presence of oleic, palmitic and stearic acids as soon as eight hours after death; these are the first phase of neutral fat breakdown. Palmitic acid increases and the oleic acid becomes reduced in amount through hydrolisation. The lipolytic enzymes produced by bacteria are more effective than the intrinsic lipases, particularly those of *Clostridia* (especially *Cl. welchii*), although other micro-organisms also take part in neutral fat breakdown. Water is necessary for both the intrinsic and bacterial enzymes to work, although there is usually sufficient water present in the fat tissue itself for this purpose. If the process continues, the neutral fat is totally converted to fatty acids which are deposited in its place. If no further chemical changes take place these fatty acids remain as adipocere. When adipocere is analysed, in addition to stearic, palmitic and oleic acids, there is also a fraction of calcium soaps (Polson, Gee and Knight, 1985, p. 24).

As well as hydrolizing, fat can also oxidize - a process that can be brought about by the action of bacteria, fungi and atmospheric oxygen. In most instances hydrolysis (rather than oxidation) dominates the fat degradation system. Fatty acids, the products of hydrolysis, will be quickly oxidized into aldehydes and ketones; however, this can only take place in the presence of oxygen. If the burial circumstances keep the oxygen levels low then the fat degradation products will remain as adipocere.

Enzyme action also serves to break down body proteins, but this does not proceed at a uniform rate throughout the body. The rate is determined by the amount of moisture, bacterial action and temperature. Moisture favours decay, and proteolysis is slowed by cooling and increased by warming. In the event of death being caused by viral or bacterial infection, not only will the body temperature be higher but bacteria may be widespread throughout the cadaver and hasten postmortem decomposition. In general, proteins break down into polypeptides and amino acids. As proteins are broken down into more simple units a greater range and number of micro-organisms can grow on the substrate. The tissues become increasingly liquid and in the case of a body buried directly in the soil, a mucus sheath will form around the corpse consisting of liquid body decomposition products and a fine silt fraction from the soil.

As a result of the rapid decomposition of intestinal contents, gas products form and the gut cavity becomes distended. Discoloured natural liquids and liquefying tissues are made frothy by the gas; some may exude from the natural orifices, forced out by the increasing pressure of gases (plate 4.2). As the skin starts to break down the body cavities will rupture. As pressure builds up within the cavities gas releases itself through the natural orifices with progressive eversion of the anus and evacuation of liquid by that route as well as through the mouth and nose. The gases formed are carbon monoxide, hydrogen sulfide, ammonia and methane.

The soft tissues ultimately liquefy and disintegrate, leaving skeletonized remains articulated by ligaments (Gresham,1973, pp. 93-96; Janssen,1984, pp. 13-22; Polson, *et al.*, 1985, p. 22). At this stage the body is skeletonized, held together by ligaments and, if clothed or wrapped in a shroud, will be surrounded by a putrescent or liquefying mass. Eventually the soft tissue degradation products will be washed down by percolating ground water and fixed into mineral complexes.

Following soft tissue decay, bone becomes susceptible to interaction with the various chemical and physical factors as well as the biological agents within the burial environment. Bone is a composite tissue (see chapter 8) having three main components: a protein fraction with collagen acting as a supportive scaffold; a mineral component, hydroxyapatite, to stiffen the protein structure; and a ground substance of other organic compounds such as mucopolysaccharides and glycoproteins (Hedges,1987; O'Connor,1987). The collagen and hydroxyapatite are strongly held together by a protein-mineral bond which gives bone its strength and contributes to its preservation (Von Endt and Ortner, 1984).

The physical condition of excavated bone will depend on the burial environment; any agent which alters the protein-mineral bond will have a destructive effect on the chemical and physical integrity of the bone. It is usual for excavated bone from aerobic, non-acidic environments to appear to be in good condition, but surface coarsening can occur in fine sands and further cracking and flaking may occur on drying. In coarser, calcareous sand or loam where it is damp and more oxygenated the bone surface will be rougher and may warp, crack or laminate on drying, while material from coarse calcareous gravels will lose much collagen and have the consistency of powdery chalk and be coated in a white encrustation of insoluble salts. Bone from acidic peat deposits can appear as interwoven

fibres, is pliable and hardens on drying. Acidic soils are the most common agent of bone destruction and work by dissolving the inorganic matrix of hydroxyapatite which produces an organic material susceptible to leaching by water. The collagen fibres are sometimes preserved by natural tannins (Cronyn,1990, pp. 277-278). It has also been suggested that collagen degradation is affected by the activity of the gas-gangrene bacterium *Clostridium histolyctium* which operates in a pH range of between seven and eight (Garlick, 1969; Rottlander, 1976). Alternative claims implicate bacterial collagenases as largely responsible for degrading bone collagen by reducing them to peptides which leach away in groundwater (Beeley and Lunt, 1980).

In archaeology there has been much recent attention concerning the degradation of bone in the soil (diagenesis; see also chapter 8). The impetus for this work has been an attempt to explain the differential survival of elements of the skeleton and differential preservation between individual burials, and to underpin more detailed biochemical analysis of archaeological bone (Price *et al.,* 1992).

At the microscopic level biological agents of decay include bacteria and fungi which mimic pathological changes in bone (Wells, 1967). Microscopic focal destruction of bone (tunnels) was first noted during the last century (Wedl, 1864) and it is now understood to be caused by invading soil micro-organisms (Hackett, 1981), possibly an unidentified mycelium-forming fungus (Hillson, 1986, p. 158). Beginning at the surface of the cortex, the organisms proceed along the microstructure creating tunnels which expand until only separated by thin bars of hypermineralised bone. In the burial environment it is believed that soil-water content and temperature are important factors in focal destruction which does not occur in wet, waterlogged or dry soils but is favoured in soils with moderate moisture in summer weather.

If there is substantial surface vegetation, bone is susceptible to plant root damage. Physical damage by plant roots can mark, warp and even break bones but the exact mechanism of biochemical plant root damage is obscure (Morse, Duncan and Stoutamire, 1983, pp. 147-148). It is probable that plant roots manufacture mucilaginous substances which promote the growth of micro-organisms when secreted. Certain of these micro-organisms, including fungi, will discharge enzymes into the soil; this catalyses the reaction that dissolves hydroxyapatite in bone and facilitates its absorption into the plant root system. A low pH will promote these chemical changes. Research conducted in Thailand has demonstrated that plants and their root systems constitute a complex of physical and chemical processes which efficiently break down the external and internal structure of human bone (Warren, 1976). While it is appreciated that plant activity in the tropics is at a greater level than in the United Kingdom the principle of vegetation acting as a decomposition vector of human skeletal remains is valid.

Postmortem injuries by animals

It is the action of meso- and macro fauna that is responsible for the more obvious changes to bone such as disturbance, breakage and complete destruction. Insects, snails and mammals have all been known to prey on buried human remains (Henderson, 1987). Insect activity depends on the conditions of the burial, season, latitude and altitude (Erzinclioglu, 1983). Soil cover is not an entirely effective barrier against the invasion of carrion feeding larvae, although it does inhibit their action (Nuorteva, 1977, p. 1078). This is because infestation may occur prior to burial, and because sarcosaprophagous insects (ie those which feed on dead animal material) generally have sense organs well adapted to locating corpses. The vertical distribution of burrowing insects can be modified by the presence of a buried corpse. Evans (1963) has reported that in graveyards Collembola have been discovered at a depth of two metres although their normal burrowing depth does not exceed ten centimetres. Insect larvae hasten liquefaction of soft tissue by the introduction of bacteria, the secretion of digestive enzymes and physical destruction by tunnelling. Their burrowing allows for the aeration of internal soft tissue (Keh, 1985). Carnivorous snails are scavengers and carrion feeders and a number of species are known to burrow, for example *Ceciliodes acicula* and *Oxychilus collarius* which were recovered from inside crania and amongst other bones from the human skeletal remains at the Neolithic long barrow of Waylands Smithy in Berkshire.

Mammals such as rodents, rabbits, dogs and foxes burrow and scavenge for food. They may disturb bones and move them away from the burial site, inflict pseudopathological marks (Patel, 1994) and even destroy bone by gnawing (see chapter 5). Primarily it is the corpse that is of interest to scavengers not the skeleton. For example, the skull of a missing man was found in Finland during April 1972 and in May the rest of the body was discovered 75 metres away. Faecal pellets from a fox were recovered from beside the body

and it was assumed that a fox was the agent of separation, digging up and removing the skull (Nuorteva, 1977).

Factors which promote or accelerate cadaveric decay

There are a large number of interrelated factors which will affect the rate and nature of cadaveric decay. These principally include the condition of the body at the time of burial and the nature and circumstances of the burial environment (Mant, 1987). A comprehensive survey of the issues has been reviewed by Mant both in forensic literature (1953) and more recently in an archaeologically orientated publication (1987). The basic work was presented as a doctoral thesis (Mant 1950) and was based on a series of exhumations carried out by Mant in his role as a war crimes investigator at the end of the Second World War. The original work is a synthesis of results from over 150 exhumations of individuals from a range of different circumstances and burial conditions. Burial, for example, was often immediately after death rather than the normal postmortem interval of several days. In most cases the dates of death and interment were known. It was not possible to carry out laboratory analyses of the tissues recovered and the results are based on gross changes, but the data made it possible to examine the influence of a variety of factors on human decomposition in buried environments. Some generalization can be made, although attention must be paid to individual circumstances.

Mant demonstrated that thin bodies will skeletonize more rapidly than more fleshy ones in the same conditions while antemortem or postmortem wounding make cadavers more susceptible to invasion by extracorporeal organisms than bodies which are buried with the skin intact; they will also have a more rapid rate of skeletonisation. The rate of decomposition of a body on the surface is more rapid than that of a buried body, a factor due to the soil limiting access by extracorporeal micro-organisms and larger animals, as well as reducing the rate of gaseous diffusion. Exposure above ground, even for a short period, will allow insects and carnivorous larvae to colonise the body and rapidly attack the soft tissue, a process which will continue after burial. Ambient temperatures above the ground are higher; there is more oxygen and less carbon dioxide, and access to the body is easier for scavenging mammals.

In the initial decomposition phase of a buried cadaver during which the soft tissues lose their morphological structure, aspects of the burial environment which affect soil biology such as oxygen availability, predominate; as a result the local soil chemistry may be modified and dominated by the biochemistry of soft tissue decomposition. When the bulk of soft tissue decay has ended, general soil chemistry may have a greater direct effect, for example on the corrosion of associated metals or in bone diagenesis. The long-term factors relate to later phases of decay in which soil chemistry has a greater effect than either soil biology or the gaseous composition of the burial atmosphere. These factors have been studied both archaeologically (Henderson, 1987; Garland and Janaway, 1989; Johansson, 1987) and forensically (Janssen, 1984; Mant, 1953; 1987).

It has been found that in the short term (up to two years) the soil type is not a particularly important factor governing cadaveric decay (Mant, 1987). However, in terms of bone preservation the nature of the soil has a greater influence (Henderson, 1987; Johansson, 1987). Bones are generally better preserved in soils with a neutral or slightly alkaline pH than in acidic soils. Dry sand is an aid to preservation as it retards bacterial decomposition, and aerobic bacteria cannot live in fine-grained soil and dense clay. Decomposition is accelerated in porous, permeable and light soils which allow a relatively free exchange of oxygen and water from the atmosphere with reductive gases such as carbon dioxide, hydrogen sulfide, ammonia and methane from the body.

The effect of temperature varies with latitude, season and depth of burial. In climates where the ground freezes in winter the burial environment during that period is one of preservation rather than decomposition. Data on putrefaction rates in a temperate climate for a cadaver of average physique have been supplied by Mant (1987). The onset of putrefaction does not appear for some forty-eight to seventy-two hours in an unrefrigerated body, during a period of average temperature, while in cold but not freezing temperatures, the first signs of putrefaction do not appear for five to seven days. In summer weather putrefaction may be pronounced after twenty four hours (*ibid*. p. 66).

Mant also observed (1950) significant retardation of decomposition in clothed bodies buried directly in the soil without a coffin. Clothing will partially negate the effects of the general soil environment and delay the process of decay. Textiles around the body also impede access of burrowing carrion scavengers. Even after two years in shallow graves those parts of the body covered by clothing frequently showed good preservation. It was also observed that adipocere formation was uniform and putrefactive liquefaction rare and that muscle tissues and muscle attachments to bone were still well preserved in areas such as the thighs and buttocks where the thick layer of fat was only in the process of hydrolysis and hydrogenation.

In general, the deeper the burial, the better the preservation of the body (Henderson, 1987). This is a result of a stable, low temperature, poor gas diffusion and inaccessibility to floral and faunal agents of decay. However, the action of soil pressure in the burial context can distort bones and this has implications for osteometric analysis in forensic anthropology. Quantifying the extent of this phenomenon is, however, virtually impossible.

Mant observed that a buried corpse surrounded by certain vegetable matter (for example, straw or pine branches) showed more rapid decomposition than others buried without this material. The straw and pine introduced additional bacteria which aided decomposition and surrounded the body with a layer of air. It is also thought that the vegetable matter acts as an insulator, retaining the heat produced by decomposition and generating heat through its own breakdown (Mant, 1987).

The shape of individual bones of the human skeleton, which may be grouped into four shape categories -flat, tubular, cubical and irregular - influence the mechanical breakdown of bone. The skull is especially prone to warping and crushing in the burial environment as are the innominate and scapula bones. Tubular bones such as the femur, fibula, tibia, humerus, radius and ulna are more resistant to soil pressure as a result of their shape. The size of the bones is also an important consideration in terms of vulnerability to decay. One study (Waldron, 1987) has shown that in archaeologically recovered human skeletal remains the phalanges and small tarsal bones are less well preserved than other bones of the human skeleton and may totally decay - a consequence of a large surface area for agents of decay to work on in relation to volume.

Bone density is also a factor as the proportions of compact and cancellous bone vary throughout the skeleton and will contribute to differential decomposition rates. The sex and age of the individual also affects bone diagenesis. Childrens' bones will be smaller, less dense and thus more prone to decay and faunal destruction. In the old, senile osteoporosis may increase the susceptibility of bone to the agencies of decay.

4.3 Preservation of soft tissue

The shorter the timescale between interment and recovery, the more likely soft tissue is to be preserved. However, it should not be assumed that the presence of extensive soft tissue will indicate a recent death, given that in certain burial environments soft tissue remains can be preserved for thousands of years. A skull recovered during commercial extraction of a peat bog in Cheshire during 1983 was examined by a Home Office pathologist who noted intact hair and skin, an identifiable eye ball and heavily decomposed matter inside the cranial vault (Garland *et al.*, 1987). Police suspicions were aroused by these well preserved human remains since a long unsolved crime was being investigated. However, archaeological dating techniques identified the skull as originating from around the third century A.D. (Turner, 1986, pp. 10-11). A further example is quoted by Bass (1984) with respect to remains from the American Civil War. Before consideration of particular circumstances that have led to soft tissue preservation over long time scales, it is necessary to consider the nature of soft tissue after it has been subject to partial decomposition. It was originally thought that natural mummification and the formation of hydrolyzed but not oxidized fat (adipocere) were mutually exclusive processes, but it has been demonstrated by Mant (1957) that both tissue types can be encountered in cadavers in forensic cases.

Adipocere itself results from the postmortem chemical conversion of neutral fats by endogenous enzymes (lipases) and micro-organisms; its formation and composition has been covered in the forensic, geochemical, microbiological and archaeological literature (den Dooren de Jong, 1961; Bergmann, 1963; Takatori and Yamaoka, 1977a and b; Cotton, Aufderheide and Goldschmidt, 1987; Evershed, 1992). Some general principles governing formation have been proposed, although adipocere formation would not appear to give reliable information on time elapsed since death. Long-term preservation of adipocere is consistent with anaerobic or oxygen-depleted environments (bogs, submerged locations, lead coffins etc.). Also warm, dry conditions promote adipocere formation. Archaeological studies have shown that under differing conditions of deposition and post-deposition, a wide range of lipid degradation products may result (Gulaçar, Susini and Klohn, 1990; Evershed, 1992). It was believed for a long time that adipocere formation was restricted to subcutaneous fat - cheeks, breasts of female and buttocks. However it is also found in internal organs such as liver, kidneys and heart, particularly if the organs had high fat levels at the time of death. When recent, adipocere is a soft greasy material which may be white or stained reddish brown. Old adipocere is white or grey, and depending on its age and condition it has been likened to suet or cheese (plate 4.3; see also Polson, Gee and Knight, 1985, p. 24; Mellen, Lowry and Micozzi, 1993).

It is also possible that putrefactive changes may be inhibited and replaced by mummification which is characterised by drying and shrivelling of the tissues. Mummification of adult cadavers most readily occurs in countries with warm dry burial conditions such as in Egypt. In temperate regions mummification generally occurs where artificial conditions will produce the same effect, and the mummification of babies or small children is more common than for adults. Mummification readily occurs in the tissues of hands and arms. The desiccation of tissue inhibits normal putrefactive changes although it is susceptible to insect attack, for example from the larvae of the brown house moth or beetles such as *Dermestes lardarius* or *Necrobia rufipes*.

Burial environments that will lead to high levels of preservation of organic materials.

Specific burial conditions can lead to the preservation of organic materials which in most circumstances would have been totally destroyed over archaeological timescales. Over shorter timescales material may be actively decaying but may not have reached the end point at the time of excavation. In general, organic materials will be preserved in situations where the relevant micro-organisms are excluded by environmental factors. For example, wood will normally decay owing to the action of fungi and bacteria unless micro-organisms are excluded by desiccation, freezing, lack of oxygen or the presence of biocidic agents such as copper ions. In the majority of burial environments a body will skeletonize, but under specific circumstances soft tissue will be preserved. The environmental conditions for soft tissue preservation are slightly more specific because the body has its own reservoir of micro-organisms in the intestinal canal and a considerable amount of water in the tissues. Thus for extensive soft tissue preservation quite extreme circumstances are necessary, although small fragments of connective tissue can be recovered from archaeological skeletons.

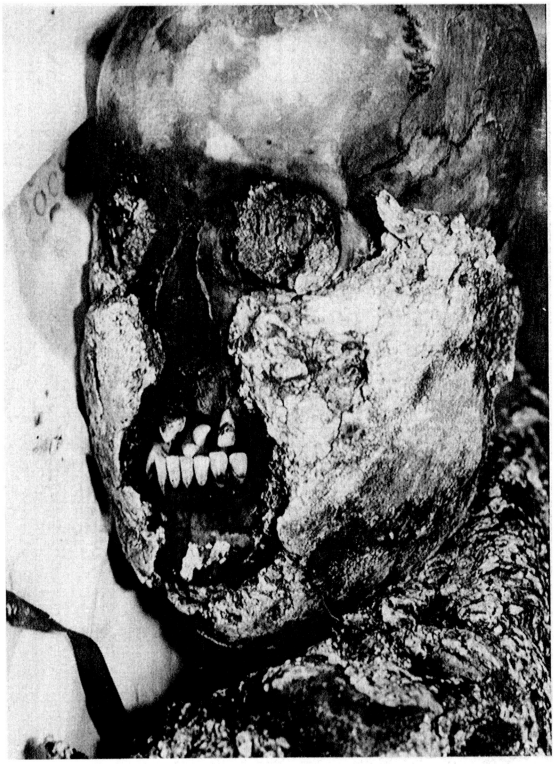

Plate 4.3 Adipocere deposits on an otherwise skeletonized body. By courtesy of the Medico-Legal Centre, University of Sheffield.

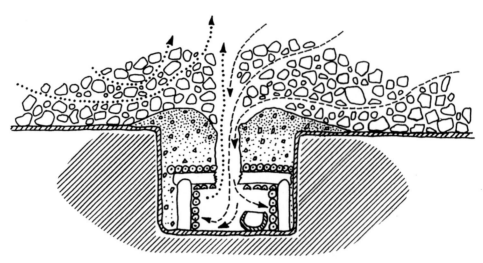

Fig 4.2 Cross-section of Siberian frozen tomb, after Barkova 1978.

Cold environments

Soft tissue can be preserved over long time periods in the frozen state. Numerous remains of mammoths dating from more than 10,000 years ago have been found in the permafrost of Siberia, many with their hair, flesh and stomach contents intact (Guthrie, 1990). Human remains, along with associated artefacts of textile, wood and leather dating to around 400BC have been recovered from the Pazyryk tombs in southern Siberia (Rudenko, 1970). The bodies had been inside wooden coffins along with the other grave goods in wood-lined, subterranean mortuary chambers which were, in turn, covered with stone cairns. When the barrows were excavated it was found that the ground under the cairns was frozen. Soon after burial a lens-shaped area of permafrost formed under the cairn. The loosely piled stones of the cairn had prevented the warmth of the summer sun penetrating down into the chamber (fig. 4.2) while the winter frost had penetrated to establish a constant sub-zero temperature. Any water in the tombs froze, and organic materials were in a high state of preservation with even the dyes in the textiles retaining their original colours. The bodies, which had been embalmed prior to burial, were well preserved with their skin tattoos clearly visible. They had been eviscerated, the brain removed by trepanation and in some instances muscle tissue had been removed from beneath the skin. The effect of this would have been to retard putrefaction during the ceremonies between death and burial, and thus to have reduced the level of decay between burial and freezing.

In the early 1980s excavations at Barrow on the north Alaskan coast revealed a driftwood and turf house which had become engulfed in ice around 500 years ago (Lobdell and Dekin, 1984; Dekin 1987) The ruined house had been infiltrated by summer melt water which had subsequently frozen. Two women and three children had been trapped in the house, the two adults being preserved by the ice, while the children who were not in a frozen area had skeletonized.

In 1984 and 1986 the exhumation of three crewmen who died on Sir John Franklin's ill-fated arctic expedition of 1845-48 revealed bodies with extensive soft tissue preservation (Beattie *et al.*, 1985, Beattie and Geiger, 1987). The graves, on the winter campsite of Beechy island, lay deep in permafrost. After the first 10cm the frozen ground had to be melted with hot water in order to proceed with the excavation. The body of John Torrington was well preserved with the exception of some distortion of the lips and eyelids (plate 4.4), although histological examination following his autopsy revealed that virtually all cellular structures were badly or completely damaged. For example, the brain had shrunk to about two-thirds of its normal size and had completely autolyzed (Amy *et al.*, 1986). The preservation of John Hartnell was similar to that of John Torrington, although the examination was complicated by the fact that the body had been subjected to an autopsy in 1846 and exhumed once before in 1852 (Beattie and Geiger, 1987). Both eyes of John Torrington were of normal size, whereas the right eye of John Hartnell was found to be shrunken when examined by Beattie and his team, which has been attributed to exposure of the right but not left side of the face

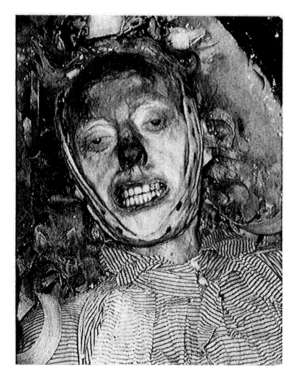

Plate 4.4 Body of John Torrington. By courtesy of Professor O. Beattie, University of Alberta.

during the 1852 investigation (*ibid*, p. 135). The body of William Braine was the least well preserved and there is some evidence that there might have been a longer time period between death and burial than was the case with the other two men (*ibid*. p. 153).

In the three preceding examples, the soft tissue and associated materials were preserved by freezing rather than desiccation associated with cold, dry conditions. However, in certain climatic conditions frozen water will sublime, that is, move straight from solid to gaseous state without becoming liquid, causing frozen organic matter to naturally freeze-dry. This property has been investigated in freeze-dried waterlogged archaeological timbers by the Canadian Conservation Institute (Grattan and McCawley, 1978; Grattan, McCawley and Cook, 1980) and has also caused a number of cadavers to freeze-dry (Brothwell, 1986). The essential condition is that water vapour pressure in the surrounding air is lower than the saturation vapour pressure (SVP) of the ice in the frozen body or object. If the SVP for water or ice is plotted against temperature, the curve is continuous and there is no break at the freezing-point. Thus ice has significant vapour pressure even at low temperatures. Relative humidity of the air is not important, but the relative temperature of the ice and the surrounding

air is significant. For example, if the temperature of the air is -20° C and that of the ice is -10° C, then the vapour pressure of the ice will exceed that of the air by about 1.5 torr and even as the relative humidity approaches 100% then sublimation will occur (Grattan and McCawley, 1978, p. 158). When ice sublimes, energy is consumed (latent heat of sublimation) and the temperature of the remaining ice will fall in much the same way as evaporating water will cause cooling. If the heat energy is not replaced then the rate of sublimation will progressively fall. Thus, in order to freeze-dry, the frozen body or object must receive some heat, for example from the sun, but without causing the ice to melt.

Cold, drying environments will suppress the activity of micro-organisms through temperature as well as desiccation, thus bodies can be preserved with extensive, desiccated soft tissue remains. For example, the Inca Period tomb at Cerra El Plomo in the high Andes produced the naturally dried body of a boy (Brothwell, 1986, p. 117). However, the term 'freeze-dried' should only be used where the body has frozen and the water sublimed directly to water vapour and this should not be confused with low humidity at low temperature which causes minimal putrefaction prior to desiccation of the tissues.

Naturally mummified bodies have also been recovered from Greenland. In about AD 1475 six women and two children were buried at Qilakitsoq, some 450 km north of the Arctic circle on the west coast of Greenland. They were discovered in 1972, the graves being partially under a rock overhang and covered with stones; the bodies had naturally mummified and their sealskin and reindeer hide clothing was exceptionally well preserved (Hansen, Meldgaard and Nordqvist, 1991). The average temperature at Qilakitsoq is below freezing, with fluctuations from -40° C in winter to +15° C in summer (Andreasen *et al.*, 1991, p. 49). The overhanging rocks protected the graves from direct sunlight, rain and snow which, with a combination of low ambient temperatures and low humidity, led to a desiccation of the bodies. However the 1924 excavations of the Norse cemetery at Herjolfsnaes, Greenland, produced well preserved clothing and wooden coffins in the permanently frozen ground, but seemingly without extensive soft tissue preservation (Hansen, Meldgaard and Nordqvist, 1991).

The most recent find of a body recovered from solid ice comes from a glacier on the Austrian/Italian border at an altitude of some 3,200 m (Hopfel, Platzer

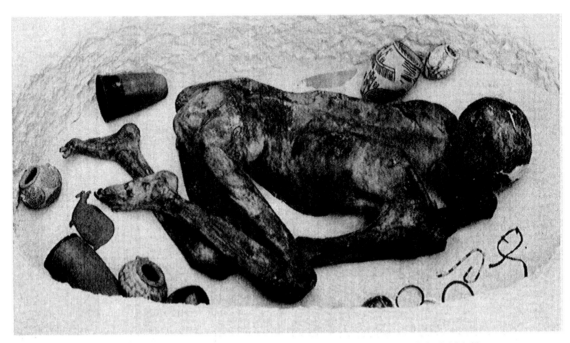

Plate 4.5 Natural mummification. Pre-Dynastic Egyptian body from Gebelein. By courtesy of the British Museum.

and Spindler, 1992; Bahn and Everett, 1993; Egg *et al*, 1993; Spindler, 1994). The man, who died several thousand years ago, dehydrated before becoming enclosed in the ice of the glacier. It is believed that the body had mummified before being enclosed in the ice on the basis that there was no evidence of adipocere, which is normal for more modern bodies recovered from glaciers. The lack of physical damage is attributed to the body being protected by a small depression in the rock (Seidler *et al*., 1992). Although more work is necessary on this find, and a single hypothesis for the mechanism of dehydration has not been universally accepted, there should be little surprise at the mummified state; nor is there a need to invoke a theory of artificial mummification (Bahn and Everett, 1993, p. 12).

Death in the vicinity of a glacier will not necessarily lead to such a high degree of preservation if, for example, a body is subject to ice movement and becomes crushed. This occurred in the instance of a soldier who died in the upper Theodulglacier in Switzerland during the late sixteenth century AD, probably by falling into a crevasse which later closed over him. The body was skeletonized and the bones broken and scattered over a distance of more than 100m (Lehner and Julen, 1991).

Dry environments

Natural mummification by rapid drying of the tissues is well attested in the forensic literature (Polson, Gee and Knight, 1985, pp.26-29). In temperate climates it usually occurs when there is good air flow and would not normally occur in bodies that have been buried. However, in areas of very dry soil such as the South Western United States, coastal Peru, the Middle East, and parts of central Asia, buried bodies can mummify (plate 4.5), although this condition cannot be guaranteed. For example, while a number of mummified bodies have been recovered from the mesa and canyon lands of Arizona, New Mexico and Colorado, dating between AD 100 and 1400, these are only a very small proportion of the number of bodies buried in these areas over that time scale (El-Najjar and Mulinski, 1980). These mummies vary in degree of preservation: some are little more than bones with patches of dry hard skin and a few ligaments; while others which have generally been more substantially preserved derive from more protected burial environments such as cist burials and caves. Burials from Pre-Dynastic Egypt (*c*.5000 years old) were buried directly in the ground and natural mummification is commonplace (Dzierzykray-Rogalski, 1986). When tomb structures were introduced in the early Dynastic period, artificial embalming practices were introduced (James, 1979, p. 157); these included evisceration and artificial desiccation using the mineral natron (a locally derived saline evaporite). The exact procedure used by the ancient Egyptians is a matter for

Plate 4.6 Lindow Man. By courtesy of the British Museum.

academic debate, although it seems most likely that the body was packed in dry natron crystals rather than a natron solution (Sandison, 1986; Garner 1986).

Bog environments

The peat bogs of northern Europe have produced over 1300 archaeological bog bodies (Glob, 1969; Brothwell, 1986; Stead, Bourke and Brothwell, 1986; Painter, 1991b; plate 4.6). The preservation of bog bodies is variable, not all tissue types being equally well preserved, although generally it is those tissues with high levels of collagen, such as the skin and the intestine, which tend to survive best. Under the skin, muscle tissue can decompose and may be reduced in size (Brothwell, 1986, p. 20) whereas tissues based on the protein keratin, for example hair and nails, tend to be well preserved in acidic bog environments. It is rare for other internal organs to be preserved although some-

Plate 4.7 Waterlogged grave from Barton-Humber. By courtesy of W. Rodwell.

Plate 4.8 The Sutton Hoo sandman. Copyright the Sutton Hoo Research Trust. Photograph by Ed Morgan.

times the brain survives, for example as in the case of the bodies of two girls from Denmark (Glob, 1969, p. 113; Glob, 1983, p. 70).The condition of the bone will depend on the degree of dissolution of the mineral content; in most cases the skeleton is extensively decalcified and in some cases the bones have completely dissolved. The mechanism of dissolution is not entirely pH driven; Painter (1991a, p. 422) has identified an anionic polysaccharide ('sphagnan') which will sequester calcium at any pH value above three, thus promoting the dissolution of bone in all but the most acidic peat bogs.

The exceptional preservation of soft tissue in peat bogs has traditionally been attributed to the anaerobic conditions, the presence of an antimicrobial substance called sphagnol and the acidic nature of peat which would therefore exclude many anaerobic bacteria. These hypotheses have recently been challenged by Painter (1991a; 1991b), who points out that while conditions are anoxic deep in peat bogs, there are still low

concentrations of bacteria present; these are probably inhibited by a lack of suitable nutrients rather than the toxic nature of the bog environment itself. He further argues that most of the bog bodies derive from low-moor peat which typically has pH values in the region 5.5 -6.5 and occasionally as high as 7.5, which would not exclude all anaerobic bacteria. It is now generally believed that the collagen fibres from the skin and other connective tissues are preserved by a process of natural tanning, probably as a result of the action of the polysaccharide spagnan, rather than the action of an unidentified polyphenol (Painter, 1991b, p. 124). However, as keratinaceous materials are generally found in anaerobic deposits provided that the pH is not too high (Cronyn,1990, p. 285), the hair and nails are probably preserved simply by environmental exclusion of the relevant micro-organisms.

There are a number of waterlogged non-peat archaeological sites which have preserved a range of organic materials but have not yielded bodies with extensive soft tissue preservation. For example, the excavations of the early medieval churchyard at St. Peter's, Barton-on-Humber produced wooden coffins, preserved by the waterlogged conditions within which were skeletonized bodies (Rodwell and Rodwell, 1982; plate 4.7).

Anaerobic environments

Soft tissue preservation can occur on archaeological bodies which are recovered from completely sealed environments. One of the best examples comes from the excavations of St. Bees Priory, Cumbria during 1991 where most of the burials in the medieval cemetery consisted of skeletonized bodies which had been placed in grave cuts in the ground and wrapped in cloth shrouds. As with most excavations of medieval burials, only the skeleton and evidence of the grave cut were preserved. However, one burial had been wrapped in a lead sheet which in turn had been placed in an iron bound wooden coffin which had been packed with grey clay. Inside, the body was well preserved as was an associated woollen shroud (Glover, 1990). The skin had a fresh pink appearance and internally the tissues were superficially in a fresh state, although there was adipocere formation and some histological changes (Tapp and O'Sullivan, 1982). Preservation had presumably been due to the rapid packing of the body in the combination coffin and to the subsequent anoxic conditions. Lead coffins are rare for earthen burials, but became more common in private and public vaults in the eighteenth and nineteenth centuries (Litten, 1991, pp. 85-119); a number have recently been examined from excavations at Christ Church Spitalfields, London, (Reeve and Adams, 1993). When first interred most lead coffins probably had good gas-tight seals, although in time these can fail. There are two main reasons for this failure: firstly, downward pressure due to the practice of stacking a large number of coffins on top of one another in communal vaults causes a bowing of the side walls which exerts strain on the seams and causes them to come apart; and secondly, highly destructive lead corrosion is precipitated by acid gases caused by air pollution, especially sulfur dioxide from burnt fossil fuels (which reached a peak in nineteenth century London) and from acetic acid released from wood in close proximity (Clark and Longhurst, 1961; Evans, 1963). As a result, when excavated, a great many lead coffins from Spitalfields were no longer gas-tight, although the contents sometimes had a greater moisture content than adjacent all-wooden coffins. Some

coffins retained a great deal of liquid, and had sufficiently low rates of gas exchange with the external environment to retain anaerobic conditions until their opening by the excavators. In extreme cases anaerobic conditions had led to a very high degree of soft tissue preservation. The inhibiting effect of lead ions on micro-organisms in this context is poorly understood.

Inhibition by metal ions

Concentrations of metal ions in the burial environment either from the weathering of ore sources or from the corrosion of buried metallic artefacts can lead to localized conditions which are highly toxic to micro-organisms. In the case of a copper alloy coin, the area affected may only be a few centimetres in diameter (Janaway, 1989) while mineral-rich sediments may affect larger areas of the buried individual. Normally this phenomenon is associated with the preservation of small areas of organic materials such as textile, wood and leather preserved in the corrosion on metal artefacts. Even when a body is buried with extensive metal grave goods, there is usually insufficient metal to result in large-scale soft tissue preservation. In archaeological inhumation graves it is usually the textile, leather or wood from organic parts of artefacts that are preserved rather than parts of the body itself (Janaway and Scott, 1989). In 1899 a well-preserved body was discovered in a collapsed shaft of a copper mine at Chuquicamata, Chile. The body, which dated to before the Spanish invasion of Chile in the sixteenth century, had extensive soft tissue preservation with flesh on the arms, legs, hands and feet, and was accompanied by woollen textiles, baskets, a rawhide pouch and wooden implements (Bird, 1975). The mine lay in an area of desert, and therefore was liable to be subject to desiccation; areas of the body had been penetrated by copper minerals to a depth of about 6mm and, although these metal ions appear to have created a very sterile environment, it is probable that the lack of moisture was a more major factor in preservation.

Burial environments that will lead to rapid decomposition of materials

In contrast to the anaerobic conditions found in sealed lead coffins, there are a number of burial environments which will result in the destruction not only of organic material and soft tissue but also of bone. In particular, well aerated, free draining, acidic sand and gravel sites will result in a very poor level of archaeological preservation. Sites of this nature that have been excavated in the last twenty years include Sutton Hoo, Suffolk (Carver, 1992), Mucking, Essex (Jones, 1975), Christchurch, Dorset (Jarvis, 1983) and West Heslerton, North Yorkshire, (Powlesland, 1986). These sites are characterized by having very heavily corroded metal-work and skeletal material which is either in a very weak and friable condition or has been completely destroyed. In the case of Christchurch X-17, the Anglo-Saxon burials were discernable only by their grave cuts and consisted of very corroded iron weapons with no skeletal material except for a few enamel tooth caps (Jarvis, 1983). In very acidic sandy and gravelly soils the body and other organic remains can be reduced to dark stains; these have been described from a number of sites including Snape, Mucking, Barrow Hill (Suffolk) and Sutton Hoo (Biek, 1969; Bethell and Carver, 1987; Bethell, 1989; Bethell, 1991; plate 4.8). Under acidic, free draining conditions the bodies are reduced to a 'stain', consisting of the residual products of the break-down of the organic parts of the body (Bethell, 1991, p. 316). It is usual for the bone mineral to be partially or totally dissolved under these conditions. If carefully excavated the stains reflect the original contours of the body in the soil.

4.3 The decay of materials associated with buried bodies

The deterioration of buried materials depends on the interaction of two factors: the chemical nature of the material itself and the nature of the burial environment. Deterioration can be divided into (a) physical decay caused by frost cracking, abrasion and distortion by the weight of overburden and (b) chemical decay which includes chemical dissolution, corrosion and digestion by microbial enzymes (Cronyn, 1990, p. 14). In general, inorganic materials survive better than organic materials over archaeological timescales. Materials such as stone or fired clay may be preserved relatively unchanged over extreme time periods; for example stone tools have been excavated which are over two million years old. Other inorganic materials such as metals and glass may interact with the burial environment and may be recoverable in an altered state. In general their condition on excavation will be determined by a number of factors including the precise level of pH and the redox potential of the soil as well as the composition of the object itself. Some glasses and metals are more sus-

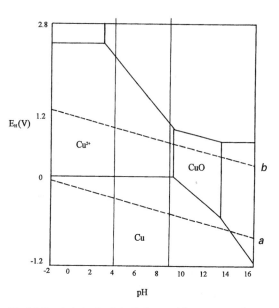

Fig 4.3 Pourbais (potential pH diagram) for copper-water system (after Pourbais, 1977, p.4). The range pH values are represented along the horizontal axis, pH7 being neutral, neither acid nor alkaline. The lower pH values are acid, while higher values are alkaline. The normal pH range encountered under burial conditions are within pH4-pH9, represented by the two vertical lines on the diagram. The vertical axis plots the redox potential- the oxidising or reducing power of the interface between the metal surface and the solution - in this case water. the more aerated the solution, i.e. the more oxygen present, the higher the redox value- the less aerated the solution the lower this value/.

ceptible to decay under specific circumstances than others. For example glass, unless of a very unstable composition, will survive in most deposits but will be totally lost in environments with a pH in excess of nine (*ibid.* p. 135). Organic materials such as wood, leather and textiles will require a specific set of burial condi-tions to be preserved over an archaeological timescale; in general, those conditions are less specialized than those which will result in extensive soft tissue preser-vation. For example, while there have been many thousands of archaeological objects made of wood, leather or textile, recovered from a whole range of waterlogged deposits in Northern Europe (MacGregor, 1982; Coles, 1984: Morrison, 1985; Hall, 1984), human bodies with extensive soft tissue require specific burial environments (for example of peat bogs) for preserva-tion over long timescales (Painter, 1991a; 1991b). As far as more modern materials are concerned, there is little archaeological experience in dealing with, for example, decayed synthetic polymers (Morse, 1983, Appendix A). The relative degradation of different 'plastic' materials in soil is a complex issue, depending to a large extent on the exact composition of the polymers, chain length, number of cross-links, nature and proportion of additives and plasticizers. The main data on this subject come from the studies of modern landfill sites usually made to assess the environmental impact of modern refuse disposal methods. The archaeologist William Rathje has studied modern refuse deposits and landfill sites (Rathje *et al.*, 1992).

Metals

The rate of corrosion of metals depends on a number of different factors, including the nature of the metal artefact itself as well as moisture, acidity and the composition of the soil atmosphere of the burial site (Goffer, 1980 p. 255). Metals can be divided into three groups according to their susceptibility to corrosion:

1. Metals that resist corrosion in all natural environments, for example gold
2. Metals that are at first easily attacked but subsequently form a corrosion-resistant film and become resistant to further attack, for example copper alloys
3. Metals that corrode rapidly and do not form a layer of protective corrosion products, for example iron (Goffer, 1980 p. 256).

In nearly all burial environments metals will be subject to aqueous corrosion which is an electrochemical reaction. Metal atoms form positive metal ions (cations) by the loss of one or more electrons (oxidation) thus

$$M \longrightarrow M^{n+} + ne^-$$
metal atom   cation   electrons

This reaction takes place at a site known as the anode and therefore the above reaction is known as the anodic reaction. The electrons released by this reaction must be consumed by a complementary (reductive) cathodic reaction; the site of the cathode can be on any part of the metal surface or an area of electrically conducting corrosion product. A typical cathodic reaction for buried objects is

$$O_2 + 2H_2O + 4e^- \longrightarrow 4OH^-$$

(after Knight, 1990, p. 38)

The metal ions released from the anode can either go into solution and be transported away from the metal object when the soil groundwater is either extremely acidic or alkaline, or they may react with negatively charged ions (carbonates, oxides, hydroxides, sulfates etc.) from the burial environment (Cronyn, 1990, p.168). In archaeological metalwork the nature and extent of solid corrosion products forming around the corroding metal core will depend on the composition of the metal, its reactivity in the chemical conditions prevalent in the burial environment, and the chemical stability of the corrosion products formed. For example, the formation of a dense layer of stable corrosion products may tend to block further activity at the metal surface thereby pacifying the potential anodic areas. Thus, with certain metals and under a number of burial conditions, an essentially sound metal core will be covered by a thin layer of relatively stable corrosion products - for example copper or silver in all but the most extreme cases. However, with metals such as iron, which do not tend to form stable corrosion products the bulk of the metallic iron will be reduced to corrosion products over archaeological timescales.

A convenient graphical method of depicting whether the metal core or any of the corrosion products are thermodynamically stable under given conditions of pH and redox potential is the Pourbaix diagram (Cronyn, 1990, p. 169; Knight, 1990, p. 37; Pourbaix, 1977; fig 4.3). The redox potential of a solution is a measure of its ability to donate or remove electrons from other substances, for example a solution with a high redox potential will more easily liberate electrons from metal atoms in the anodic reaction, while a metal in a lower redox environment will be less likely to form ions and remain as unaltered metal. The presence of a substance on the Pourbaix diagram does not necessarily indicate that it will be present in the system, nor that other products cannot be formed in the short-term, but it does indicate which substances will be stable in the long term under the conditions specified.

Most soils range between pH 4 and pH 9 (Knight, 1990, p. 37). The dotted lines marked *a* and *b* on the diagram indicate the upper and lower limits for the stability of water. Below line *a* water may be reduced to hydrogen, while above line *b* water may be oxidized to oxygen. Therefore, in effect, the area of the Poubaix diagram that is relevant to buried metal objects is bounded by the upper and lower limits for the stability of water (lines *a* and *b*) and the pH range 4-9. It should be noted that it is possible for the solutions at the bottom of corrosion pits in the metal surface to reach pH values greatly different from those in the prevailing soil water.

Leather

Leather is manufactured from animal skin which has been chemically treated to inhibit degradation. In addition, various colours, finishes and waterproofing treatments may be added. Skin is composed almost entirely of connective tissue fibres which are mainly collagen fibres. These are arranged in long, wavy bundles which vary from 1 - 20 microns in diameter (Reed, 1972, p. 29). In fresh skin the fibrous and cellular elements are surrounded by the ground substance which consists of a sticky viscous fluid, comprising a highly complex aqueous system of mucopolysaccharides and proteins. During the tanning process blood, fat and much of the lubricating ground substance will be lost. A tanning agent will be introduced which reacts with the collagen, preventing bacterial attack which would normally take place in untreated skin. Lubricating fats or oils are usually also used to make the leather pliable. In antiquity the most common method of leather production used vegetable-based tanning agents derived, for example, from oak bark. However, since the nineteenth century a greater range of tanning processes have become available including methods using iron, chromium and aluminium as well as a greater range of synthetic dyes. The result is that modern leathers are more generally resistant to decay in the ground than most 'archaeological' leathers. For example archaeological leather is usually only recovered in desiccated or waterlogged environments. Recent material recovered from the Overton Down Experimental Earthwork (Bell and Fowler, forthcoming) demonstrated that over a period of thirty two years chromium-tanned leather buried under a turf and chalk bank showed very little deterioration compared to adjacently buried samples of vegetable-tanned leather. In addition to the leather itself, many modern items such as shoes will contain elements of metal, cloth and synthetic materials.

Wood

The main structural materials of wood cell walls are cellulose, hemicellulose and lignin. In favourable environments wood will be totally decomposed by a combination of bacteria, fungi and wood-boring insects. Generally, however, in aerated damp soils the action of fungi and bacteria will transform wood into a soft, damp rotten material prior to further degradation and incorporation into the soil as amorphous organic matter (Hudson 1972, pp. 9-16). The speed and nature of wood decay will depend on the species as well as the age and the part of the tree from which it derived. In general, soft woods such as pine will decay at a much faster rate than hardwoods such as oak or beech (Cartwright and Findlay, 1958; Stamm, 1971). In aerated soils all the cell wall components are vulnerable to microbial attack, although in conditions with reduced oxygen levels the aerobic fungi cannot operate, leaving the anaerobic bacteria as the main vectors of decay. The latter cannot attack lignin, so in waterlogged deposits wood may be preserved as a soft, decayed material composed mainly of a lignin skeleton held up by water, organic debris and silt (Grattan, 1987). It is wood in this condition that has been recovered from a number of archaeological sites (Coles, 1984; Coles and Coles, 1989; Taylor, 1992).

Textiles

The discussion of the degradation of textile materials in the soil is complicated by the range of different fibres and fibre blends that are used in modern textiles (Textile Institute, 1970). In the past, a greater range of plant and animal fibres may have been used, for example goat hair, but owing to the absence of synthetic polymers such as nylon and polyester, the range liable to be recovered from an archaeological site is much more limited (Walton, 1989; Barber, 1990). While in soil burial there is differential degradation of a number of organic materials, for example between soft wood and hardwood, animal bone from different parts of the skeleton, and between different species, the effect is much more pronounced with textiles. For example, the condition which will promote the preservation of a cellulosic based textile material such as cotton may not be favourable to the proteinic fibres of wool (Jakes and Sibley 1983; 1984). It is also important to note that the nature of certain dyes and finishes, as well as rot-proofing treatments, will affect the degree of microbial attack on textile materials. Because of the problems with modern synthetics, data from archaeological textiles are likely to be rarely used in forensic contexts. There have been studies related to the deterioration of scene of crime materials in Florida (Morse,1983), although these should be viewed with caution as the trends reported can only be related to the specific fabrics used (including their dyes) in the specific range of burial conditions applicable. Nine different burial locations were used, with cloth samples being recovered at time intervals between one and sixty months. The cloth tested included, rayon, cotton, triacetate, cotton/polyester, nylon, silk and wool.

An important source of data on organic materials that have decayed in the burial environment can be derived from the corrosion products of metal artefacts. In certain substances, metals such as iron and copper alloys will preserve organic materials such as wood, leather and textiles in their corrosion (Janaway and Scott, 1989). The preservation of textiles, or of other organic materials, in association with metal artefacts, is dependent on two decay rates: the rate of degradation of the organic material and the rate of release, transport and deposition of metal ions onto or into that material. If the former rate is faster then the organic material will not be preserved in the corrosion. With copper alloys the metal ions act as localized biocidic agents preventing microbial action, while with iron, a cast of corrosion products is formed around the organic structure which may then decay away leaving a negative cast replica of any microstructure (Janaway, 1987; 1989). Although examination of structures in corrosion products has largely been confined to archaeological materials, the application of the cleaning methods of the archaeological conservator can also yield suitable information in a forensic context. For example, it has been demonstrated that cellulosic textile materials, which normally decay very rapidly in acid soils (such as upland moorland), can decay completely in a matter of months except when preserved by corrosion products (Janaway, 1987, pp. 142-146; 1989). The author has found that corroded metalwork recovered during forensic enquiries can be successfully investigated by applying the methods of cleaning, micro-excavation and microscopy used with archaeological metalwork.
In a recent case a heavily corroded watch, recovered from a body, was cleaned of corrosion products to enable its type to be identified; at the same time the process recovered evidence of associated decayed textile materials.

References

Amy, R., Bahatnagar, R. Damkjar, E. & Beattie, O. (1986), The last Franklin expedition: report of a postmortem examination of a crew member, *Canadian Medical Association J.* 135: 39-52.

Andreasen, C. Gullv, H. C., Hansen J. P., Lyberth, J. and Tauber, H. (1991), The find, in J. P. Hansen, J. Meldgaard & J. Nordqvist,(eds), *The Greenland Mummies*, London: 37-52.

Bahn, P. G. & Everett, K. (1993), Iceman in the cold light of day, *Nature*, 362, 4 March: 11-12.

Barber, E. J. W. (1990), *Prehistoric Textiles*, Princeton.

Barkova, L. L., (1978), The frozen tombs of Altai, in *Frozen Tombs: the Culture and Art of the Ancient Tribes of Siberia*, London: 23.

Bass, W. M. (1984), Time interval since death, in T. A. Rathbun & J. E. Buikstra, (eds), *Human Indentification: Case Studies in Forensic Anthropology*, Springfield, Illinois:136-147.

Beattie, O. B., Damkjar, E., Kowal, W. & Amy, R. (1985), Anatomy of an arctic autopsy, *Medical Post* 20 (23): 1-2.

Beattie, O. & Geiger, J. (1987), *Frozen in Time: The Fate of the Franklin Expedition*, London.

Beeley, J. G. & Lunt, D. A. (1980), The nature of the biochemical changes in softened dentine from archaeological sites, *J. Arch Sci.* 7: 371-377.

Bell, M. & Fowler, P. J. (forthcoming). *The Experimental Earthwork, Overton Down, Wiltshire 1960-1992*. Council for British Archaeology Research Report.

Bergmann, W. (1963), Geochemistry of lipids, in I. A. Berger (ed), *Organic Geochemistry*, Oxford: 503-42.

Bethell, P.H. (1989), Chemical analysis of shadow burials, in C. A. Roberts, F. Lee & J. Bintliff, (eds), *Burial Archaeology: Current Research, Methods and Developments*, British Archaeological Reports (British Series) 211: 205-214.

Bethell, P. H. (1991), Inorganic analysis of organic residues at Sutton Hoo, in P. Budd, B. Chapman, C. Jackson, R. C. Janaway, & B. Ottaway, (eds), *Archaeological sciences 1989: Proceedings of a Conference on the Application of Scientific Techniques to Archaeology*, Bradford, September 1989,Oxford: 316-318.

Bethell, P. H. & Carver, M. O. H. (1987), Detection and enhancement of decayed inhumations at Sutton Hoo, in A. Boddington, A. N. Garland & R. C. Janaway, (eds), *Death, Decay and Reconstruction: Approaches to archaeology and forensic science*, Manchester: 10-21.

Biek, L. (1969), Soil silhouettes in, D. Brothwell & E. S. Higgs, (eds), *Science and Archaeology*, London (second edition): 118-123.

Bird, J. B. (1975),*The Copper Man: A Prehistoric Miner and His Tools from Northern Chile*, Dumbarton Oaks Conference on Pre-Colombian Metallurgy of South America, Washington D.C.

Boddington, A., Garland, A. N. & Janaway, R. C. (eds), (1987), *Death, Decay and Reconstruction: Approaches to Archaeology and Forensic Science*, Manchester.

Brothwell, D. (1986), *The Bog Man and the Archaeology of People*, London.

Burges, A. (1967), The soil system, in A. Burges & Raw, F. (eds),

Soil Biology, London: 1-14.

Cartwright, K. St.G. & Findlay, W. P. K. (1958), *Decay of timber and its preservation*, London (second edition).

Carver, M. O. H. (1992), The Anglo-Saxon cemetery at Sutton Hoo: an interim report, in M. O. H. Carver, (ed), *The Age of Sutton Hoo*, Woodbridge: 343-372.

Clark, F. E. (1967), Bacteria in soil, in, A. Burges & F. Raw (eds), *Soil Biology*, London: 15-49.

Clark, S. G & Longhurst, E. E. (1961), The corrosion of metals by acid vapours from wood, *J. of Applied Chemistry* 11: 435-443.

Coles, J. (1984), *The Archaeology of Wetlands*, Edinburgh.

Coles, B. and Coles, J. (1989), *People of the Wetlands: Bogs, Bodies and Lake Dwellers*, London.

Cotton, G. E., Aufderheide, A. C. & Goldschmidt, V. G. (1987), Preservation of human tissue immersed for five years in fresh water of known temperature, *J. Forensic Sci*, 32 (4): 1125-30.

Courty, M. A., Goldberg, P. & Macphail, R. (1989), *Soils and Micromorphology in Archaeology*, Cambridge.

Cronyn, J. M. (1990), *The Elements of Archaeological Conservation*, London.

Dekin, A. A. (1987), Sealed in time: ice entombs an Eskimo family for five centuries, *National Geographic*,171 (6): 824-36.

den Dooren De Jong, L. E., (1961), On the formation of adipocere from fats, contribution to the microbiology of systems containing two liquid fats, *Antonie von Leeuwenhoek J. Microbiology and Serology*, 27: 337-61.

Duncan, S. J. & Ganiaris, H. (1987), Some sulphide corrosion products on copper alloys and lead alloys from London waterfront sites, in J. Black, (ed), *Recent Advances in the Conservation and Analysis of Artefacts*, Jubilee Conservation Conference Papers, Summer Schools Press, University of London, Institute of Archaeology: 109-118.

Dzierzykray-Rogalski, T. (1986), Natural mummification in Egypt, in David, A. R. ed. *Science in Egyptology*, Manchester: 101-112.

Egg, M., Goedecker-Ciolek, R., Waateringe, W. G-van, & Spindler, K. (1993), *Die Gletschemumie von Ende der Steinzeit aus den Otztaler Alpen*, Jahrbuch des Romisch-Germanischen Zentralmuseums 39, Mainz.

El-Najjar, M.Y. & Mulinksi, T. M. J. (1980), Mummies and mummification

practices in the southwestern and southern United States, in Cockburn, A. and

Cockburn, E. eds., *Mummies, Disease and Ancient Cultures*, Cambridge: 103-17.

Erzinclioglu, Y. Z. (1983), The application of entomology to forensic medicine, *Med Sci Law*, 23 (1):57-63.

Evans, W. E. D. (1963), *The Chemistry of Death* , American Lecture Series, Springfield, Illinois.

Evans, J. G. (1978), *An Introduction to Environmental Archaeology*, London.

Evershed, R. P. (1992), Chemical investigation of a bog body adipocere, *Archaeometry* 34 (2): 253-65.

Fitzpatrick, E. A. (1980), *Soils: their Formation, Classification and Distribution*, London.

Garland, A. N., Denton, J., Chandler, N. P. & Freemont, A. J. (1987), Anatomical, radiological and histological investiga-tions of Worsley Man, *Acta Anatomica*, 130: 35

Garland, A. N. & Janaway, R. C. (1989), The taphonomy of inhu-mation burials, in C. AΩΩ

Garlick, J. D. (1969), Buried bone: the experimental approach in the study of nitrogen content and blood group activity, in D. R. Brothwell & E. Higgs (eds), *Science in Archaeology*, London: 503-512.

Garner, R. C. (1986), Experimental mummification of rats, in A. R. David, (ed), *Science in Egyptology*, Manchester: 11-12.

Glob, P. V. (1969), *The Bog People*, London.

Glob, P. V. (1983), *The Mound People*, London.

Glover, J. M. (1990), The conservation of medieval and later shrouds from burials in north west England, in S. A. O'Connor & M. Brooks, (eds),

Archaeological Textiles, United Kingdom Institute for Conservation Occasional Paper No.10: 49-58.

Goffer, Z. (1980), *Archaeological Chemistry: a Source Book on the Application of Chemistry to Archaeology*, New York.

Grattan, D. W. (1987), Waterlogged wood, in C. Pearson, (ed), *Conservation of Marine Archaeological Objects*, London: 55-121.

Grattan, D. W. & McCawley, J.C. (1978), The potential of Canadian winter climate for the freeze-drying of degraded waterlogged wood: Part I, *Studies in Conservation*, 23 (4): 157-167.

Grattan, D. W., McCawley, J. C. & Cook, C. (1980), The potential of Canadian winter climate for the freeze-drying of degraded waterlogged wood: Part II, *Studies in Conservation*, 25 (3): 118-136.

Gresham, G. A. (1973), *A Colour Atlas of Forensic Pathology*, London.

Gulaçar, F. O., Susini, A. & Klohn, M. (1990), Preservation and postmortem transformations of lipids in samples from a 4000-year-old Nubian mummy, *J. Arch. Sci.*, 17: 691-705.

Guthrie, R. D. (1990), *Frozen Fauna of the Mammoth Steppe*, Chicago, Illinois

Hackett, C. J. (1981), Microscopical focal destruction (tunnels) in exhumed human bones, *Med. Sci. Law*, 21: 243-265.

Hall, R. (1984), *The Viking Dig; The Excavations at York*, London.

Hansen, J. P., Meldgaard, J. & Nordqvist, J. (eds), (1991). *The Greenland Mummies*, London.

Hedges, R. E. M. (1987), Potential information from archaeological bone, its recovery and preservation, in K. Starling & D. Watkinson, (eds), *Archaeological Bone, Antler and Ivory*, United Kingdom Institute for Conservation Occasional Paper No. 5: 22-23.

Henderson, J. (1987), Factors determining the preservation of human remains, in A. Boddington, A. N. Garland & R. C. Janaway, (eds), *Death, Decay and Reconstruction: Approaches to Archaeology and Forensic Science.* Manchester: 43-55.

Hillson, S. (1986), *Teeth*, Cambridge.

Hopfel, P., Platzer, W. & Spindler, K. (1992), Der Mann im Eis. Band 1 *Bericht uber das Internationale Symposium 1992*, Vol 1, Innsbruck.

Hudson, H. E. (1972), *Fungal Saprophytism*, Studies in Biology No. 32, London.

Jakes, K. A. & Sibley L. R. (1983), Survival of cellulosic fibres in the archaeological context, *Science and Archaeology*, 25: 31-38.

Jakes, K. A. & Sibley L. R. (1984), Survival of protein fibres in the archaeological context, *Science and Archaeology*, 26: 17-27.

James, T. G. H. (1979), *An Introduction to Ancient Egypt*, London.

Janaway, R. C. (1987), The preservation of organic materials in association with metal artefacts deposited in inhumation graves, in A. Boddington, A. N. Garland, & R. C. Janaway, (eds), *Death, Decay and Reconstruction: Approaches to Archaeology and Forensic Science*, Manchester: 127-148.

Janaway, R. C. (1989), Corrosion preserved textile evidence: mechanism, bias and interpretation, in R. C. Janaway & B. Scott, (eds), *Evidence Preserved in Corrosion Products: New Fields in Artefact Studies*, United Kingdom Institute for Conservation Occasional Papers No. 8, London: 127-148.

Janaway, R. C. (1993), The textiles, in J. Reeve & M. Adams, (eds), *The Spitalfields Project; Volume 1 - The Archaeology*, CBA Research Report no. 85, London: 93-119.

Janaway, R. C. & Scott, B. (eds), (1989), *Evidence Preserved in Corrosion Products: New Fields in Artefact Studies*, United Kingdom Institute for Conservation, Occassional Papers No. 8, London.

Janssen, W. (1984), *Forensic Histopathology*, Berlin.

Jarvis, K. S. (1983), *Excavations in Christchurch 1969-1980*, Dorset Natural History and Archaeological Society, Monograph No.5, Dorchester.

Johansson, L. U. (1987), Bone and related materials, in H. W. M. Hedges, (ed), *In Situ Archaeological Conservation,* Getty Conservation Institute and Instituto Nacional de Antropologia y Historia de Mexico: 132-137.

Jones, M. U. (1975), Mucking: the Anglo-Saxon cemeteries, *Current Arch.* 5 (3): 73-80.

Keh, B. (1985), Scope and applications of forensic entomology, *Ann. Rev. Entomol.*, 30: 137-154.

Knight, B. (1990), A review of the corrosion of iron from terrestrial sites and the problem of post excavation corrosion, *The Conservator*, 14: 37-43.

Lehner, P. & Julen, A. (1991), A man's bones with 16th-century weapons and coins in a glacier near Zermatt, Switzerland, *Antiquity*, 65: 269-73.

Limbrey, S. (1975), *Soil Science and Archaeology*, London.

Litten, J. (1991), *The English Way of Death: The Common Funeral since 1450*, London.

Lobdell, J. E. & Dekin, A. A. (1984), The Frozen Family from the Utqiagvik site, Barrow, Alaska. *Arctic Anthropology*, 21 (1): 1-154.

MacGregor, A. (1982), *Anglo-Scandinavian finds from Lloyds Bank, Pavement, and other sites,* London.

Mant, A. K. (1950), A Study in Exhumation Data, Unpublished M.D. Thesis, University of London.

Mant, A. K. (1953), Recent work on postmortem changes and timing death, in K. Simpson, (ed), *Modern Trends in Forensic Medicine*, London: 147-162.

Mant, A. K. (1957), Adipocere - a review, *J. Forensic Medicine*, 4: 18-35.

Mant, A. K. (ed), (1984), *Taylor's Principles and Practice of Medical Jurisprudence*, (13th edition), London.

Mant, A. K. (1987). Knowledge acquired from post-war exhumations, in A. Boddington, A. N. Garland, & R. C. Janaway, (eds), *Death, Decay and Reconstruction: Approaches to Archaeology and Forensic Science*, Manchester: 65-78.

Mellen, P. F., Lowry, M. A. & Micozzi, M. S. (1993), Experimental observations on adipocere formation, *J. Forensic Sci.*, 38 (1):91-93.

Molleson, T. & Cox, M. (1993), *The Spitalfields Project; Volume 2 - The Anthropology*, CBA Research Report No. 86, London.

Morrison, I. (1985), *Landscape with Lake Dwellings*, Edinburgh.

Morse, D. (1983), Appendix A, in D. Morse, J. Duncan & J. Stoutamire, (eds), *Handbook of Forensic Archaeology* and Anthropology, Tallahassee, Florida.

Morse, D., Duncan, J. & Stoutamire, J. (eds), (1983), *Handbook of Forensic*

Archaeology and Anthropology, Tallahassee, Florida.

Nuorteva, P. (1977), Sarcosaprophagous insects as forensic indicators, in C. G. Tedeschi, W. G. Eckert & L. G. Tedeschi, (eds), *Forensic medicine: a Study in Trauma and Environmental Hazards*, Vol II, Philadelphia: 1072-1095.

O'Connor, T. P. (1987), On the structure, chemistry and decay of bone, antler and ivory, in K. Starling, K. & D. Watkinson, (eds), *Archaeological Bone, Ivory and Antler*, United Kingdom Institute of Comservation, Occasional Paper No. 5: 6-8.

Painter, T. J. (1991a), Preservation in peat, *Chemistry and Industry*, 17 June 1991: 421-424.

Painter, T. J. (1991b), Lindow Man, Tollund Man and other peat-bog bodies: the preservative and antimicrobial action of spagnan, a reactive glycuronoglycan

with tanning and sequestering properties, *Carbohydrate Polymers*, 15: 123-142.

Patel, F. (1994), Artifact in forensic medicine -postmortem rodent activity, *J. Forensic Sci.*, 39 (1): 257-260.

Polson, C. J., Gee, D. J. & Knight, B. (1985), *The Essentials of Forensic Medicine*, (fourth edition), London.

Pourbaix, M. (1977), Electrochemical corrosion and reduction, in B. F Brown,

H. C. Burnett, W. T. Chase, M. Goodway, J. Kruger & M. Pourbaix, (eds), *Corrosion and Metal Artefacts: A Dialogue between Conservators, Archaeologists and Corrosion Scientists*, NBS Special Publication 479, Washington D. C.: 1-16.

Powlesland, D. (1986), Excavations at Heslerton, North Yorkshire, 1978-82, *Arch. J.*, 143: 53-173.

Price, T. D., Blitz, J., Burton, J. & Ezzo, J. A. (1992), Diagenesis in prehistoric bone: problems and solutions, *J. Arch. Sci.*, 19 (5): 513-530.

Rathje, W. L., Hughes, W. W., Wilson, D. C., Tani, M. K., Archer, G. H., Hunt, R. G. & Jones, T. W. (1992), The archaeology of contemporary landfills, *Amer. Antiquity*, 57 (3): 437-447.

Reed, R. (1972), *Ancient Skins, Parchments and Leather*, London.

Reeve, J. & Adams, M. (eds), (1993), *The Spitalfields Project; Volume 1 - The Archaeology*, CBA Research Report No. 85, London.

Rodwell, W. and Rodwell, K. (1982), St. Peter's Church, Barton-on-Humber: excavation and structural study, 1978-81, *Antiquaries J.*, 62 (2): 283-315.

Rottlander, R. C. A. (1976), Variation in the chemical composition

of bone as an indicator of climatic change, *J. Arch. Sci.*, 3:83-88.

Rudenko, S. I. (1970), *Frozen Tombs in Siberia. The Pazyryk Burials of Iron Age Horsemen*, London.

Russell, E. J. (1950), *Soil Conditions and Plant Growth*, (eighth edition), London.

Sandison, A. T. (1986). Human mummification technique in ancient Egypt, in A. R. David, (ed), *Science in Egyptology*, Manchester: 1-8.

Seidler, H., Bernhard, W., Teschler-Nicola, M., Platzer, W. Nedden, D. zur, Henn, R., Oberhauser, A. & Sjovold, T. (1992), Some anthropological aspects of the prehistoric Tyrolean ice man, *Science*, Vol 258, 16 October 1992: 455-457.

Spindler, K. (1994), *The Man in the Ice*, London.

Stamm, A. J. (1971), Wood deterioration and its preservation, in G. Thompson, (ed), *Conservation of Stone and Wooden Objects* (Preprints of New York Conference), June 1970, London: 1-12.

Stead, I. M., Bourke, J. B. and Brothwell, D. (1986), *Lindow Man: The Body in the Bog*, London.

Takatori, T. and Yamaoka, A. (1977a), The mechanism of adipocere formation I. Identification and chemical proper-ties of hydroxy fatty acids in adipocere, *Forensic Sci. Int.*, 9: 63-73.

Takatori, T. and Yamaoka, A. (1977b), The mechanism of adipocere formation II. Separation and identification of oxo fatty acids in adipocere, *Forensic Sci. Int.*, 10: 117-25.

Tapp, E. and O'Sullivan, D. (1982), St. Bees Man: the autopsy, *Proc. Paleopath. Assn.*, 4th European Meeting, Middelberg: 178-82.

Taylor, M. (1992), Flag Fen: the wood, *Antiquity*, 66: 476-498.

Textile Institute (1970), *Identification of Textile Materials*, Manchester (sixth edition).

Turner, R. L. (1972), Important factors in soil burial test applied to rotproofed textiles, in A. H. Walters & E. A. Huek-van-der Plas,(eds), *The Biodeterioration of Materials*, Vol 2, Essex: 218-226.

Turner, R. C. (1986), Discovery and Excavation of the Lindow Bodies, in I. M. Stead, J. B. Bourke & D. Brothwell, (eds), *Lindow Man: The Body in the Bog*, London: 10-13.

Von Endt, D. W. & Ortner, D. J. (1984), Experimental effects of bone size on bone diagenesis, *J. Arch. Sci.*, 11: 247-253.

Waldron, T. (1987), The relative survival of the human skeleton: implications for palaeopathology, in A. Boddington, A. N. Garland & R. C. Janaway, (ed), *Death, Decay and Reconstruction: Approaches to Archaeology and Forensic Science*, Manchester: 55-64.

Walker, N. I., Harmon, B. V., Gobe, G. C. & Kerr, J. F. R. (1988),

Patterns of cell death, *Methods and Achievements in Experimental Pathology*, 13: 18-54.

Walton, P. (1989), *Textiles, Cordage and Raw Fibre from 16-22 Coppergate*, London.

Warren, C. P. (1976), Plants as decomposition vectors of skeletal human remains, *Proc. Indiana Acad. Sci.*, 85: 65 (abstract).

Wedl, C. (1864), Ueber einen Zahnbein und Knochen keinenden, Pilz. Sber. Akad. Wiss Wein, Vol 1 (1), 50: 171-93

(Translation in the Library of the Institute of Orthopaedics, London).

Wells, C. (1967), Pseudopathology, in D. Brothwell & A. Sandison, (eds), *Diseases in Antiquity*, Springfield, Illinois:5-19.

White, R. E. (1979), *Introduction to the Principles and Practice of Soil Science*, London.

Chapter five

Locating buried remains

J. R. Hunter
with contributions by A. L. Martin

Advice for the detection of buried human remains has occupied a small but important part of the forensic anthropology literature in the United States. Many papers serve as introductions to more detailed anthropological topics (for example, Krogman and Iscan, 1986) while others are more complete (for example, Morse, Duncan and Stoutamire, 1983; Killam, 1990), the latter being the most comprehensive and providing a detailed discussion of individual methods, including parapsychology, and a useful series of appendices and checklists for use in practical situations. Practitioners of parapsychological techniques (for example, in divining and spiritualism) frequently offer their services in the search for buried remains, but their methods are not discussed further here. A succinct guide to the location of buried remains (France *et al.*, 1992) has since been based on the controlled burial and systematic detection of pig carcasses in Colorado - an experiment necessitated by a need for local law enforcement officials to locate and recover a number of reportedly buried victims. The total United States literature is based on a case load in excess of anything so far experienced in the United Kingdom and the derived methodology therefore warrants attention, despite potential differences between the American and British landscapes. These include soil and climatic differences as well as distinctions in plant and animal species which may facilitate or inhibit detection. Nevertheless, given the importance and long-standing of the existing literature, it seems appropriate to retain at least part of the developed terminologies, notably those selected from Duncan (1983, p. 4) and France *et al.* (1992, 1457f):

1. **Search area** - all of the terrain to be searched
2. **Burial site** - the grave itself together with the area of localized disturbance

3. **Grave** - the pit used for burial
4. **Search** indicators - specific abnormalities used for detection of the burial site
5. **Climax vegetation** - the plant community that will reproduce itself on a given site; the end point of succession

Work in the United States has also shown the need to differentiate between the landscape adjacent to, and at a distance from the grave in order to identify more clearly influences that directly impose on the burial; the terms 'near-field' and 'far-field' respectively have been coined for this purpose (France *et al.*, 1992) but are not used in Britain. The United States literature also tends to use the word 'dirt' as a simplified definition for most soils. In burial contexts this usually requires redefinition into 'upcast' (i.e. earth which has been taken out of the ground during the digging of the grave) and 'backfill' (i.e. earth which is returned into the grave as part of the burial process).

Although much of the United States literature pertains to human remains which are *buried*, there is now significant attention paid to those which lie on the *surface*, particularly with regard to scatter and decomposition (for example, Haglund, Reay and Swindler 1989; Haglund, Reichert and Reay 1990). The discovery of both buried and surface types is aided by remote prospection (which is why regular updating of detection methods becomes increasingly necessary), but the basic techniques are otherwise those of fieldcraft - the understanding of geology, landscape and environment -which lies at the core of the archaeologist's experience and training.

Surface changes

The anomalous nature of any burial within the surrounding subsoils is likely to have implications for the vegetation growing within or around the area of disturbance. These can materialise even when the burial has become old and consolidated or when the upper components have become established in a subsequent ground surface caused, for example, by ploughing. In the shorter term, the vegetational change may be species-distinctive (see below), but over the longer term the effect will be for the surrounding plant communities to absorb the disturbed area and produce a climax vegetation which is ostensibly indistinguishable. However, the disturbance created by the burial will have a number of implications for growth factors (see also Killam, 1990, pp. 131-37). It may, for example, provide a better growth medium for some of the surrounding species than for others and hence provide a concentration. This might be most visible during the summer flowering period or in early spring when vegetational differences are more easily observed; its occurrence depends on several variables including soil matrix, depth of disturbance and climate. The Colorado experiment was able to identify a number of these factors in the development of a climax vegetation (based on the vegetational analysis of eight burials), notably the occurrence of distinctive species during the process of recolonisation (France *et al.*, 1992, p. 1452). Knowledge of the local flora in a search area was considered to be a major and desirable advantage.

However, a more frequent consequence of burial can be in the *degree* of vegetational growth. A burial committed into a good growing matrix such as soil will, by the nature of the backfilling, provide a looser, more water retentive medium for vegetational growth than the surrounding undisturbed ground (fig 5.1). As decomposition of the victim takes place this growth environment can become more enriched by decay products (see chapter 4), one result being the increased stature of the affected vegetation in relation to the surrounding vegetation, or a differential in the time of ripening and flowering. The converse can also occur. In circumstances where the burial context provides a poorer growth medium than that of the surrounding soils, for example if a victim is covered with stones or wrapped in polythene, the relatively low moisture retention and nutrient supply may produce a surface vegetation which is lower and weaker, and, again with different ripening and flowering times than elsewhere (fig 5.1). These relative differences in height are not always apparent at ground level, but can

become increasingly obvious from a higher position, ideally from the air or even from the vantage point of a tree; this is because the differential is best identified by its shadow. The technique is at its optimum with a low sun, either in the morning or in the evening; it is equally dependent on the growing season, which has the advantage of being an annual event providing that the vegetation regime is unchanged. Burials of many years' standing will continue to offer this potential even though the growing season, and the critical points within it, are relatively brief.

Shadow marks may also be used as search indicators in more closed environments, or where

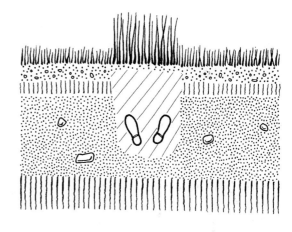

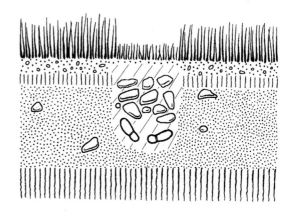

Fig 5.1 Extremes of burial type showing exaggerated vegetational implications. Top: burial providing wet nutritious growth environment. Bottom: burial providing moisture restricted growth environment.

vegetational factors are less useful. Digging a grave, or for that matter any type of pit or hole in the ground, always tends to generate more upcast than can be easily used for backfilling; this problem is compounded by the presence of a victim who will absorb a considerable volume of grave space. Compression of the surface, for example by stamping or beating with a spade, may partly rectify this but in any event will bring about a significant vegetational anomaly. This anomaly may also be evident in the area immediately around the grave where upcast earth has been temporarily deposited during the digging process and where leverage for digging has caused compression marks. Duncan has shown that there is likely to be a direct and logical relationship between the depth of a grave and the area of associated surface disturbance (1983, fig 1.1). The deeper a grave is dug, the greater the amount of upcast and hence the wider the surface area affected. The examples on which these observations were based also suggested that burials in remote or mountainous areas tended to be relatively shallow (0.6 - 1.0m) while those detected near inhabited places tended to be approximately twice as deep, subject to soil conditions. In many parts of the United Kingdom this latter depth might be difficult to achieve in view of the geology. In an experiment conducted to train English police dogs, control cadavers (pigs) were buried at various depths between 0.15 - 0.5m from top of animal to ground surface. This was argued to be 'generally at a significantly greater depth, buried with better visual concealment than is likely to arise with a typical murder victim' (Walker and Payne, 1973, p. 45).

Another solution to concealment is to spread or dump the excess earth; this should be immediately apparent in the short term but probably impossible to identify in the longer term. In the backfilling of any pit or grave there is a tendency to create a low mound to cater for the excess backfill - a usual practice by sextons in official graveyards. In time, this mound will subside through a combination of consolidation of the grave-fill and collapse of the skeletal structure within, and probably develop as a shallow depression, depending particularly on climate and moisture content. Depth is also a factor; a deeper grave is likely to become more compacted and therefore exhibit a greater depression than a relatively shallow grave. As compaction occurs it may produce tell-tale cracking or splitting at the ground surface where the backfill meets the undisturbed surface (Duncan, 1983, p. 9). It is virtually impossible for a perpetrator to calculate how much backfilling or consoli-

dation will be required to prevent this happening, particularly in circumstances which are both hurried and clandestine. The main unknown is the degree of skeletal collapse of the buried victim; in some cases the collapse of the abdominal cavity may even produce a secondary depression, particularly in shallow burials (*ibid*, p. 11). In most circumstances, therefore, the outcome tends to be the creation of both shorter and longer term detectable topographical anomalies. In instances of relatively shallow graves where the victim is buried in little more than topsoil a low mound is almost inevitable and other forms of concealment such as branches may have to be used. Consolidation of the fill is likely and the mound might also be detectable for longer. Shallow burials, however, are more prone to animal disturbance (see 5.4 below).

Low mounds or depressions will also both lend themselves to shadow detection, but only if the light angle is low. The method was used successfully in the Colorado experiment (France *et al.*, 1992, p. 1451). In reality, burial sites tend to occur in more closed environments (woods, field edges, gardens etc.) for which aerial photography is largely unsuited. However, in pronounced form, they may be detected by systematic ground search, particularly if other factors such as vegetational or soil differences are involved. Another option, and one which has been successfully applied to archaeological work (Carver, 1984), is to simulate a low sun by using a powerful light source at night. This has the advantage of being controllable (unlike the sun) for both height and position and is particularly useful for searching small or closed areas.

Shadows can also be effectively simulated by lightly blown snow. This has the effect of highlighting even the most minor of ground contours and has long been used as a valuable, if unpredictable method of defining archaeological sites. Snow conditions tend to coincide with seasons of low vegetational growth and the combination can therefore be particularly effective.

Drought conditions may also emphasise the nature of burial deposition. In conditions of extreme dryness, vegetation overlying non-moisture-retentive features will parch in advance of the surrounding area. In archaeological terms this is particularly useful for detecting buried walls which become identifiable as linear brown parch marks against an otherwise non-parched landscape. The same principle can apply to buried human remains in instances where the burial is compacted with stones under the soil or wrapped in a manner which will inhibit any moisture retention in the surface soils. These instances are, however, extreme and are only likely to occur when the depth of topsoil above the stones or wrapping is thin.

At various times of the year another method might also be usefully applied. Other than in superficial, and presumably hurried burials where the body lies largely within the topsoil component (the 'shallow grave' of most newspaper reports), the grave will inevitably cut through lower strata of the soil profile. Some of these are likely to be purely natural geology depending on the region concerned, with the lowest cut natural stratum being, for example, of clay, chalk or soft stone. Other than in the unlikely event of these different strata being separated out in the upcast during the digging of a grave, the upcast will contain a mixture of the various layers. In circumstances where cultivation occurs, notably at field edges, the surface discolouration of the grave which results from this will be readily visible. Annual ploughing may continue to enhance this discolouration, although with some spreading. According to United States evidence the survival of a burial depression, which forms readily within the light soils of cultivated land, is unlikely to outlast a single season's harvest (Duncan, 1983, p. 13). By contrast, the survival of the soil discolouration or mixing is longer lasting and therefore of some importance. The same effect may also be evident in non-cultivated areas where the presence of surface stones, clay patches etc. may immediately point to ground disturbance and have a long-term effect on the vegetational density in the area of the grave.

5.2 Aerial reconnaissance

In more open locations aerial photography has traditionally been the vehicle for detecting archaeological sites and landscapes on the basis of shadow, crop and soil marks brought about by the factors discussed above. Depending on land-use these can survive for centuries or even millennia, but their detection is dependent on a number of seasonal, climatic and timing factors. Photographs taken of the same part of the landscape will reveal different features according to the angle of photograph, time of day and angle of the sun. This is well illustrated in a comparison of two photographs of the same site taken during different months of the year (plate 5.1). Many larger archaeological sites are plotted out from a number of photographs taken over several years as different climatic circumstances offer different opportunities for detection. Plans of the whole site can be compiled by using rectification techniques (see

Plate 5.1. Comparative aerial photographs of Glenlochar Roman fort, Scotland. One, taken with inappropriate crop and ground conditions, fails to shows any traces of the monument. British Crown Copyright/MOD.

below). The principles, however, offer some merit in forensic contexts where the main advantage is the longevity of the evidence, even although the location is likely to be less exposed and the features somewhat smaller. The general uses of aerial photography in archaeology have been well discussed (for example, Wilson, 1982; Riley, 1987; Bewley, 1993) and can be directly applicable to forensic contexts (Killam, 1990, ch. 8).

These elements of seasonality are hardly ideal in instances of very recent crime when a suspect is held in custody but not yet charged, the maximum period currently being thirty six hours in England without a court appearance (this can be extended to seventy two hours with the court's consent). However, in the experience of the author, the majority of requests for advice normally occur some months or even years after the crime when the suspect has been through the commital stage or is serving a sentence without the victim having yet come to light. In most of these instances extensive searching using a task force or equivalent has already taken place and the time factor is less critical. In any event, the process of search requires careful planning and implementation and 'cannot generally be considered as an emergency' (Duncan, 1983, p. 6). In some cases, even the recovery of a body may not be necessary for legal reasons (*corpus delicti*) but is normally desirable for family or for emotional purposes and to allow the case to be finally closed. The increased use of DNA evidence in homicide cases is almost certain to increase the number of instances in which recovery, although always preferable, is no longer essential. At the present time, however, convictions without a body are extremely rare.

For forensic work the use of aerial reconnaissance may not necessarily entail the use of cameras other than for infra-red or thermal purposes, although if a potential scene is located it is often helpful to take record photographs. This recognises the fact that the same light and growth conditions may not be replicated on a future occasion and, perhaps more importantly, it may be difficult to find the exact place on the ground without known reference points. An anomaly visible from the air is not necessarily visible from the ground. Most photographs taken for reconnaissance purposes are taken obliquely (i.e. at an angle from the ground) by a hand-held camera from either a helicopter or a small high-wing aircraft. Archaeological features tend to be either large or in groups and therefore altitude of reconnaissance must be flexible; but in forensic contexts, altitude (i.e. scale of coverage) may need to be both lower and consistent for the detection of individual burials. There is merit too, in circular coverage of a search area in order to maximise shadows and angles of visibility (Killam, 1990, fig. 8.6). In most archaeological cases features identified obliquely from the air will need to be transcribed into a mapping format so that they can be defined accurately on the ground surface. In regions where landmarks are dense (for example, walls, buildings, tracks, trees etc.) this poses no real problem. However, where the anomalies are identified in moorland or even general rural environments there may only be a

few landmarks such as fence lines, and these may lie at a distance from the burial site. In such circumstances it is essential that the photographer checks the general location with a suitable scale of Ordnance Survey (OS) map and identifies reference points which are common to both map and visible landscape. Whenever photographs are taken they must include as many reference points as possible together with the probable site. Oblique photographs, particular those taken with a 35mm lens, can produce considerable distortion. This can only be rectified in transcription if a *minimum* of three reference points, common to both photograph and map, can be found. Computerised rectification, now a common feature of archaeological field research, will transcribe the feature(s) on the basis of three sets of grid co-ordinates and enable them to be plotted accurately against OS reference points to a selected scale. This subsequently allows the feature to be located by simple measurement on the ground.

Archive photographs may sometimes be of use for detection purposes. Most county SMRs (sites and monuments records), usually kept in planning departments, possess catalogued reference collections of aerial photographs. These have been collected from a variety of sources and include both oblique and vertical photographs. Unlike obliques which are usually 'one-off' photographs, verticals are systematic and usually taken in overlapping runs across huge tracts of landscape, both urban and rural. Vertical photographs are normally the product of specially designed and mounted cameras which take a series of continuous exposures in parallel runs across a defined sector of landscape. The overlap between each exposure is usually approximately 60% both in sequence and between adjacent runs. Best results are obtained by viewing adjacent, overlapping pairs stereoscopically, but basic information can also be obtained from the study of single photographs. Both verticals and obliques are normally archived according to the OS grid. Potential users would be well advised to familiarize themselves with the OS system before commencing an archive search.

The post-war history of vertical photographs shows diverse interests: land use; census; planning or military use; or by commission for local authority record purposes. Much of the country has been covered in this way by commercial photographic companies (for example, Aerofilms Ltd, Meridian etc.) since the 1960s. Additionally there are good post-war military runs which provide earlier cover. Although sometimes of limited archaeological use in view of their higher altitude and lack of seasonal sensitivity, they have the advantage of showing a changing landscape over time and can be crucial in the not uncommon searches for human remains of ten or twenty years ago. They also illustrate the nature of the landscape and land-use at various times; this information can be used to narrow down or to expand search areas accordingly. For example, what may be an ideal burial location in 1994 from the point of view of cover, foliage and general dereliction may have been quite different even five years earlier.

One such example occurred with the disappearance of a young woman in London in 1987. A report of her abduction, murder and burial in an area of Worcestershire was subsequently given to a newspaper in 1991. The area in question consisted of some thirty two hectares of abandoned military barracks and land which, by then, was wholly overgrown, thick with brambles, rubble and dumped material and virtually impossible to search in any detail without vast expenditure. However, a potential purchaser of the property had taken the trouble to photograph the area from the air in 1988 for redevelopment and publicity purposes. This photograph, taken shortly after the woman went missing, clearly showed the landscape and vegetation at the time, and, more pertinently, showed that within the thirty two hectares only a small number of places could have provided an appropriate burial location. Investigation on the ground narrowed this down to one place according to criteria of suitable soil and geology (see 5.3 below). No remains were detected and the newspaper report was discounted in a highly cost-effective way. This aerial photograph was essentially a 'one-off' which was not formally archived. However, similar types of information can be gained more systematically; vertical runs in particular provide some of the few controls available to assess landscape change.

Although aerial photographic cover is to some extent in regional collections, there are a number of resources which may be worth pursuing, both nationally and locally. The Royal Commission on the Historic Monuments of England holds the major national archive in its Swindon office - the National Library of Aerial Photographs (NLAP) - although this includes a substantial duplication of regional material. The Royal Commission for Wales and Scotland likewise hold national collections in Aberystwyth and Edinburgh respectively. Another important source is the Cambridge University Committee for Aerial Photography (CUCAP) collection; this dates from 1949 and has extensive British coverage, including current survey work using vertical runs. As an idea of

size, the English Commission now holds in excess of half a million prints, the CUCAP slightly fewer. Other sources may include local archaeological societies or professional archaeological units, although in most cases these may duplicate the resources of the SMRs. The existence of the National Association of Aerial Photographic Libraries (NAPLIB) now provides a directory of sources and libraries where aerial photographs can be found. Although this might be useful for an exhaustive search, the first port-of-call, and the most efficient method of evaluating local resources lies within the county-based archive, from where any necessary further direction can be given.

Multispectral and thermal imaging

Recent developments in aerial reconnaissance in archaeology have involved both multispectral image survey and thermal survey of ground surfaces, although neither have been widely used. The former has a more established track-record in the fabric study of standing buildings, particularly churches (Brooke, 1986) but can be extended to emphasize soil and vegetational disturbances. Based on the ability of materials to show varying absorption and reflectance characteristics according to different bands of the electromagnetic spectrum, the method has the potential to enhance the visible contrast between, for example, adjacent surface deposits (Brooke, 1989, p. 6f.). Moisture retention which can characterise burial fills also has the potential to be highlighted in the same manner and is an area which merits further development.

The potential of thermal analysis of soil for the location of archaeological features was first recognized over twenty years ago and evolved from techniques of geological survey. In theory, thermal detection can exploit two phenomena; firstly, the differential in heat-loss at the ground surface between soil in which there are buried features and the surrounding undisturbed soil (Scollar et al., 1990, p. 591 f.); and secondly, the heat emitted from the biological decay processes of a buried victim or animal. Despite the limitations of operational cost, complex interpretation and the need for specific climatic conditions, aerial thermography has also been used to reveal buried archaeological structures. A photo-conducting detector mounted on the underside of an aircraft was successfully used to survey several Neolithic enclosures near Seine et Marne in France (Perisset and Tabbagh, 1981).

The prospective utility of aerial thermal detection in police operations had already been tried (Dickinson, 1977). A Royal New Zealand Air Force helicopter fitted with an infra-red camera was used to search for the body of a missing hitch-hiker in the winter of 1975. It was suspected that the body was hidden or buried in scrub country and, as the air temperature was low, the rate of decay would be slow and a temperature differential would exist between the body and its surroundings. An infra-red search was initiated at an altitude of 60m using a camera which scanned the target area for invisible infra-red energy. With the temperature range set at 2° C, anomalies were produced from targets less than 2° C above the normal background; detected features included dead sheep, half-buried sacking and plastic sheeting, moss, decaying vegetation and disturbed soil.

The victim's body was not located during the search and the survey was compromised by wet and foggy weather conditions which blocked the ground-to-air infra-red signal. Later experiments using a buried possum demonstrated that after seventeen days the buried remains were still detected as a "hot-spot" on the ground surface, registering 1-3° C higher than the surrounding soil. Controlled experimentation with buried human remains has since shown that heat generated by decomposition can lie well within the detectable limits of infrared thermal scanning; even at a depth of four feet the temperature of the cadaver was recorded as having a differential of more than 3.4° C, and at a depth of one foot from the surface the differential was more than 10° C (Rodriguez and Bass, 1985). Although it is difficult for the technique to discriminate between disturbed soil, decaying organic matter and graves it offers an important, if expensive, forensic role which Killam places first in his list of recommended techniques (1990, p. 236).

5.3 Landscape and geological factors

Most county planning departments will undoubtedly possess geological data in the form of geological maps held for planning or resources purposes; in addition, local public libraries will usually hold more detailed information regarding drift and bedrock geology produced regionally by the British Geological Survey. In many senses this type of resource, used in conjunction with standard Ordnance Survey maps, should be the first port-of-call; they can instantly provide added definition to a search area by showing those areas in which burial is feasible according to soil profile, land-use and underlying geology.

One recent case in Kent involved the searching of several hectares of landscape (both open and wooded) for buried remains on the basis of information received.

The local geological maps showed the bedrock to be of chalk and this transpired to be virtually impenetrable using a spade. Additionally, the County Council's recent aerial photographic coverage showed that the topsoil was so thin that in places the chalk could be seen underneath. Any burial would have been so shallow as to have been immediately apparent and therefore unlikely; as a result, considerable tracts of landscape could be given a low search priority.

Given that most enquiries are undertaken on limited budgets the ability to define areas of relative priority is becoming increasingly essential. In such circumstances the archaeologist has a specific contribution to make within the overall equation. Other parts of the team will provide input regarding, for example, areas of necessary cover for burial, known movements of the suspect, likely time available for burial, psychological or profiling factors, likelihood of the victim being carried/dragged to the grave, soil type on suspect's tyres etc. All these will narrow down the number of areas to be searched. Killam has also introduced other useful factors into the equation on the basis of United States 'dump-site analysis', namely the propensity for disposals to fall into one of two broad categories: those bodies which are dumped quickly within a locality little known or unknown to the perpetrator; and those where the landscape is well-known to the perpetrator, either through ownership, holidays or visits (1990, pp. 15f.). Figures are also cited to suggest that some 90% of victims are recovered downhill (i.e. for facilitation of carrying) from vehicular access points or trackways. Another factor to consider may be the importance of landmarks or sighting lines, particularly in remoter rural parts, which may have been important if the perpetrator had cause to revisit the site. This may have been necessary if, for example, the grave had been prepared earlier so that the burial could be effected very quickly. Psychological reasons may also necessitate revisiting. The archaeologist's contribution will probably cover burial feasibility, preferable detection methods and recovery potential.

The primary input is likely to be one of landscape appraisal - an assessment of what is or what is not likely to have been possible and the subsequent delimitation of target areas. The process is short-term, assuming availability of appropriate maps and photographs, and may involve some trial excavation in order to ascertain soil character, chemistry and depth. The result of the assessment will be to make recommendations regarding more detailed investigation of the target areas, for example the use of specific geophysical survey techniques, augering,

Plate 5.2 Investigations on Saddleworth Moor (late 1980s). The strategy involved lateral excavation across the target areas.

aerial photography or excavation. This is a longer-term exercise which will have cost and manpower implications and may need a considerable degree of planning. One of the most important factors at this stage of the enquiry is that of recording which areas have been targeted, which have been subjected to trial excavation or where work has already been carried out as part of the enquiry. In investigations of long duration (of which the Moors Murders is a classic example) personnel regularly change and although files are kept they rarely detail, other than in memory, precise locations of activity. A formal and updated plan of the area will prevent police (or archaeological) activity being misconstrued or confusing later investigation. Even over the shorter term it is important to know what has been done and where, if only to prevent duplication of effort.

In another recent case the area search was prioritized according to this general approach, two very different areas being earmarked. One, a relatively open but easily accessible headland contained a shallow soil profile over a hard bedrock, but the soil depth increased considerably around sporadic clumps of trees and bushes owing to the formation of leaf-mould. There was also increased depth within a series of natural gullies which sloped away from the line of public access. In the other location which lay in an area of sand dunes, much of the area could be dismissed on the basis of the height of the water table. This was ascertained by experiment.

Sand occurs in many forms and poses a number of particular problems during search (Duncan 1983, pp. 14f.).Other parts were then targeted according to different input factors.

Similar factors were eventually used in the Moors Murders re-investigation of 1986-1988 where the recovery of victim Pauline Reade on Saddleworth Moor was based on the systematic excavation of those parts of the moor where potential depth was thought to have best facilitated burial (gullies, edges etc), with the general area outlined by one of the perpetrators. In scenarios such as this progress is inevitably slow, and is necessarily systematic. The methodology is geared to the location of the body in the first instance; recovery and the maximization of the available evidence becomes secondary. Under ideal circumstances the two are of equal priority; this may indeed be the case where a small area of land (for example, a garden) is concerned, but in a wider environment the methodology often has to reflect costing factors. It is interesting to see that the conclusions drawn by those conducting the Colorado experiment were of a similar philosophy: they recognized that it was 'important to follow a progression from completely non-destructive to increasingly invasive procedures such that evidence collection is optimized while evidence disturbance is minimised' (France *et al.*, 1992, p. 1454). The same line is followed by Killam (1990, Appendix 7) who considers intrusive methods to be a last resort.

In the case of the 1986-1988 Saddleworth Moor investigations, the approach was by systematic line spading; this effectively produced a slowly moving section across the target areas (plate 5.2). Lateral excavation of this type is immensely preferable to vertical excavation in those circumstances where there are no surface characteristics to focus attention. The advantages are twofold: firstly, that the target area can be seen to be exhaustively covered *in toto* and need not be returned to (vertical excavation, unless gridded, invariably leaves gaps); and secondly, that neither the body nor any stratigraphy to which it belongs are likely to be seriously damaged by being approached from the side (both are particularly vulnerable to an unguarded vertical approach), providing that the body is subsequently excavated vertically according to stratigraphic laws (see chapter 3).

In an ideal situation a search team will possess reasonable field skills with respect to vegetation, soil and topographic change. In such circumstances detailed gridding can be employed to maximize available staff resources. As any landscape archaeologist will confirm, the best detection results derive not from walking in one direction, but by taking a series of different perspectives of any given area. This allows the landscape to be viewed with the light source in different places and from different angles. Walking uphill, for example, can often reveal vegetational changes that are not apparent when walking downhill. Gridding systems, particularly those which require searchers to 'interlock' by searching the same defined area of ground from different directions (for example, Killam, 1990, fig. 3.4) are devised for that very reason.

However, in most situations search teams are inexperienced in landscape change and are directed towards the detection of obvious features, usually recently disturbed earth or surface remains such as clothing. The danger here is that unless the appropriate archaeological parameters are brought into the formula at this primary stage of the investigation certain types of evidence may be inadvertently destroyed. These include minor vegetational changes, the occurrence of loose soil, subtle undulation, compactness factors and even dragging marks. The undoubted skills of a task force or similar group in surface recovery unfortunately tend to be accompanied by a pronounced trampling factor on the ground surface. This problem can be reduced if a rapid scanning of the ground surface to identify areas of possible disturbance can be undertaken ahead of the line search. Only minimal planning is required and the process can be assisted by the setting up of a system-

atic grid system however crude; the methods can then be viewed as being properly complementary rather than in conflict. One such example took place in the Greater Manchester area where dismembered human remains were noticed by a member of the public in scrubland at the top of a motorway embankment. The pieces had been bagged and buried but had been unearthed by foxes and left on the surface adjacent to the place of burial. The burial spots were excavated and a further part of the body was eventually recovered, but the majority of the body, notably the torso, was missing. Line searching was undertaken but this was preceded by systematic scanning for the detection of minor surface changes, any 'hot spots' being marked for more detailed attention.

In some circumstances when visual location procedures have drawn a blank, a programme of invasive probing can be implemented. Success can depend on a number of factors: these include the interval since burial, the nature of the subsoils and any wrapping of the remains. Probing can be conducted using a metal rod typically 2cm in diameter and around 1m in length with a T-shaped handle at the top and a sharp point at the base. Its function is to determine the nature of, or differences between sub-surface materials. The operator pushes the probe into the ground at regular intervals within the search grid, noting the ease or difficulty of penetration. Regular soil will require more pressure to penetrate a given distance than disturbed or foreign soil associated with a grave. Thus 'soft spots' can be identified, marked and explored in more detail by probing to determine the nature of the anomaly. As soft areas can also be created by decaying vegetation, animal burrows or water coursing, the size and shape of the detected area needs to be established by more dense probing in an attempt to 'chase' any grave wall. Duncan suggests that the initial approach should be by personnel probing in a line approximately 4 - 5m apart taking close-spaced readings diagonally within a roped grid until all the ground has been covered (1983, p. 17). More closely-set systems based on finding avalanche victims are illustrated by Killam (1990, pp. 46f.). However, as all these methods depend on relative and subjective resistance to the probe, there is an argument to suggest that, time-permitting, it should be carried out by a single person, ideally at 1m intervals across a roped grid. This provides a slower but arguably more consistent approach to detection. An adult grave will typically be in the order of two metres long and one metre in width and is theoretically detectable by probing at 1m intervals. A greater level of confidence lies at 0.75m intervals but this involves more complex gridding unless the search area is relatively small.

More sophisticated, although more arduous to operate, are probing methods which include sampling of the sub-soils, usually by taking a narrow core of the sub-strata with an auger or similar device. This is a method commonly used by soil scientists to investigate soil properties or formation processes and can be adapted to test for chemical indicators of decay such as localised alkali levels by using litmus paper (Imaizumi, 1974) or even the spread of fats within the soils (see chapter 4) although this requires more detailed analysis. At a more routine level, the use of coring also enables the user to observe any visual changes in the sub-surface stratigraphy that might result from burial. There is the additional factor of smell which will be self-evident from cores taken at or immediately around a decomposing body. The main disadvantages are of relative slowness and of the physical effort required, depending on the soil profile, of boring and lifting the core.

There are, however, inherent dangers in using probes of any type: soil differences may be too slight for the operator to notice any anomaly; and more importantly, when dealing with human remains the probe may strike the body and damage clothes, soft tissue or even bone thus leaving marks that could be confused with stab wounds or evidence of other trauma. Although sometimes seen as a last resort, it has the great advantage of being (or potentially being according to operation) totally systematic and comprehensive. Providing that searched areas are logged accurately, it can be continued as and when time and manpower permit according to need.

The use of specially trained dogs is another factor to be considered, preferably within the overall framework of the investigation and within the same spatial gridding. Like all techniques they are best used systematically and within defined target areas. 'Body dogs' as they tend to be known are normally trained to dig and/or scratch on detection and, in the process of achieving the appropriate standards of detection, will have experienced a range of control graves in which the depth, age and mass of buried material (usually pigs) has been deliberately varied. Dog training is a highly specialized field and only takes place within a small number of police forces in the United Kingdom (Lancashire, West Yorkshire, Strathclyde and the Metropolitan). The potential of body dogs was realized in the Near East after the Arab/Israeli war when they were successfully used to recover bodies of soldiers some of whom were buried to a depth of approximately 1m. Their operational value is considerable (Greene, 1982; Killam, 1990, pp. 37-41) but is to some extent climate-dependent: research has shown the dogs tend to be less effective at extremes of temperature but prefer moist soil conditions (Walker and Payne, 1973, pp. 41; France *et al.*, 1992, p. 1453). Wind strength and direction is also significant and may determine the direction from which the search commences.

5.4 Surface scatters

In some instances the victim is left unburied, usually in a location which is well screened and remote, and effectively becomes a surface artefact. This situation evokes a more explicit search routine than with buried individuals, although analysis of the remains, to some extent, rests more heavily on spatial recording. Case studies have shown that human remains which are left exposed or partially exposed are subject not only to natural processes of decomposition but also to a catalytic process of degeneration brought about by scavengers, typically rats, foxes and carrion birds, although insects may also be included. These have the effect of moving and scattering the skeletal components, even those still bearing soft tissue. The literature on these animal effects has been well compiled by Haglund, Reay and Swindler (1989) who found it possible to denote the degree of scavenging, for practical purposes, on a scale of between 0 and 4. The lowest score (0) represents the 'removal of soft tissue with no disarticulation', and the highest (4) the 'total disarticulation and scattering, with only cranium and assorted skeletal elements of fragments recovered' (*ibid*, p. 589).

In the United States where scatter patterning has been studied most, there has been seen to be a useful correlation between time since death and extent of disarticulation (for example, Haglund, Reay and Swindler, 1989, table 1; Morse, 1983, table 6.1). Data from individual cases show scatter beginning to occur from about five weeks since death. In another case, after seven months most bones lay within an area of 3-4m although some had been moved further and, in another example, after a year the area of distribution had increased significantly and a number of bones were never recovered. Degree of scatter is best seen as a working guide rather than an absolute measure of elapsed time. Other dependent factors include clothing (or wrapping), climate (see Galloway *et al.*, 1989), season, population density and environment, not to mention species and size of predators. An analagous study has been made of scavenged animal material in Africa (for example, Blumenschine, 1986) although there the predators are likely to be larger than those encountered in Northern Europe (for example, lions) and the prediction of specific bone groups being scavenged in single units less applicable.

Consideration has also been given to the manner in which bone damage can occur by various types of predator - a field which has long been the domain of archaeologists in identifying gnawing species or in attempting to distinguish between animal gnawing and human workmanship. Correlation of this literature together with laboratory experimentation has since provided useful sets of control data (for example, Morse, 1983, pp. 148-153; Krogman and Iscan, 1986, table 2.3). Although these contain some species not present in Britain (notably alligators, bears and vultures), many species are relevant, most commonly dogs (coyotes), rodents and crows. The general scatter trends are presumably also similar.

A further degree of difficulty may be encountered in the longer term when the individual skeletal components become self-buried, that is when they become wholly or partially covered by topsoil as a result of rainfall and general settling. This may be particularly prevalent in restricted or closed areas where movement of the remains is minimized, and where the decomposition products of the body itself may combine with natural organic matter such as leaves, twigs and droppings to produce added burial material (see also chapter 3). The greatest problems, however, occur where partial remains of the same individual become recovered in different locations and at different times (Haglund and Reay, 1993).

A number of scenes have provided useful case experiences for detection of surface remains, notably the so-called Green River murders in King County, Washington, United Staes, where (to date) some 40 individuals have been recovered with a range of interval between death and recovery of between 2 days and 6 years (Haglund, Reichert and Reay, 1990). The majority of the remains were recovered from the ground surface remains and involved the recording of over 8,500 different items of evidence (see also chapter 5). Detection methods utilized dogs and search personnel, including experts in entomology, botany, geology and anthropology (the distinction between animal bone and human bone, particularly if small and splintered, is often hazardous; see also chapter 6), and showed the importance of recognizing local indicators of decomposition. These included the yellowing of vegetation caused by ammonia, human hair within birds' nests and pronounced insect activity on the ground surface. On detection of the remains the search area was divided into a series of perimeters with the innermost zone requiring the most detailed search, the outer zones being searched in progressively less detail. On recovery of further remains or concentrations of remains, the zoning focus could be shifted accordingly.

5.5 Geophysical prospection

Geophysical prospection methods are now widely used in archaeology, particularly in evaluation studies (Gaffney, Gater and Ovenden, 1991; Gaffney and Gater, 1993) and have a long history of applied technical development (for example, Scollar *et al.*, 1990). Their forensic application in the United States has also been considered and a variety of methods discussed and ranked (Killam, 1990, ch 5), although only those which are most widely available and proven in the United Kingdom are discussed here. Notable advances for both archaeological and forensic purposes can be seen in automated data logging systems and in computerized data processing and graphics. It is now possible, for example, to survey a relatively large area, say one hectare (100 x 100m), and produce a preliminary interpretation from contour plots in a single day. According to method, geophysical survey can be carried out with as few as two people and is a highly cost-effective and unobtrusive approach, but it is one best suited to small rather than large search zones and has a valuable role to play as a detailed detection method in target areas.

All reputable geophysical surveyors operate according to a grid system, usually 20 x 20m with readings being taken at 1m intervals for archaeological survey. The Colorado experiment considered a range of between 1 and 3m (France *et al.*, 1992, p. 1450). In forensic contexts, and if the search area can be narrowed down, this interval is probably best reduced to 0.5m. It is important that the geophysics grid can be related to any other search grid being used, especially as some topographical features may also elicit or indirectly cause a geophysical response. Although archaeologists tend to use geophysical methods in open landscapes, they can also be used in more closed areas and in most climates, including snow, subject to the limitations of individual methods (see below). Theoretically, extensive or overgrown vegetation provides no difficulty other than in impeding the progress of the operator; however, in practice it creates difficulty in gridding and in maintaining, where necessary, a consistent instrumental height.

In archaeological contexts, geophysical methods are particularly useful in that they are able to detect not only features which have been cut through the existing ground surface, but also features which have become well-sealed or buried by later layers, notably plough soil, depending on size and depth. In fact this type of buried anomaly constitutes the majority of all archaeological features recorded by geophysical means -typically buried ditches, walls, hearths and pits. Few of these are evident visually and can only be relocated on the ground surface for excavation purposes if precise gridding control is maintained. The characteristics of graves which have implications for vegetational change also have implications for detection by geophysical means, particularly if the intervention of the burial has penetrated through the local bedrock. The two most commonly used methods of detection, soil resistance and magnetometry (fluxgate gradiometry), both rely on the difference (i.e. the *anomaly*) between the relevant characteristics of the grave fill and those of the surrounding undisturbed soil.

A number of other methods have also been developed, although not all are sufficiently advanced or appropriate for forensic purposes. Seismic refraction surveys are better suited to geological and large archaeological features (Goulty *et al.*, 1990). Induced polarization measurements proved largely unsuccessful in defining test graves during Home Office experiments (Lynam, 1970, pp. 199ff), and the detection of soil gas (methane), although useful, is limited to the period of decomposition and warmer temperatures. The Colorado experiment additionally noted the method to be labour intensive (France *et al.*, 1992, p. 1453). Thermal probing, as yet unrefined for forensic purposes, shows some potential in the development of a thermistor probe for recording the temperature of the ground 0.2m below the surface (Noel and Bellerby, 1990). Geologists and archaeologists at Sheffield University have since collaborated on a series of test experiments to assess the viability of thermal probing for geoarchaeological prospection (Bellerby, Noel and Branigan, 1990). Results from trials at the Roman town of Verulamium indicated that the probe could detect thermophysical anomalies such as walls at depths of up to 1.3m, although the detection of individual graves is currently beyond technical capability.

Soil resistance and magnetometry

In the case of resistance survey, an electrical current is

Plate 5.3 Archaeological resistance survey in progress with readings taken at one metre intervals across a grid. Copyright Jean Williamson/Mick Sharp.

passed between two metal probes pushed into the ground surface. Measurement is taken of the resistance to the current as it passes beneath the surface between the probes (plate 5.3) As water is a good conductor, moist subsoils tend to give a lower resistance response than stonier or drier subsoils. Detection depends on the grave fill being of different structural character to that of the ground through which it has been cut, for example being more porous in the case of a burial back-filled with the original soil (fig. 5.1), or less moisture-retentive in the case of a burial back-filled with stones or wrapped in polythene. By varying the probe separation it becomes possible to discriminate between the size and depth of individual anomalies. A useful example of relevant resistance survey is that of All Hallows Hill, South Yorkshire (plate 5.4), a field showing no obvious topographical features but which, according to the resistance data, contained the foundations of a documented church together with associated burials in the immediate environment. The display method used is based on contours indicating the various degrees along the scale of resistance measurements recorded. The identification of burials is especially valid from a forensic point of view.

Magnetometer survey detects localized changes to the earth's magnetic field. Again these can be detected systematically, in this case by taking readings across a grid. Magnetometers are expensive and sensitive devices which will also detect adjacent ferrous matter including that surrounding the operator, for example zips, buttons, fastenings, boot nails and the contents

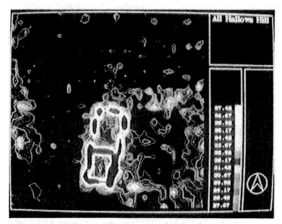

Plate 5.5 Resistance survey at All Hallows Hill, South Yorkshire. The processed data show not only the location of the buried structure, but also the surrounding graves. By courtesy of Dr A Aspinall.

of pockets. They operate by being carried at a constant height above the ground and will thus detect any changes of a ferrous character within the soil or subsoil, the response depending on a number of factors. A grave cut into iron-bearing soils will therefore emerge as a specific anomaly in that the grave fill (including the victim) will contain a comparatively lower density of 'magnetic particles'. If the burial is cut through iron-rich bedrock, for example igneous granite, this effect is likely to be even more emphazised. The reverse type of anomaly can occur if, for example, the grave is partially infilled with iron-bearing stone which is in greater density than that of the surrounding soils. In other words the method, like that of resistance measurement, detects change within otherwise undisturbed soils. Furthermore, the Colorado experiment suggested that even the backfilling of the grave was sufficient to bring about a reorientation of the magnetic particles in the soil and thus produce a detectable anomaly (France *et al.*, 1992, p. 1452). Magnetometry is used extensively in archaeological fieldwork and has also been shown to be able to distinguish between different types of anomaly, for example between burials, settlements and cultivated soils (Clark, 1990).

The disadvantages, however, are that both soil resistance and magnetometry methods are unsuited to land which has been subjected to considerable disturbance; in the case of magnetometry even small amounts of surface iron rubbish will create awkward background interference, and the proximity of metal fences or (fired) brick walls may severely limit the area of usefulness. In the case of resistance survey the pres-

ence of moisture-drawing features such as trees may cause problems; severe frost, ice and even extensive localized radio transmission may negate its usefulness altogether. Both technologies are the product of considerable experience and development and, as no two sites and conditions are likely to be the same, their operational advantages and limitations should be clearly explored before work commences. The Colorado experiment confirmed the need to test the response and appropriate settings of individual methods in order to establish optimum background levels in the vicinity before any work was undertaken (France *et al.*, 1992, p. 1452). Either method might be used to locate a small number of appropriate-sized anomalies each of which can be tested or excavated individually (chapter 3).

Both methods are also useful in providing *negative* evidence in an enquiry, for example a witness account or other information can be disproved by survey. In 1992 a police force in the East Midlands received a report that a body had been buried many years ago in a domestic garden. The garden was subsequently gridded out and a resistance survey undertaken using two different probe arrays. On-site computer processing identified a small number of anomalies of which one was sufficiently large to merit further investigation. This was carefully excavated in three places and found to be a natural drainage depression. The case was subsequently closed. In another enquiry, this time in the north of England, a victim was thought to have been buried within a large area of wasteland. This had been searched intensively without success; the geology was also inappropriate for burial. Nearby, however, was a cultivated field which had been under plough at the time of the murder and which would have provided a better opportunity for burial. Resistance survey was carried out along a 5m strip at the edge of the field against the hedgeline. No anomalies were recorded and that particular area was subsequently deleted from the search area. In both instances the only other search alternative was to dig systematically from one end to the other - an alternative which would have been more costly, more labour-intensive and considerably less efficient.

Metal detectors

Resistance and magnetometry (and their variants) effectively detect the *disturbance* brought about by the intrusion of burial, not the body itself. In fact during early Home Office trials a soil resistance survey was able to register test graves but was unable to differentiate between graves containing pig cadavers and control graves refilled with soil (Lynam, 1970, pp. 199ff). Simple hand-held electromagnetic induction machines (metal detectors), which have a limited role in this type of work, may be able to detect metal associated with the body itself, for example jewellery, a watch, coins or other small items. They will also detect metal objects not associated with a body or a grave, particularly on the surface, and will elicit no response from a burial in which metal objects are either too small, too deep or not present at all. Detection will be improved by the size of object and proximity to surface. Metal detectors have a more useful role to play once a grave has been identified, both in the systematic search for surface clues and in the gradual excavation and recovery of the victim (Stoutamire, 1983).

Ground penetrating radar

Significant developments in geophysical prospection for both archaeological and forensic purposes occurred in ground penetrating radar (GPR) during the 1970s (Alongi, 1973; Bevan and Kenyon, 1979). In this method detection is accomplished by transmitting a short pulse of electromagnetic energy into the ground and receiving a characteristic reflection from the target object or layer. The target is registered as an anomaly because it represents a discontinuity in electrical properties of the soil. Information is presented to the operator as a visible image of changing pulse shapes. Although not originally devised for archaeological prospection GPR has found applications in certain fields such as the location of subterranean chambers at the ancient city of Sepphoris, Israel (Batey, 1987), the investigation of burial vaults in Japan (Imai, Sakayama and Kanemori, 1987), the surveying of the complex urban sites in York (Stove and Addyman, 1989) and the attempt to locate graves at a sixteenth century Basque whaling station in Labrador (Vaughan, 1986). Recent archaeological work at Gloucester was able to identify intact skulls as target points using GPR, but only with hindsight and reprocessing and it was admitted that it was not possible to locate skeletons as such below 1.3m. The practicalities and problems of GPR (including cost implications) for archaeological purposes have since been reviewed (Atkin and Milligan, 1992), but assessment of the technique for the location of buried human remains by British police forces has not been made public. The apparent and well-publicised success of GPR leading to the recovery of nine buried victims in Cromwell Street, Gloucester may change this situation.

Early research in the United States produced encouraging results under test conditions, for example in the detection of a freshly buried dog in both 0.3m of heavy clay and 0.6m of dry sand with the assertion of being able to show such details as the chest cavity, head, rear legs and grave cut (Alongi, 1973). These early tests were the subject of later criticism, but the method was successfully used to locate a twin grave (burial dates 1920 and 1939) at Marble Falls, Texas. The advantages of the system are claimed to be its speed of operation, non-invasive nature and straightforward interpretation, one particular benefit being the 'real time' display of data as the equipment moves across a transect (France *et al.*, 1992, p. 1452).

The method has been successfully used in the United Kingdom notably in locating a hoard of bank notes (around £150,000) buried in a Lincolnshire field. The money had been handed over as the ransom for the safe return of an estate agent, Stephanie Slater, and its recovery in 1992 was in many respects a classic example of landscape search and the pinpointing of a target area. West Yorkshire police, who were conducting the enquiry as part of an earlier murder investigation, used evidence of the suspect's known movements and witness accounts as well as a psychologist's report and both military and archaeological advice regarding feasibility. As a result, the search area was narrowed down to a thin strip of land which appeared to satisfy all the information and advice given. The hoard was likely to have been too small for the burial disturbance to be detectable by either soil resistance or magnetometry and GPR was used. Using systematic transects of the strip the operators (*Oceanfix* of Aberdeen) detected a number of buried phenomena, the hoard eventually being recovered amid much excitement.

References

Alongi, A. V. (1973), A short pulse, high resolution radar for cadaver detection, *Proc. lst Int. Elec. Crime Countermeasure Conference*: 79-97.

Atkin, M. & Milligan, R. (1992), Ground-probing radar in archaeology - practicalities and problems, *The Field Archaeologist*, 16: 288-291.

Batey, R. A. (1987), Subsurface interface radar at Sepphoris, Israel, 1985, *J. Field Archaeology* 14: 1-8.

Bellerby, T. J., Noel, M. & Branigan, K. (1990), A thermal method for archaeological prospection: preliminary investigations, *Archaeometry*, 32 (2): 191-203.

Bevan, B. & Kenyon, J. (1979), Ground probing radar for historical archaeology, *MASCA Newsletter*, University of Pennsylvania, 11: 2-7.

Bewley, R.H. (1993), Aerial photography for archaeology, in J. R. Hunter & I. B. M. Ralston, (eds) *Archaeological Resource Management in the UK: An Introduction*, Stroud: 197-204.

Blumenschine, R. J. (1986), Carcass consumption sequences and the archaeological distinction of scavenging and hunting, *J. Human Evolution*, 15 (8): 639-659.

Brooke, C. J. (1986), Ground-based remote sensing for the archaeological study of churches, in L. A. S. Butler & Morris, R. K. (eds) *The Anglo-Saxon Church*, Council for British Archaeology, Research Report No 60, London: 210-217.

Brooke, C. J. (1989), *Ground-Based Remote Sensing*, Institute of Field Archaeologists Technical Paper No 7, Birmingham.

Carver, M. O. H. (1984), Techniques: throwing light upon the past, *The Field Archaeologist*, 2: 19.

Clark, A. (1990), *Seeing Beneath the Soil: Prospecting Methods in Archaeology*. London.

Dickinson, D. J. (1977), The aerial use of an infra-red camera in a police search for the body of a missing person in New Zealand, *J. Forensic Sci. Soc.*, 16: 205-211.

Duncan, J. (1983), Search techniques, in D. Morse, J. Duncan & Stoutamire, J. (eds) *Handbook of Forensic Archaeology and Anthropology*, Tallahassee: 4-19.

France, D. L., Griffin, T. J., Swanburg, J. G., Lindemann, J. W., Davenport, G. C., Trammell, V., Armbrust, C. T., Kondratieff, B., Nelson, A., Castellano, K.& Hopkins, D. (1992), A multidisciplinary approach to the detection of clandestine graves, *J. Forensic Sci.*, 37 (6): 1435-1750.

Gaffney, C. F. & Gater, J. G. (1993), Practice and method in the application of geophysical techniques in archaeology, in J. R. Hunter & I. B. M. Ralston, (eds) *Archaeological Resource Management in the UK: An Introduction*, Stroud: 205-214.

Gaffney, C. F., Gater, J. G. & Ovenden, S. M. (1991), *The use of Geophysical Techniques in Archaeological Evaluations*, Institute of Field Archaeologists Technical Paper No 9, Birmingham.

Galloway, A., Birkby, W. H., Jones, A. M., Henry, T. E. & Parks, B. O. (1989), Decay rates of human remains in an arid environment, *J. Forensic Sci.*, 34 (3): 607-616.

Goulty, N. R., Gibson, J. P. C., Moore, J. G. & Welfare, H. (1990). Delineation of the vallum at Vindobals, Hadrian's Wall, by a shear-wave seismic refraction survey, *Archaeometry*, 32 (1): 71-82.

Greene, M. A. (1982), Air scent dogs in search and rescue, *Law and Order*, May 1982: 46-50.

Haglund, W. D. and Reay, D. T. (1993), Problems of recovering partial human remains at different times and locations - concerns for death investigators, *J. Forensic Sci.*, 38 (1): 69-80.

Haglund, W. D., Reay, D.T. & Swindler, D.R. (1989), Canid scavenging/disarticulation sequence of human remains in the Pacific Northwest, *J. Forensic Sci.*, 34 (3): 587-606.

Haglund, W. D., Reichert, D. G. and Reay, D. T. (1990), Recovery of decomposed and skeletal human remains in the Green River murder investigation: implications for medical examiner/coroner and police, *Amer. J. Forensic Med. and Pathology*, 11 (1): 35-43.

Imaizumi, M. (1974), Locating buried bodies, *F.B.I. Law Enforcement Bulletin*, 43 (8): 2-5.

Imai, T., Sakayama, T. & Kanemori, T. (1987), Use of ground-probing radar and resistivity surveys for archaeological investigations, *Geophysics*, 52 (2): 137-150.

Killam, E.W. (1990), *The Detection of Human Remains*, Springfield, Illinois.

Krogman, W. M. & Iscan, M. Y. (1986), *The Human Skeleton in Forensic Medicine*, Springfield, Illinois.

Lynam, J. T. (1970), *Techniques of Geophysical Prospection as Applied to Near Surface Structure Determinations*, Unpublished Ph.D thesis, University of Bradford.

Morse, D. (1983), The time of death, in D. Morse, J. Duncan & J. Stoutamire, (eds), *Handbook of Forensic Archaeology and Anthropology*, Tallahassee, Florida: 124-144.

Morse, D., Duncan, J. and Stoutamire, J. (eds), (1983), *Handbook of Forensic Archaeology and Anthropology*, Tallahassee, Florida.

Noel, M. and Bellerby, T. J. (1990), Thermal archaeological surveying: a recording soil temperature probe, *Archaeometry*, 32 (1): 83-90.

Perisset, M. C. and Tabbagh, A. (1981), Interpretation of thermal prospection on bare soils, *Archaeometry*, 23 (2): 169-187.

Riley, D. N. (1987), *Air Photography and Archaeology*, London.

Rodriguez, W.C. and Bass, W. M. (1985), Decomposition of buried bodies and methods that may aid in their location, *J. Forensic Sci.*, 30 (3): 836-852.

Scollar, I., Tabbagh, A., Hesse, A. and Herzog, I. (1990), *Archaeological Geophysics and Remote Sensing*, London.

Stoutamire, J. (1983), Excavation and recovery, in D. Morse, J. Duncan & J. Stoutamire, (eds) *Handbook of Forensic Archaeology and Anthropology*, Tallahassee, Florida: 20-47.

Stove, G.C. & Addyman, P.V. (1989), Ground-probing impulse radar: an experiment in archaeological remote sensing at York, *Antiquity*, 63: 337-342.

Vaughan, C. J. (1986), Ground-penetrating radar surveys used in archaeological investigations, *Geophysics*, 51 (3): 595-604.

Walker, R. W. & Payne, C. D, (1973), The use of trained police dogs for corpse detection, *Police Research Bulletin*, 21: 37-47.

Wilson, D.R. (1982), *Air Photo Interpretation for Archaeologists*, New York.

Chapter six

Forensic anthropology 1: the contribution of biological anthropology to forensic contexts

C. A. Roberts
with contributions on the use of teeth for age at death determination by A. M. Pollard and D. Lucy

6.1 Background

Anthropology is an umbrella term which covers five categories of study: physical (or biological) anthropology, cultural and social anthropology, linguistics and archaeology. Biological anthropology concentrates on human evolution (primatology and palaeoanthropology) and variation (differences between and within populations). Within biological anthropology, forensic anthropology is a specialized sub-discipline which uses the methods developed in biological anthropology in crime scene investigations to identify individuals and establish cause and manner of death. According to Reichs (1992) today in the United States it is a discipline utilized by most law enforcement, coroner and medical examiner systems.

There are currently around forty individuals in the United States and Canada who are practising certificated forensic anthropologists (*ibid.* p.152), having passed a series of examinations in the discipline. It was not until 1972 that a physical (biological) anthropology section of the American Academy of Forensic Sciences was established and, by 1987, of the 2,843 members of the Academy, 3.2% (91) were biological anthropologists (Iscan, 1988, p.204). In 1973 the Forensic Sciences Foundation was formed to set standards for practitioners. With this organisation in place, the American Board of Forensic Anthropology could certify anthropologists as Diplomates. Prior to 1972 biological anthropologists had developed methods over many years in skeletal biology for the analysis of skeletal remains by studying 'known' relatively modern skeletal reference collections such as the Terry Collection, curated in the Department of Anthropology, Smithsonian Institution, Washington DC and the Hamman Todd collection at the Cleveland County Museum, Ohio, both in the United States.

These methods are seen to be invaluable in the identification of skeletonized bodies in a forensic context, although some of the collections on which they have been based have inherent biases. For example, the individuals represented are often from populations of low socio-economic status and older age groups. The effect of these factors on expressions of age, sex, race, stature etc. in the skeleton and the dentition are difficult to measure. Biological anthropologists also use these methods commonly in the analysis of human remains from archaeological sites and are generally comfortable with interpreting skeletal data from an archaeological context with these techniques even though there are a number of inherent problems.

Although the numbers of incidents requiring identification of human remains in a forensic setting are relatively large in the United States compared to the United Kingdom, few forensic anthropologists make a living out of crime scene investigations. Fortunately, from the point of view of training biological anthropologists, the number of skeletons excavated from archaeological sites is larger than from forensic contexts.

In the United Kingdom, there is no equivalent organization which functions to enhance the role of the biological anthropologist in forensic contexts; all human remains from forensic cases are identified by the forensic pathologist. The structure of university departments focuses on archaeology as the umbrella term; biological anthropology sometimes does, and sometimes does not, feature as a sub-discipline. Within that sub-discipline the level of training in biological anthropology is very dependent on the availability of staff and resources. Forensic anthropology is only practiced occasionally by university employees and freelance biological anthropologists when approached by local police forces. Often the request is to distinguish non-human from human bone. However, there is increasing interest from the police for biological anthropologists to become involved in their work in appropriate and relevant scenes of crime. This chapter, together with chapter 7, discusses the nature of the work of the forensic anthropologist in the identification of victims of crime discussing the contrast between North American and British crime scene investigations, and including case studies. The main theme is the similarity between the work a biological anthropologist may undertake on an archaeological cemetery and the work needed for the identification of a crime victim.

Reliable Information?

In the United States the forensic anthropologist seeks to provide information about individuals under examination which may help to identify the person. In most cases the anthropologist deals with the skeleton and its dentition if available; bodies (i.e., those with soft tissue preserved), are usually examined by the forensic pathologist. The biological anthropologist in an archaeological context also seeks to identify individuals in a cemetery when an accurate identification is *desirable*, although rarely possible. In a forensic setting, however, accurate identification is, by necessity, *essential*.

In an archaeological context, data on age, sex, stature, metrical and non-metrical features and pathological abnormalities for each individual are recorded within the limits of the methods available. Beyond these data more rigorous investigation is not necessary because the biological anthropologist is not (in the vast majority of cases) identifying a known or missing individual and therefore has no opportunity to compare features on the skeleton with those in records, for example radiographs. Exceptions exist, however, in relatively later time periods in archaeology. For example, Stirland (1990) confirmed the identity of Sir Thomas Reynes by comparing skeletal with historical data, and in another case two individuals could be excluded in the quest for the identification of a woman known to have been pressed to death in the sixteenth century (Roberts, Manchester and Storey 1992). There has been, in recent years, an increase in the availability of documented skeletal material particularly in the United Kingdom. For example, The Spitalfields Project excavated 968 individuals from the crypt at Christ Church in London (Molleson and Cox, 1993) and of those, 389 had legible coffin plates giving details of name, age and date of death. This presented a unique opportunity to test methods of analysis against known parameters and provided archaeologists with a population for which historical documentation on lifestyle existed. However, for the majority of archaeological contexts this is not the case.

The biological anthropologist, by using the basic data, aims to reconstruct the living population for a specific area and time period, and the cemetery may contain hundreds of skeletons spanning several hundred years. By comparing cemetery populations from different areas and time periods, it is the aim to trace the evolution, variation and change in human populations through time. The data obtained from other forms of evidence (for example settlement patterns or subsistence economy) used in combination with the skeletal data can then be assessed to envisage how social, political and economic factors have shaped this structure. For example, what happens to populations at the transition from hunter-gathering to agriculture (Cohen and Armelagos, 1984) or how may rural or urban environments affect a population's health (Cohen, 1989)?

Biological anthropologists have developed methods of analysis of age, sex, stature and race based on 'modern' populations with associated data on these attributes. Primarily these data were, and are, used in the analysis of past human populations. Many of the methods developed, it is argued, should only be applied to individuals from the same population and period of time and this may be one of the reasons that forensic anthropology in North America developed; large sets of osteological data and methods developed on known North American populations were available to apply to forensic cases. The application of these methods within a forensic context allows them to be further refined. Unfortunately, in Britain, there is relatively little equivalent data available and consequently North American data tend to be applied to European populations. Whilst in an archaeological situation it could be argued that accurate identification of an individual is not of paramount importance, the establishment of the identity of a person who is a victim of crime and the recording of events surrounding the case are the ultimate aim and may lead to the prosecution of a criminal. The report which the forensic anthropologist produces is a legal document which can be presented in the court proceedings; all statements need to be supported by evidence together with the limitations of those methods used (Galloway *et al.*, 1990). Some of the techniques may be subjective and their confidence limits should be outlined. The situation is very different in archaeology where the data from the biological anthropologist is often taken at face value and not questioned. In the United States, credibility for the forensic anthropologist can be gained by certification, which involves rigorous testing of the individual's abilities. The accuracy of the data being applied to human remains in crime scene investigations can only be assessed when the identity of the individual is successfully established. This may be a long drawn-out process where many records of missing persons are checked against the identity of the individual as determined by the forensic anthropologist. It is sometimes the case that the person is never given a true identity either because the forensic anthropologist may have been unable to match the remains with a missing person (perhaps through poor preservation), that the person was never reported missing, or that the methods of identification were not appropriate to the individual concerned.

What information is retrievable?

The range of information potentially retrievable from human remains is extensive but this information is heavily dependent on the condition of the body. In archaeology the completeness of the skeleton is a pre-requisite for examination and accurate reporting within the limits of the methods used. It is not the purpose of this chapter to outline the potential processes which a body undergoes before, during and after burial as this is covered elsewhere (see chapter 4) but a few points will illustrate their relevance. Deposition, burial, excavation and processing of material can all affect the final 'product' (plate 6.1). Acidic soils are particularly prone to accelerate decay of bone in the ground and pathological bones may be more fragile; nor do the bones of subadult individuals tend to survive as well in the ground. In addition, in some archaeological periods infants and children were sometimes buried away from the main cemetery.

Bodies may survive intact, for example the famous North European bog bodies of the Iron Age (Stead, Bourke and Brothwell, 1986); alternatively they may only be represented by a stain in the ground. Duration of burial will also affect survival rate and for archaeology these time periods are lengthy, whilst in forensic contexts human remains may only be buried for a few months or years. The adult skeleton normally has 206 bones. However, because parts of the main skeletal elements remain unfused until certain ages during the individual's growth there are more individual bone elements in subadult skeletons. It is important to retrieve all the bones carefully (for detail on excavation and post-

Plate 6.1 Example of good preservation in an archaeological context. The Anglo-Saxon cemetery at Addingham, West Yorkshire, UK. By courtesy of West Yorkshire Archaeology Service.

excavation treatment of human remains see McKinley and Roberts, 1993). Notable absences from the archaeological skeletal record often include hyoid bones (a bone in the neck area which can be damaged in strangulation or hanging), and small bones of the hands and feet including sesamoid bones. These latter bones can be affected in certain diseases and may be identified on X-rays of the suspected victim. Careless damage of the skeleton during burial and excavation may also produce breaks in bones which may be difficult to distinguish from perimortem injuries and gall, bladder and kidney stones can also be easily missed in the grave.

Most of the time biological anthropologists are dealing with relatively large numbers of individuals compared to the forensic setting where in most cases one individual is being considered. In the latter, it becomes more difficult to identify an individual due to the lack of other comparative material with which to establish unambiguous and distinguishable features, for example in the sexing of an individual.

The forensic anthropologist's remit (Wolf, 1986, p. 4) is to:

1. Identify the individual from their remains
2. Determine the cause and manner of death
3. Document events occurring before, during and following the death of the individual

In many instances the forensic anthropologist may work directly with the forensic pathologist or odontologist when detailed analysis of associated soft tissue and dental remains is needed. In all cases, the anthropologist is part of a multidisciplinary investigatory team which views the case holistically. This is also seen in archaeological contexts where the biological anthropologist represents one member of the team who contributes to the final interpretation of the site, provides relevant data for other members and uses information to expand on the skeletal data. The forensic anthropologist often deals with skeletal and dental remains and establishes whether the remains are human or animal, the number of individuals represented, age at death, sex, racial characteristics, stature, medical and dental history, individual characteristics, for example occupation, and attempts to assess the cause and manner of death. The forensic anthropologist (like the biological anthropologist on archaeological sites) should always be involved from the early stages of the investigation, particularly during the excavation of any human remains discovered. Examining the human remains within their environment of deposition is essential to the interpretation of the data retrieved. For example, the association of artefacts and clothing with the body may help identify the individual and contribute to investigations of cause of death. In the United Kingdom a visit to the crime scene before the body is removed is made by the forensic pathologist and this duty is often included as part of the contract of service (Knight, 1991, p.3; see also chapter 2). The identification of unknown human remains is necessary for the following reasons (*ibid*, p.57):

1. The ethical and humanitarian need to know which individual died especially for the information of surviving relatives.
2. To establish the fact of death in respect of that individual (or individuals) for official, statistical and legal purposes.
3. To record the identification for administrative and

ceremonial purposes in respect of burial or cremation.
4. To discharge legal claims and obligations in relation to, for example, property, estate and debts.
5. To allow legal investigations, inquests and other tribunal...and accident enquiries to proceed with a firm knowledge of the identity of the decedent.
6. To facilitate police enquiries into overtly criminal or suspicious deaths, as the identity of the deceased person is a vital factor in initiating investigations.

(Knight, 1991)

Identification of individuals is, of course, easier if the skeletal remains are associated with soft tissue but this becomes more difficult the closer to skeletonization or the more fragmented the body becomes. The act of burning of remains also affects the material available for study. Whilst before the 1960s few archaeological cremated remains were collected as it was believed that the bone was unidentifiable (McKinley, 1989, p.67), it is now demonstrated that data, for example, regarding age, sex, stature, ritual and technology is now recoverable (plate 6.2). Indeed, recent reports in the literature (Fairgrieve, 1994; Owsley, 1994) have indicated that skills have been developed by forensic anthropologists for the identification of cremated skeletal material. Cremated material is inherently fragile and requires even more care on excavation. Biological anthropologists are experts in dealing with fragmentary skeletal material, distinguishing non-human from human bone, dealing with skeletons (not bodies) and sorting mixed burials.

6.2 Human or non-human?

According to Owsley and Mann (1990, p. 623) 15-25% of the medico-legal cases involving forensic anthropologists represent non-human remains. In the United Kingdom, physical anthropologists are frequently called upon to determine whether bones found by civilians, often dug up in their gardens, are human or not, and for the anthropologist this is not normally a difficult process. In their routine work they deal with skeletonized remains on a daily basis and distinguish between non-human and human bone fragments, the latter often being found in graves on archaeological sites. It is also often the case that archaeologists not trained in the discipline of human osteology sometimes mistake human for non-human bone and *vice versa*. For example, complete dog skele-

Plate 6.2 Cremated bone from an archaeological context.

tons have sometimes been mistaken for human baby skeletons on archaeological sites. A common mistake in the United States is to attribute bear bones to a human origin (*ibid*. 1990). Morphologically, elements of the skeleton can initally appear similar, but the biological anthropologist's expertise in comparative anatomy and in distinguishing human from non-human bone is invaluable and can save much time in a forensic case. Owsley and Mann (1990) also note that a bear's paw was taken to three podiatrists in Maryland, USA, all of whom ruled out the possibility of the foot being human. In Britain, the author was recently asked to give an opinion on a skeletonized body in a sack dumped in a river. There was no doubt that the skeleton was that of a dog but this was a second opinion following that of the forensic pathologist who was uncertain whether the bones were human or not. If the remains are very fragmentary and difficult to identify, features apart from gross morphology may be useful. For example, the outer layer of bone or cortex microstructure is distinctive in human and non-human bone, where the arrangement, size and number of features varies between species (Owsley, Mires and Keith, 1985). However, some species of animal do have similar bone microstructures and disease can affect the histological appearance of bone (Harsanyi, 1993) which can make this method of identification difficult.

Radiography has also been shown to be useful in distinguishing non-human from human long-bone fragments (Chilvarquer *et al.*, 1991). Differences between the spongy or cancellous bone appearance in the midshaft area were noted, as was the demarcation line between cortical and cancellous bone. Thirteen dentists and eleven archaeologists were asked to test the method on twenty radiographs. For both archaeologists

Plate 6.3 Late and post-medieval charnel house deposit, Rothwell parish church, Northamptonshire, UK.

and dentists 80% of the sample was correctly identified. In the case of tooth fragments found at a crime scene, natural disaster or accident, species identification may be necessary and Whittaker and Rawle (1987) describe a method of extracting antigens from the powdered teeth of both rats and humans. Although the method requires further work and will probably be superseded by DNA techniques (see Gaensslen *et al.*, 1992 for recent developments), the research showed that this technique was viable for specimens stored at different temperatures and humidities for between one and six months.

6.3 Minimum number of individuals

Often, physical anthropologists are faced with collections of skeletal remains which are comingled and fragmentary. For example, the Tudor warship Mary Rose which sank off the south coast of England in 1545 (Stirland, 1984) became the grave for dozens of unfortunate sailors and required the osteologist to reconstruct individuals from mixed remains. Plague pits and charnel houses or bone crypts (Roberts, 1984; plate 6.3) in the United Kingdom also provide comingled remains with the problems of analysis that this entails. In addition,

Plate 6.4 Intercutting burials. The Anglo-Saxon cemetery at Addingham, West Yorkshire. By courtesy of West Yorkshire Archaeology Service.

complex urban cemeteries may have more recent graves intercutting older graves often with the consequences that burials become mixed and scattered (plate 6.4). These examples illustrate the expertise which biological anthropologists acquire from the examination of archaeological sites, an experience which is directly relevant to forensic scenes, for example in major disasters where fragmentary or mixed remains of many individuals may be scattered over a large area.

One of the first tasks is to establish the *minimum* number of individuals (MNI) by counting the most commonly occurring bone. Care in not counting two fragments of the same bone twice, for example, is negated by detailed knowledge of skeletal anatomical landmarks. Whole bones do not present a problem, but it is often difficult to establish whether two or more fragments are from the same bone. A simple example will illustrate the MNI calculation: if there are six left femurs and five right femurs there is a minimum number of six people represented. In many cases, however, the forensic anthropologist deals with individual burials. At the forensic scene, establishing the number of individuals represented is crucial to the investigation. Reconstructing individuals from mass comingled deposits may start with the forensic anthropologist separating bones on the basis of age and sex characteristics, colouring of the bones, anatomical landmarks and pathological lesions (for example, two bones of a joint both showing skeletal changes of joint disease or arthritis) which may help allocate the bones to individuals. In an archaeological context knowing the number of individuals will go some way towards reconstructing the population size for that period in that particular geographical area, but this has its limitations.

6.4 Age and sex

Determining the age and sex of human remains is vital in the identification of an individual in a forensic setting. Biological anthropologists have developed methods of ageing and sexing skeletal remains by using skeletal populations of known age, sex and race. Most of these studies have been in the United States and are most appropriate to identification of individuals in a contemporary forensic context in North America. Being based on relatively modern populations, these methods are less appropriate to archaeological material. Work of a similar nature has been more limited on other continents (but see Workshop of European Anthropologists, 1980 for example) and this is perhaps due to lack of availability of appropriate skeletal and dental material. It is therefore inevitable that some of the methods used, especially for ageing adults, are not wholly appropriate for European populations either in a forensic or archaeological sense. For example, applying methods of ageing based on the Terry Collection to a population from the Anglo-Saxon period in England with 1,200 years difference in time emphasises this point. Diet, living conditions, lifestyle etc. will affect how and at what rate the body ages.

Sex determination

In a forensic context the anthropologist is often identifying single individuals whereas in an archaeological setting the numbers are greater. For example, excavation of the Medieval cemetery site of St. Helen-on-the-Walls, Aldwark, York, England (Dawes and Magilton, 1980) revealed over 1,000 individuals. Skeletal features for determining sex, and methods for assessing age at death, may be specific to that population alone and in this event mistakes could be made. For example, large mastoid processes and prominent brow ridges in a skull may, for that population, indicate a female when normally the biological anthropologist would consider these as male characteristics; the difference in size and prominence of traits may be small. If one individual from the site was being assessed in isolation the incorrect sex may be attributed to them, and on some archaeological sites it is often difficult to sex many of the individuals because the features observed have equal male and femaleness.

There are three areas of the skeleton on which biological anthropologists concentrate to ascertain sex: the pelvis; skull; and metrical data of specific skeletal and dental elements of the body. The methods selected are determined by the completeness of the skeleton. The problems inherent in the assessment of sex are often related to the fragmentary or isolated nature of the remains in forensic contexts, the age of the individual (which may affect the expression of sexually dimorphic characteristics) and, most importantly in recent times, the effect of diet, environment and lifestyle, for example, on the skeletal features used for sex determination. It is necessary to know how each feature manifests itself in the bone, that is, what shapes its appearance, what its range of variation is in racial/ethnic groups and whether there are any secular changes (St Hoyme and Iscan, 1989). More recent studies use both morphological and morphometric aspects of the skeleton to assess sex especially when individual cases are proving difficult in forensic contexts. In an archaeological setting skeletons are often fragmentary and therefore the biological anthropologist becomes experienced in recognizing, firstly, the relevant areas of the fragmented skeleton in order to ascertain sex and, secondly, in interpreting those data recorded.

The pelvic girdle is believed to be the most sexually dimorphic part of the skeleton (for example, see Krogman and Iscan, 1986, pp. 200-26) which obviously reflects the childbearing capacity of the female. For sexing purposes it is maintained that a complete skeleton gives a near 100% accuracy, the pelvis alone 95% and the skull alone 90%, the skull and pelvis together 98%, long bones alone 80-90%, the long bones and skull together 90-95% and the pelvis and long bones together 95% (*ibid*. p. 259). There are many areas of the pelvis used for determining sex; Table 1 summarises some of the main features used (see also plate 6.5). The ventral arc, subpubic concavity and medial aspect of the ischiopubic ramus comprise features of a method of sex determination described by Phenice (1967). The ventral arc (or elevated ridge of bone on the ventral part of the pubic bone) in particular is related to muscle origin attachments of some of the adductor muscle mass in females (Anderson, 1990); Phenice found a high accuracy (95.56%) in sexing 275 known individuals and emphasised that any form of ridge found in males was much more medial than the female ventral arc. A more recent study tested the method (Lovell, 1989) and found a lower accuracy (*c.* 83%) especially with older individuals. In 1991 Sutherland and Suchey refined the use of the ventral arc by stating that its presence should only be considered if the ridge was palpable. The same study recorded a 96% accuracy for a documented sample of 1,284 known individuals. It is notable that some of the features used in sex attribution have been questioned

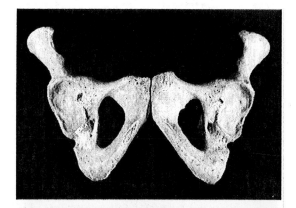
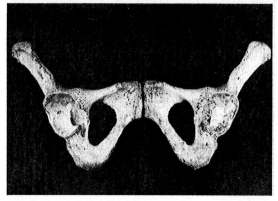

Plate 6.5 Sex determination from the pelvis. Pelves of males (top) and females (bottom).

with regard to their applicability to populations of different ethnic and temporal origins, questions more regularly asked of adult ageing techniques. MacLaughlin and Bruce (1986) reported pubis length and sciatic notch width to be different even between two populations of European origin. Again, this emphasizes that applying methods based on one group may not be valid for another group.

	Male	Female
Pubic bone	shorter	longer
Subpubic angle	narrower	wider
Subpubic concavity	absent/rare	present
Ventral arc	absent/rare	usually present
Ischiopubic ramus	wide	narrow
Sciatic notch	narrow	wide
Preauricular sulcus	less common	more common
Pelvic basin	heart-shaped	circular,elliptical
Obturator foramen	oval	triangular
Sacrum (lateral)	curved	flatter

Table 1: features of the pelvis used for sex attribution

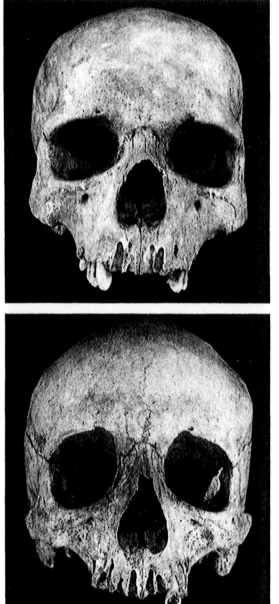

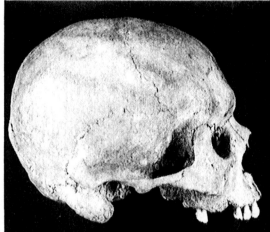

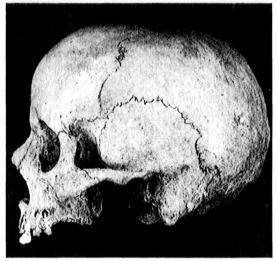

Plate 6.6. Sex determination from skulls. Skull of male (top) and female (bottom) showing anterior and lateral views.

The skull also reveals areas which can be differentiated on the basis of sex (for example, see Krogman and Iscan, 1986, pp. 191-200). The features of the skull used are summarised in Table 2 (see also plate 6.6). The majority of the features used pertain to relative differences in size between the two sexes. Meindl et al. (1985) assessed the accuracy of sexing a skeleton by independently examining 100 adult skulls of known sex from the Hamann-Todd Collection. They found that female skulls, unlike male skulls, are rarely misclassified and that there was no single cranial feature which was a hallmark of gender (ibid. p. 84). Nevertheless, assessment of relative size differences in a large population should still be possible. Furthermore, when dealing with a single individual in a forensic setting the process becomes more difficult. Teeth, however, which are accepted as being larger in males, are seen by many researchers to be sexually dimorphic (for example, Nageshkumar et al., 1989) although provide only variable accuracy. However, if a tooth is all that is available to the forensic anthropologist for analysis, this method of sex attribution may be the only one possible.

	Male	**Female**
Supraorbital ridges	prominent	less prominent
Frontal sinuses	larger	smaller
Superior orbit	blunter	sharper
Muscle ridges	more prominent	less prominent
Frontal bone	sloped	more upright
Zygomatic process/ extension to supra meatal crest	yes	no
Mastoid process	larger	smaller
Anterior mandible	square	pointed
Cranial capacity	larger	c. 200cc smaller

Table 2: Features of the skull used for sex attribution

For both pelvis and skull it is common to find a mixture of male and female traits. Increasingly there have been many metrical studies to discriminate between the sexes; there are few bones of the body on which this has not been attempted (see Krogman and Iscan, 1986, pp. 226-47). For example, measurement of the skull (Giles and Elliot, 1962) and the pelvis (Washburn, 1948; Ali and MacLaughlin, 1991) have revealed varying degrees of accuracy. However, if the skull and pelvis do not survive, the use of osteometric criteria may be the only clue to assigning a possible sex to the individual (for example, femora from the Medieval charnel house at Rothwell, Northamptonshire were measured to ascertain sex; Roberts, 1984). Unfortunately the measurement range for specific osteometric criteria for males and females usually has an overlap; this makes distinguishing males and females impossible if the measurement falls in the overlap zone. In addition, environmental, occupational, racial and dietary factors, for example, may affect the 'normal' accepted dimensions of the skeletal elements. The most commonly used bone is the femur, especially the femoral head and bicondylar width (Bass, 1987, pp. 218-21). In common with the morphological methods of sexing, the great majority of these studies are considered to be population specific and should not strictly be used on other skeletal populations. In recent years, use of more sophisticated methods to determine sex have been applied to cases in forensic contexts (eg Naito, *et al* 1994) but these methods refer usually to tissues other than bone.

In addition to osteological criteria the circumstances of disposal of the body may help with sex identification, for example associated clothing or jewellery, preservation obviously being dependent on burial and environmental conditions. However, although archaeologists, use grave goods to interpret the sex of an individual they recognize that these are not always accurate indicators (Henderson, 1989). In a forensic context the anthropologist should be equally wary of false deposited evidence. Fortunately, the morphology of the pelvis and skull (if available) should indicate sex. Foetal bones in the abdominal area of a skeleton would also guide the anthropologist to sex attribution (for example, Wells, 1978), and certain diseases are more likely to occur in females, for example, rheumatoid arthritis. Bodies with substantial amounts of soft tissue surviving may also provide sexually dimorphic features, but this depends very heavily on the state of preservation.

The assessment of the sex of individuals who have not attained adulthood is not possible with any great accuracy with currently available osteological methods. Secondary sexual characteristics which appear during puberty have not developed, even though sexual differentiation begins very early in foetal life. There are also few collections of subadult individuals on which to develop methods. Several authors have attempted to sex subadult individuals. For example, Boucher (1955) describes the foetal sciatic notch index of the pelvis and suggests its use in sex differentiation. Fazekas and Kosa (1978, p. 383) supported this view with significant sex differences in length and depth of the sciatic notch. They stated that the sexual characteristics of pelvic measurements which they took are connected to the type of sciatic notch; a 70-80% accuracy was claimed. Hunt and Gleiser (1955) suggested that assessment of sex in subadults could be undertaken by comparing dental development with postcranial development (i.e. long bone diaphyseal length) on the basis that males mature more slowly than females. Unfortunately, long bone length standards are based on relatively modern healthy populations; they are therefore not the most appropriate for analysing archaeological populations, but are better for forensic contexts. More recently De Vito and Saunders (1990) used five measurements of the deciduous teeth and first permanent molar to assign sex correctly in between 76% and 90% of dental casts taken from 162 children aged three to four years. It cannot be stressed too strongly that these methods should ideally only be applied to individuals from populations of the same geographic region, time period, race, health and socio-economic status. In archaeology, methods for assessment of subadult sex would be especially valuable; this part of the population remains absent from the gender profile of the cemetery and assessment of the relative mortality of subadult males:females is therefore impossible.

Likewise, although methods have been developed for the determination of the parity of an individual by examining 'scars of parturition' on the dorsal and ventral surfaces of the pubic symphysis of the pelvis, and the preauricular sulcus (a groove which runs parallel to but outside of the joint linking the sacrum to the pelvis in the area of the back), it is generally agreed that pelvic scarring does not always correlate with documented childbirth (see Krogman and Iscan, 1986, pp. 247-57 for a history of work in this area; also Cox and Scott, 1992 for a recent study on a known population). In an examination of ninety four documented skeletons from the excavations at Christ Church, Spitalfields, London (dated 1729-1859) Cox and Scott (1992) found that 'parturition scars' were not significantly related to parity status. Again, knowing about parity in past populations would be useful for reconstructing fertility and reproduction rate through time; it would also be useful for identification of individuals in a forensic context. However, non-parous individuals can have 'scars' and parous people can have no 'scars'.

Age at death

Age at death estimation is relatively straightforward for the subadult skeleton but is much more difficult for the adult. In the latter, the forensic anthropologist assesses the relative degeneration of the skeleton which can vary between individuals. Again, the methods used are those developed by biological anthropologists on populations of known age at death. The populations used for method development derive from different areas of the world, particularly in the United States, and are of recent origin; they may therefore be of different socio-economic status than the people being identified in a forensic or archaeological context.

The age of a skeleton is its biological not its chronological age. The subadult skeleton provides the most precise age estimation in terms of narrow age ranges, whereas adult ageing methods assess the process of degeneration of the skeleton once maturity has occurred; maturity can be extremely variable between and within populations. In archaeology the aim of ageing individuals is to reconstruct a mortality profile for the population (fig. 6.1) to see at what age individuals were dying and to what extent age at death may be influenced by lifestyle or disease. Ages for adults are usually given in broad ranges or as general terms, for

example 'old adult', which reflects the problems of ageing adults. In a forensic setting the attribution of age is to help make a positive identification of the body.

(i) subadults

In the subadult the examination of dental development, calcification and eruption, long bone diaphyseal length and appearance and union of ossification centres are a pre-requisite to determining age (Ubelaker, 1987). Postcranial length-for-age standards have been developed on a variety of both relatively modern (by measurement of bones on X-rays) and ancient populations of subadults which are then applied to individuals from appropriate populations (Maresh, 1943, 1955 on X-rays of modern Denver children; Johnston, 1962 on the Indian Knoll archaeological populations from Kentucky; Sundick, 1978 on a Medieval German population;

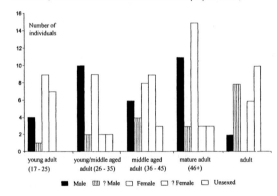

Fig 6.1 Mortality profile from an Anglo-Saxon cemetery. Data by courtesy of A. Boylston.

Hoffman, 1979 on X-rays of modern Colorado children; Scheuer, Musgrave and Evans, 1980 on modern Bristol and London foetus and neonates; Fazekas and Kosa, 1978 on modern foetuses). In modern instances the principle of this method is a comparison of the length of the diaphyses of the long bones, macroscopically and/or radiographically, with the known age of the individual. In archaeological populations age is assessed by a correlation of long bone length with dental development, the latter being based on modern development and eruption standards. Long bone length is a particularly useful method of ageing subadults if no teeth survive.

Order and timing of appearance and fusion of centres of ossification in the skeleton are assessed by comparison with data acquired from known-aged skeletal material and/or radiographs. There are a number of sources of data available, developed from relatively modern populations and summarised in Ubelaker (1987).

The ages given for these events can, once again, vary within and between populations, and the age-range in which, for example, an epiphysis fuses may be several years. Females also mature one to two years earlier than males; this presents a problem since it is not possible to sex a subadult skeleton, but use of these data may help to assign sex. Ubelaker (1987) suggests that in this case both male and female data should be used and the range of variation stated. It is emphasized that it is important to be confident of the state of epiphyseal union that is being recorded; studies based on epiphyseal union data derived from radiographs may underage an individual due to the retention of the epiphyseal line up to several years after union has taken place macroscopically.

Dental calcification and eruption comprise the third area of the skeleton used for age estimation in the subadult; it is accepted that there is less influence from the environment on developing teeth compared to bone, although again, female teeth develop a little earlier than those of males. Dental remains are amongst the most resistant parts of the human body and will survive most decompositional processes, and even moderate periods of burning. They are therefore potentially an extremely valuable source of information both forensically and archaeologically; indeed, they may be the only evidence that survives. In a forensic setting, dental records may aid identification of an individual by the teeth. Furthermore human teeth undergo continuous change from an age of approximately 20 weeks *in utero* through to death (or complete loss of dentition) making them a likely source of ageing information (Costa, 1986). However, genetic, hormonal, environmental, nutritional and social factors must be considered as elements affecting the rate of dentition development (El-Nofely and Iscan, 1989). Radiological and clinical studies have contributed significantly to our knowledge of the rate of dental development in various populations. These studies have examined dental calcification and eruption sequences in people of known age; according to Ubelaker (1987, p. 1256) dental eruption is considered to be less reliable for ageing than calcification as the former is affected by so many factors. Schour and Massler's (1944) study on white children provides an extremely useful source of data for forensic anthropology by identifying twenty one phases of tooth eruption. Moorees, Fanning and Hunt (1963a and b) studied dental calcification timing in deciduous and permanent teeth in North American schoolchildren whilst Nielsen and Ravn (1976) provide data on Northern European children;

studies are abundant and cover different ethnic groups and areas of the world. In a forensic situation consideration should be given to the problem that skeletal and dental development and maturation is highly population-specific and may be determined, for example, by the sex and nutritional status of the individual. Methods of analysis should be selected according to the population under consideration.

(ii) adults (fig. 6.2)

Maples (1989, p. 323) comments that, 'age determination is ultimately an art, not a precise science' which illustrates the problems with ageing adult skeletons from around the age of 20-25 years at death when bone and tooth development and maturation are normally complete. After maturity the biological anthropologist has to deal with the inconsistencies in skeletal and dental degeneration but he/she has learnt to tackle these problems by using the multifactorial approach. The use of multiple methods of analysis of skeletal and dental material is advocated throughout the assessment of age and sex of an individual; this is even more important in the ageing of adults. The effect of ageing on two different people can vary (Iscan, 1989), and several authors have used the multiple method approach to assess how age changes in one part of the body relate to another (for example, Lovejoy et al., 1985a; Saunders et al., 1992; Bedford et al., 1993). This multifactorial approach is also helpful in situations of fragmentary skeletal material; if most parts of the body can be used for age estimates, the more likely a fragmented skeleton is to be aged (of course, the more methods that are used, the more accurate one would expect the age to be). Dental wear, cranial suture closure, pelvic pubic symphyseal and auricular surface degeneration, sternal rib-end metamorphosis, radiography and histology of bone and teeth reflect the main areas of the skeleton used for ageing the adult (fig. 6.2) and the multitude of macroscopic and microscopic methods perhaps reflects the often desperate quest to find accurate adult ageing methods. It should be noted that the majority of these methods demand knowledge of the sex of the individual before they can be used. The theory that the majority of people died young in antiquity may not hold true if documentary sources recording old age are correct. In addition, work at Spitalfields (Molleson and Cox, 1993) showed that macroscopic methods of ageing often overaged the young and underaged the old. This emphasizes that ageing methods may be more appropriate to forensic rather than archaeological contexts.

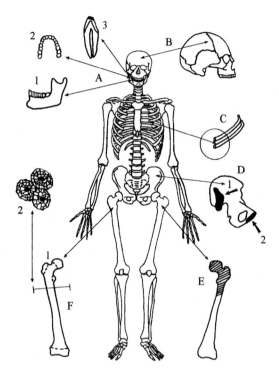

Fig 6.2 Areas of the skeleton used mainly for ageing adults

- **A.** 1. Dental development and eruption
- 2. Dental attrition
- 3. Dental histology
- **B.** Cranial suture closure
- **C.** Degeneration of sternal ends of ribs
- **D.** 1. Degeneration of pelvic auricular surface
- 2. Degeneration of pubic symphysis
- **E.** Radiography of femur
- **F.** 1. Epiphyseal fusion
- 2. Histological structure of cortical bone

In the young adult skeleton some of the epiphyses fuse late and provide useful markers for that age interval. The sternal end of the clavicle, heads of the ribs, superior and inferior epiphyseal rings of the vertebral centra, the iliac crest, sacral segments and basilar suture of the skull all fuse approximately between the ages of 25 and 35 years. Some recent work (Owings Webb and Suchey, 1985) has established fusion age-ranges for specific epiphyses. However, there is a need for more studies of this kind on well-documented modern populations of both sexes in different ethnic groups and geographic areas to account for changes through time, for example, in lifestyle, diet and health, thus making the data more applicable to forensic cases. Even so, these data are more applicable to a forensic than to an archaeological situation.

Utilization of the dentition for age assessment in the adult has concentrated on dental attrition, histology and more recently the analysis of amino acids. Dental attrition or wear as a function of age is usually measured in archaeological populations when all the permanent teeth have erupted (Brothwell, 1989) and is one of the most common methods used by physical anthropologists. However, in modern forensic cases it is considered inappropriate for ageing adults. The changes which have occurred in diet through time from coarser to softer foodstuffs makes the occurrence of dentine exposure in modern populations a rare event, at least in westernized societies. Diet is one of a multitude of factors which affect rate and pattern of tooth wear. Individual patterns of tooth wear, however, may be specific to an individual and prove useful for identification in a forensic context (see chapter 7). For example, in some archaeological cases evidence for pipe smoking in the form of attrition in a circular pattern in the upper and lower teeth can be identified. Once a human tooth has reached maturity, there are a number of degenerative changes which occur with age. Histological methods of ageing using teeth have provided some of the more reliable criteria for age assessment in the adult dentition. These methods are time-consuming, expensive and destructive, needing special expertise. Even though they are accepted as being generally more accurate, they are rarely used archaeologically because of these factors.

Gustafson (1950) pioneered the detailed study of age determination of teeth using the development of six degenerative features on the tooth: attrition of the occlusal surface; gingival recession; secondary dentine formation in the pulp cavity; cementum apposition; root resorption, and root transparency. In order to produce a numerical score which could be regressed on age, Gustafson divided each of the six variables into four semi-quantitative states to give a point system. In each case a score of zero was allocated to the absence (or expected level, in the case of cementum thickness) of each criteria. He developed the method on forty one Scandinavian teeth of known age with an error of estimation of +/- 3.6 years. Since then, researchers have criticised and refined his method or have concentrated on one or more of the age-related features described above (see Xiaohu *et al.*, 1992 for a summary). Johanson (1971) refined his categories by introducing half points for intermediate stages; he additionally considered the sex of the individual and used multivariate regression techniques to show that cementum thickness and root transparency were the variables most correlated with age. Many later studies have shown that root transparency is the most reliable method of age estimation; for example Bang and Ramm (1970) report an accuracy of +/- 4.7 years in 58% of cases and +/-10 years in 79% of cases. Root transparency occurs when dentine in the root tubules is replaced by minerals and is observed histologically, which requires the tooth to be sectioned longitudinally. Typical correlation coefficients for this type of measurement are claimed to be as high as 0.7, giving good age estimates up to seventy five years. Lucy (1993) has critically reviewed these three approaches, and tested them on a range of both modern and archaeological teeth. He also used a range of techniques for estimating the degree of root transparency and concluded that the best results are to be obtained by a combination of Gustafson's method (without an estimation of root transparency) and Bang and Ramm's method for root transparency. When comparing all three methods on a modern data set of thirty five teeth from seventeen individuals, Lucy showed that age predictions made using Gustafson's method are as accurate as those made using Johanson's technique, and better than Bang and Ramm's method. A quoted error of +/- 5.16 years is reasonable for either of the better techniques. There could, however, be a problem when applying any of these techniques to archaeological teeth, in that interaction with groundwater may, for example, result in the loss of sclerotic dentine. These problems have been discussed by Hillson (1986).

Cementum annulation, or the accumulation of layers of cement around the root of the tooth with age, has also received attention in the literature both for archaeological and forensic work (Stott, Sis and Levy, 1982; Lipsinic et al., 1986; Charles et al., 1989). However, there appears to be a high error in estimating age in older age groups (Miller, Dove and Cottone, 1988).

There is also an alternative, chemical approach to the derivation of age at death from teeth. The amino acids which make up proteins exist in two chemically stable forms related to each other as mirror images. Conventionally they are labelled L- and D- enantiomers, and the conversion of one to the other is termed racemization (see also chapter 8, appendix). Most living systems (higher plants and all animals), however, only synthesize proteins which contain the L-form, and therefore if proteins from living tissue are analysed they should yield only L-amino acids. It is known that D-amino acid residues (particularly the D- form of aspartic acid) accumulate *in vivo* with time due to *in vivo* racemization of L- residues, in tissues including dental enamel and dentine at approximately 0.1% per year relative to L-aspartic acid levels (Masters, 1986a); for modern freshly extracted teeth the age at death estimate provides accuracies comparable to other methods. Unreliability of the method has been reported (Masters, 1986b; Gillard et al., 1990; 1991; Child et al., 1993a). These studies show that the method may fail when applied to older (and therefore potentially degraded) collagen although all the error cannot be attributed to this factor alone. It has been postulated (Child, Gillard and Pollard, 1993b) that the problem is caused by selective microbial attack on the collagen, possibly *via* collagenase activity, resulting in fragmentation of the molecule and subsequent variation in the rate of terminal amino acid racemisation. This has initiated a study of microbiological attack on collagen at ambient temperatures (*ibid*.). In light of this, it may be possible to improve the reliability of age estimations *via* amino acid racemisation by being more selective about the collagen fraction extracted, thus turning a potentially useful technique into a reliable tool. It is recommended that multiple methods of histological and chemical assessment of the teeth for age assessment should be used to provide the most reliable ages.

Commonly used macroscopic methods in the assessment of adult age are the closure of the cranial sutures, degeneration of the pubic symphysis and auricular surface of the innominate (hip bone) and the sternal ends of the ribs. Endocranial and ectocranial suture closure as an age assessor has a long history of use with varying degrees of success stemming back to the sixteenth century (Masset, 1989). Pioneers in the study include Todd and Lyon (1924, 1925a; 1925b; 1925c) whose work was used by many anthropologists with little regard to the inaccuracies it produced for ageing adults. Sexual, racial and geographic differences in the rate and pattern of suture closure have been recorded in some studies (for example, Zivanovic, 1983) whilst in 1985 Meindl and Lovejoy recorded a new method of age assessment using ectocranial suture closure based on 236 crania of known age from the Hamann-Todd Collection. Ten points on the sutures were recorded and the results showed that the lateral-anterior sutures were the most reliable, that ectocranial suture assessment was superior to endocranial sutures, and that age estimation was independent of sex or race. Although not without its problems, cranial suture closure provides a method of age estimation to be used in conjunction with other age markers but never in isolation.

Degeneration of the surface of the pubic symphyseal face of the innominate has also provided a popular method of age assessment (see Meindl and Lovejoy, 1989 for a history of study), with differences in pubic symphyseal ageing being documented between the sexes and races. Todd (1920, 1921) was the first researcher to establish a method of ageing in this area, developing phases to the age-related changes. Since then, the method has been the most commonly used for adult ageing. McKern and Stewart (1957) developed a three component numerical scoring method on 450 males who had died in the Korean War. Gilbert and McKern (1973) then devised a similar system based on 103 known-aged females, although its accuracy has since been criticised (Suchey, 1979). It is clear that different methods are necessary for males and females owing to differences in the rate of the degeneration of the pubic symphyseal face, and that racial differences are also apparent (Katz and Suchey, 1989). A revision of the Todd and McKern and Stewart methods has now been made (Suchey, Wiseley and Katz, 1986; Katz and Suchey, 1986) based on 739 males between the ages of fourteen and ninety two years autopsied in Los Angeles County. The pubic symphysis is often incomplete and damaged both in forensic and archaeological contexts; it is one of the first areas of the skeleton to be reached during excavation. Therefore, the use of another area of the innominate which survives better, the auricular surface, is recommended by some authors. The method, which assesses the degeneration of the area, is beneficial for biological anthropologists as it can age a skeleton to sixty years and beyond whereas most of the other macroscopic methods do not extend beyond forty and fifty years. It is therefore a useful tool in forensic cases where it is known that victims may be very old. The method (Lovejoy *et al.*, 1985b) was developed on 500 specimens from the Hamann-Todd Collection and 250 archaeological skeletons from the Libben population; eight phases were defined. No sex differences were observed in the rate of degeneration except in females who had well-defined preauricular sulci. The method's accuracy is claimed to be at least as accurate for the prediction of age at death as the pubic symphysis. A recent test of the method by Murray and Murray (1991) suggests that it has potential. The method could equally be applied to males and females with a small but statistically insignif-

icant difference in the rate and pattern of change, both in whites and blacks. However, underestimation of older individuals and overestimation of younger individuals (seen also on skeletal material assessed from Spitalfields for the pubic symphysis) suggests that the method should be used in conjunction with other techniques.

Degeneration of the sternal ends of the ribs as a measure of age has been one of the most recent developments in adult ageing on white males and females (Iscan, Loth and Wright, 1984, 1985; Loth and Iscan, 1989). It is, again, important to know the sex of the individual to use this method which has been developed on individuals of known age from adolescence to old age. Eight phases of ageing are assigned for both males and females according to the depth and shape of the sternal end pit, and to the condition of the walls of the rib end. The method has the advantage that the ribs are not subject to the stresses and strains of lifestyle unlike the pelvis, for example; therefore these factors will not have any influence on age related changes in this area of the skeleton. Independent tests also show the method to be superior to the pubic symphyseal changes for some populations. The problems with the method may be survival and/or identification of the 4th rib which is recommended for the method although recent work has suggested that other ribs could be used (Dudar, 1994; Loth, Iscan and Scheuerman, 1994). Mann (1993) has developed a method of sequencing the ribs in the human rib cage which may help with identification of specific ribs. In archaeological contexts ribs are often very fragmentary and brittle once buried for long periods of time; it is consequently difficult to identify specific numbered ribs.

Radiographic and microscopic methods of bone ageing have been considered for both archaeological and forensic purposes. Radiography has the advantage of being able to assess not only age related demineralisation of the bone but also age specific disorders (Sorg, Andrews and Iscan, 1989, p. 89). In forensic contexts the use of radiography and histology to age an individual may not be affected by the state of preservation of the bone to the same degree as in an archaeological context. However, postmortem changes to bone structures in the skeleton can affect assessment of age using these methods and Bell (1990) records the preservation of bone structure and its effect on the interpretation of skeletal remains. A method incorporating six phases for the assessment of osteoporosis or loss of bone mass with age was described by Ascadi and Nemeskeri (1970) for the proximal humerus and femur. However, this method could only provide wide age-ranges. Walker and Lovejoy (1985) developed a method for the clavicle and proximal femur based on 130 individuals from the Hamann-Todd Collection, finding the clavicle to be the most reliable. However, osteoporosis has often been diagnosed in archaeological material based on relative bone weight when, in fact, loss of bone due to postmortem effects on the skeleton can cause its weight loss. Like dental histology, some microscopic methods of age assessment provide more accurate estimations than others, but good preservation is essential for all methods.

Histological methods of age assessment of thin sections of cortical bone were pioneered by Kerley (1965). He used transverse sections from the femur, tibia and fibula and examined the numbers of osteons (Haversian systems), osteon fragments, percentage of circumferential lamellar bone and number of non-Haversian canals in four fields of the bone section; the four variables were added and regression formulae applied to produce standards for ageing of up to ninety five years at death. Developments of the method followed: Kerley and Ubelaker provided a correction factor for field size assessment (1978); and Ahlqvist and Damsten (1969) located their observation fields midway between Kerley's points to avoid the linea aspera on the femoral posterior surface; they also used a square rather than a circular field of observation. There have been other studies of more recent date concentrating either on other parts of the skeleton or on minimizing destruction of the bone (see Stout, 1992 for summary). Suggestions to minimize the effects of variation in age changes in cortical microstructure include examining two sections from the same bone and/or different bones to avoid differences in bone remodelling at different sites, using a whole section rather than a core, and using as many sampling sites as possible (Stout, 1992, p. 34). The use of bone histomorphometry in order to age an individual in a forensic case can be illustrated in Stout (1986) where the histological results supported the historical records for age of Francisco Pizarro.

The methods of ageing adults are many and varied and the preceding dialogue has attempted to summarize the currently available literature on the subject. The use of any of these methods should always take into account the original population on which the method was developed and should consider their applicability to a forensic identification. Differences in rates and patterns of ageing in people of different sex, race, region and socio-economic status (and even between people of the same population) are factors which are difficult to quantify; even if a method based on a population of the same race and region is used it is difficult to control for differences in diet and health. A further consideration is the ease of use of the methods available. Histological methods of age determination in both bone and teeth need considerable expertise but provide the most accurate ages and should be used by biological anthropologists for forensic cases. However, these methods need time and money and are destructive; in a forensic setting these factors would represent less of a hurdle for determining an accurate age and identification. In addition, experience in the use of morphological methods of ageing is also necessary to avoid errors in final age estimates. More tests of the methods currently used should be made on populations of different ethnic groups and regions of the world. The final word is use as many methods as can be applied to the case in question. In an archaeological setting most methods will provide a similar age range, but there could be one method which may not fit with the rest.

6.5 Stature

The calculation of a person's height from their skeletal remains helps in the identification process. Numerous techniques have been developed and these can be categorized into either the anatomical or mathematical methods (Krogman and Iscan, 1986, pp. 302-51 for a summary).

The anatomical method needs a near complete skeleton in order that the basio-bregma height (bottom to top) of the skull, height of the vertebral column and length of the lower limbs can be measured and summed. A correction factor (which is believed not to differ between populations) is added to allow for soft tissue of the scalp, sole of the foot, cartilage of joints and intervertebral discs. Although some authors consider it to be the most accurate method of predicting stature (Lundy, 1985), in forensic and archaeological cases it is often the situation that the skeleton is incomplete. The mathematical method is therefore the most often used and consists of measuring the long bones and applying regression formulae developed on populations of known height, race and sex to determine actual height (Trotter and Gleser 1952; 1958; 1977; Trotter, 1970). Based on individuals from World War II (height taken at induction into the army) and the Terry

Collection the six long bones were measured and regression formulae applied to account for the relationship between long bone length and total living height. The 1958 study re-evaluated earlier work by testing the regressions on Korean War dead. Lower limb bones were considered to give the best estimate compared to the upper limb bones, but regression formulae are available for all the long bones. In both forensic and archaeological contexts it is therefore possible to estimate stature even if the lower limb bones are missing, although the standard deviation will be greater. Height is determined by many factors especially nutritional status; and in archaeology, studies of stature have tried to relate diet to height (for example, Nickens, 1976).

Trotter and Gleser provided regression formulae for American whites and blacks, Mexicans and Puerto Ricans. There have been many studies using long bone lengths from populations from different continents, for example, by Pan (1924) on East Indian Hindus, by Breitinger (1937) on Germans, by Telkka (1950) on Fins, by Allbrook (1961) on Britons, and by Genoves (1967) on Central American Indians. However, the formulae of Trotter and Gleser are considered by most to provide the most reliable estimates and in the United Kingdom biological anthropologists use these formulae in archaeological contexts. Formulae using bones other than long bones are limited but Musgrave and Harnega (1978) found only a 3% difference between their stature estimates and those obtained by Trotter and Gleser by using the length of the metacarpals. Byers, Akoshima and Curran (1989) also presented data on stature estimation using the metatarsal length and claimed a similar accuracy as for the metacarpal. These formulae could be used in situations when long bones were unavailable.

The preceding discussion relates to adult skeletons. In foetal and older subadults it is more difficult to calculate stature because of accelerated growth which makes precise estimation almost impossible at any one point in time for the child's development. In addition, sex and age need to be known in order to account for their effect on growth, as well as considerations of nutritional status and health. Little information exists for these age groups. However, Fazekas and Kosa (1978), amongst others, provide formulae for foetal skeletal height, Feldesman (1992) provides some data on femur/stature ratio estimation in children and Himes, Yarborough and Martorell (1977) give data on metacarpal length and stature in children. Fragmentary bones and their use in stature estimation have been approached by, for example, Steele (1970) and Holland (1992), and provide data

for use in both archaeological and forensic contexts.

There are a number of problems highlighted in the literature related to stature calculation. Concern about collection of the original data and how people were measured antemortem is common (for example, Snow and Williams, 1971). If the person's living height was measured inaccurately/ inconsistently then how can postmortem stature compare to it? The time of day at which the height was measured (people are shorter at the end of the day), postural slump, age (height is lost with age - for example, see Galloway, 1988), nutritional status, genetic makeup and environment will all affect final stature. More recently, Jantz (1992) has modified the original Trotter and Gleser formulae for females to account for modern changes in stature. Applying the most appropriate formulae to individuals in both an archaeological or forensic context is essential if a close approximation of antemortem to postmortem height is to be achieved.

6.6. Race

The concept of biological race has different meanings to many people and often becomes confused with social, political and religious concepts of race. Biological race is the result of an adaptive response to success (Gill, 1986, p. 143) with resulting physical variation. Race can be described in terms of appearance (phenotype) and genetics or units of inheritance (genotype). The biological anthropologist examines skeletal remains to assess human racial variation assigning individuals to three main races, Caucasoid, Negroid and Mongoloid; subdivisions of these racial groups are many (see Jurmain and Nelson, 1994, pp. 190-91). Today, however, with extensive interbreeding of original racial groupings no one skeleton usually shows all the characteristics accepted as belonging to one specific group. In the forensic context this is especially true and attribution of race often cannot be made with any certainty. In archaeology the obsession with skulls stemming back to the nineteenth century encouraged the analysis of the skull for racial characteristics. Biological anthropologists today are still prone to chart migrations of people from one population to another based on skull shape and compare populations with one another on this basis (for example, Dawes and Magilton, 1980). In a forensic context, however, the attribution of an individual to a racial group is desirable, not least because missing persons lists include racial affinity, but may be complicated to undertake.

The skull is considered to be the most indicative part of the skeleton for race determination by morphological and metrical methods of assessment, including discriminant function analysis of multiple measurements. The reader is referred to Gill (1986, Table 1) for a list of traits and their appearance in the skull for the different racial groups. Skull and face shape, nasal aperture, interorbital width and nasal root, palatal dental arch, and morphology of the molar and incisor teeth are all accepted as features which may indicate race. With respect to metrical analysis of the skull for race identification, Giles and Elliot (1962) analysed seven skull measurements on blacks and whites from the Terry and Hamann-Todd Collections and reported an accuracy of 80-88% in assignment of race. Gill and Rhine (1986) assessed the mid-face in different racial groups taking six measurements and calculating three indices to separate whites from the rest of the sample, but not blacks from Indians and Eskimos. It is important to remember that none of the traits observed are unique to a particular racial group, or have equal weighting; there is also a wide range of variation in both males and females (Stewart, 1979, pp. 227-8). For example, features of the skull in blacks such as low orbits, wider interorbital distance, broader nasal aperture and pronounced alveolar prognathism may not all be present in one skull or be as pronounced as expected. However, the facial region is accepted as being the best indicator of racial characteristics.

Other bones of the skeleton have also been used to assess race, particularly by using metrical data. Todd (1929) provided useful data on black and white pelves, with Iscan (1983) and Schulter-Ellis and Hayek (1984), for example, applying discriminant function analysis to the same area of the skeleton and giving between 80-90% accuracy. Combinations of bones are also used by some researchers (for example DiBennardo and Taylor, 1983 on the femur and innominate with an accuracy of 97%) as a means to greater accuracy in race determination because the proportions of bones of the skeleton to one another are believed to be good indicators of race; these methods, however, present problems if a near complete skeleton is not available.

6.8 Conclusion

The identification of age, sex, stature and race of individuals in a forensic context has been made possible because of the development of methods of analysis by biological anthropologists on known populations for application to archaeological populations. A natural step has been to use these methods in forensic cases to aid positive identification. Biological anthropologists aim to reconstruct the population structure and its lifestyle during past periods of time; positive identification is not possible because, with few exceptions, records for comparison do not exist for these individuals. However, in forensic contexts the need for individual identification is more pressing. Knowing the age, sex, stature and race of an individual is only the first step. Detailed factors of individual identity are covered in the next chapter.

References

Ahlqvist, J. and Damsten, O. (1969), A modification of Kerley's method for the microscopic determination of age in human bone, *J. Forensic Sci.*, 14 (2): 205-12.

Ali, R. S. & MacLaughlin, S. M. (1991), Sex identification from the auricular surface of the adult human ilium, *Int. J. Osteoarchaeology* 1: 57-61.

Allbrook, D. (1961), The estimation of stature in British and East African males: based on tibial and ulnar bone lengths, *J. Forensic Med.*, 8: 15-28.

Anderson, B. E. (1990), Ventral arc of the os pubis: anatomical and developmental considerations, *Amer. J. Phys. Anthrop.*, 83: 449-58.

Ascadi, G. & Nemeskeri, J. (1970), *History of Human Life Span and Mortality*, Budapest.

Bang, G. & Ramm, E. (1970), Determination of age in humans from root dentine transparency, *Acta Odontol. Scand.*, 28: 3-35.

Bass, W. M. (1987), *Human Osteology. A Laboratory and Field Manual*, Missouri.

Bedford, M. E., Russell, K. F., Lovejoy, C. O., Meindl, R. S., Simpson, S. W. & Stuart-Macadam, P. L. (1993), Test of the multifactorial ageing method using skeletons with known ages-at-death from the Grant Collection, *Amer. J. Phys. Anthrop.*, 91: 287-97.

Bell, L. (1990), Palaeopathology and diagenesis: an SEM evaluation of structural changes using backscattered electron imaging, *J. Arch. Sci.*, 17: 85-102.

Boucher, B. J. (1955), Sex differences in the foetal sciatic notch, *J. Forensic Med.*, 2 (1):51-4.

Breitinger, E. (1937), Berechnung der koperhohe aus den langen gliedmassenknochen, *Anthropol. Anzeiger*, 14: 249-74.

Brothwell, D. (1989), The relationship of tooth wear to ageing, in M. Y. Iscan, (ed), *Age Markers in the Human Skeleton*, Springfield, Illinois: 303-16.

Byers, S., Akoshima, K. & Curran, B. (1989), Determination of adult stature from metatarsal length, *Amer. J. Phys. Anthrop.*: 79: 275-279.

Charles, D. K., Condon, K., Cheverud, J. M. & Buikstra, J. E. (1989). Estimating age at death from growth layer groups in cementum, in M.Y. Iscan (ed), *Age Markers in the Human Skeleton*, Springfield, Illinois: 277-301.

Child, A. M., Gillard, R. D., Hardman, S. M., Pollard, A. M., Sutton, P. & Whittaker, D. (1993a), Preliminary microbiological investigations of some problems relating to age at death determinations in archaeological teeth, *Proceedings of the 4th Australian Archaeometry Conference*, ANU, Canberra, 29th-31st January 1991.

Child, A. M., Gillard, R. D. & Pollard, A. M. (1993b), Microbially induced promotion of amino acid racemisation in bone: isolation of microorganisms and detection of their enzymes, *J. Arch. Sci.*, 20: 159-68.

Chilvarquer, I., Katz, J. O., Glassman, D. M., Prihoda, T. J. & Cottone, J. A. (1991), Comparative radiographic study of human and animal long bone patterns, *J. Forensic Sci.*, 32 (6): 1645-54.

Cohen, M. N. (1989), *Health and the Rise of Civilization*, London.

Cohen, M. N. and Armelagos, G. J. (eds), (1984), *Paleopathology at the origins of agriculture*, London.

Costa, R. L. (1986), Determination of age at death: dentition analysis, in M. Zimmerman & J. L. Angel, (eds), *Dating and Age Determination of Biological Material*, London: 248-69.

Cox, M. & Scott, A. (1992), Evaluation of the significance of some pelvic characters in an 18th century British sample of known parity status, *Amer. J. Phys. Anthrop.*, 89: 431-40.

Dawes, J. D. & Magilton, J. R. (1980), *The Cemetery of St Helen-on-the-Walls, Aldwark*, The Archaeology of York: The Medieval Cemeteries 12/1, London.

De Vito, C. & Saunders, S. R. (1990), A discriminant function analysis of deciduous teeth to determine sex, *J. Forensic Sci.*, 35 (4): 845-58.

DiBennardo, R. and Taylor, J. V. (1983), Multiple discriminant function analysis of sex and race in the postcranial skeleton, *Amer. J. Phys. Anthrop.*, 61: 305-314.

Dudar, J. C. (1994), Identification of rib number and assessment of intercostal variation at the sternal rib end, *J. Forensic Sci.*, 38 (4): 788-797.

El-Nofely, A. & Iscan, M. Y. (1989), Assessment of age from the dentition in children, in M.Y. Iscan (ed) *Age Markers in the Human Skeleton*, Springfield, Illinois: 237-54

Fairgrieve, S. I. (1994), SEM analysis of incinerated teeth as an aid to positive identification, *J. Forensic Sci.*, 39 (2): 557-565.

Fazekas, I. Gy. & Kosa, F. (1978), *Forensic Fetal Osteology*, Budapest.

Feldesman, M. R. (1992), Femur/stature ratio and estimates of stature in children, *Amer. J. Phys. Anthrop.*, 87: 447-59.

Gaensslen, R. E., Berka, K. M., Grosso, D. A., Ruano, G., Pagliaro, E. M., Messina, D. & Lee, H. C. (1992), A PCR method for sex and species determination with novel controls for DNA template, *J. Forensic Sci.*, 37 (1): 6-20.

Galloway, A. (1988), Estimating actual height in the older individual, *J. Forensic Sci.*, 33 (1): 126-36.

Galloway, A., Birkby, W. H., Kahana, T. & Fulginiti, L. (1990), Physical anthropology and the law: legal responsibilities of forensic anthropologists, *Yearbook of Forensic Anthropology*, 33: 39-57.

Genoves, S. (1967), Proportionality of the long bones and their relationship to stature among Mesoamericans, *Amer. J. Phys. Anthrop.*, 26: 67-77.

Gilbert, B. M. & McKern, T. W. (1973), A method for ageing the female os pubis, *Amer. J. Phys. Anthrop.*, 38: 31-8.

Giles, E. & Elliot, O. (1962), Race identification from cranial measurements, *J. Forensic Sci.*, 7: 147-57.

Gill, G. W. (1986), Craniofacial criteria in forensic race identification, in K. M. Reichs, (ed), *Forensic Osteology. Advances in the Identification of Human Remains*, Springfield, Illinois: 143-59.

Gill, G. W. & Rhine, J. (eds), (1986), *Skeletal Race Identification: New Approaches in Forensic Anthropology*, Albuquerque.

Gillard, R. D., Pollard, A. M., Sutton, P. A. & Whittaker, D. W. (1990), An improved method for age at death determination from the measurement of D-aspartic acid in dental collagen, *Archaeometry*, 32: 61-70.

Gillard, R. D., Hardman, S. M., Pollard, A. M., Sutton, P. A. & Whittaker, D. K. (1991), Determinations of age at death in archaeological populations using the D/L ratio of aspartic acid in dental collagen, in E. Pernicka & G. Wagner, (eds), *Archaeometry '90*, Birkhauser Verlag, Basel: 637-44.

Gustafson, G. (1950), Age determination on teeth, *J. Amer. Dent. Assoc.*, 41: 45-54.

Harsanyi, L. (1993), Differential diagnosis of human and animal bone, in G. Grupe & A. N. Garland, (eds), *Histology of Ancient Human Bone: Methods and Diagnosis*, London, Springer Verlag: 79-94.

Henderson, J. (1989), Pagan Saxon cemeteries: a study of the problem of sexing by grave goods and bones, in C. A. Roberts, F. Lee & J. L. Bintliff, (eds), *Burial Archaeology: Current Research, Methods and Developments*, British Archaeological Reports British Series 211, Oxford: 77-83.

Hillson, S. W. (1986), *Teeth*, Cambridge.

Himes, J., Yarborough, D. & Martorell, R. (1977), Estimation of stature in children from radiographically determined metacarpal length, *J. Forensic Sci.*, 22:. 452-6.

Hoffman, J. M. (1979), Age estimations from diaphyseal lengths: 2 months to 12 years, *J. Forensic Sci.*, 24: 461-9.

Holland, T. D. (1992), Estimation of adult stature from fragmentary tibias, *J. Forensic Sci.*, 37 (5): 1223-39.

Hunt, E. E. & Gleiser, I. (1955), The estimation of age and sex of preadolescent children from bones and teeth, *Amer. J. Phys. Anthrop.*, 13: 479-87.

Iscan, M. Y. (1983), Assessment of race from the pelvis, *Amer. J. Phys. Anthrop.*, 62: 205-8.

Iscan, M. Y. (1988), Rise of forensic anthropology, *Yearbook of Physical Anthropology*, 31: 203-30.

Iscan, M. Y. (1989), Research strategies in age estimation: the multiregional approach, in M. Y. Iscan, (ed), *Age Markers in the Human Skeleton*, Springfield, Illinois: 325-39.

Iscan, M. Y., Loth, S. R. & Wright, R. K. (1984), Age estimation from the rib by phase analysis: white males, *J. Forensic Sci.*, 29: 1094-1104.

Iscan, M. Y., Loth, S. R. & Wright, R. K. (1985), Age estimation from the rib by phase analysis: white females, *J. Forensic Sci.*, 30: 853-63.

Jantz, R. L. (1992), Modification of the Trotter and Gleser female stature estimation formulae, *J. Forensic Sci.*, 37 (5): 230-35.

Johanson, G. (1971), Age determinations from human teeth, *Odontologisk Revy*, 22 (Supplement).

Johnston, F. E. (1962), Growth of the long bones of infants and young children at Indian Knoll, *Amer. J. Phys. Anthrop.*, 20: 249-54.

Jurmain, R., Nelson, H. (1994), *Introduction to Physical Anthropology*, (sixth edition), New York.

Katz, D. & Suchey, J. M. (1986), Age determination of the male os pubis, *Amer. J. Phys. Anthrop.*, 69: 427-35.

Katz, D. & Suchey, J. M. (1989), Race differences in pubic symphyseal aging patterns, *Amer. J. Phys. Anthrop.*, 80: 167-72.

Kerley, E. R. (1965), The microsopic determination of age in human bone, *Amer. J. Phys. Anthrop.*, 23: 149-63.

Kerley, E. R. & Ubelaker, D. H. (1978), Revision in the microscopic method of estimating age at death in human cortical bone, *Amer. J. Phys. Anthrop.*, 49(4): 545-6.

Knight, B. (1991), *Forensic pathology*, London.

Krogman, W. M. & Iscan, M. Y. (1986), *The Human Skeleton in Forensic Medicine*, Springfield, Illinois.

Lipsinic, F. E., Paunovich, E., Houston, G. D. & Robison, S. F. (1986), Correlation of age and incremental lines in the cementum of human teeth, *J. Forensic Sci.*, 31 (3): 982-9.

Loth, S. R. & Iscan, M. Y. (1989), Morphological assessment of age in the adult: the thoracic region, in M.Y. Iscan, (ed), *Age Markers in the Human Skeleton*, Springfield, Illinois:105-35.

Loth, S., Iscan, M. Y. & Scheuerman, E. H. (1994), Intercostal variation at the sternal end of the rib, *Forensic Sci. Int.*, 65 (2): 135-143.

Lovejoy, C. O., Meindl, R. S., Pryzbeck, T. R. & Mensforth, R. P. (1985b), Chronological metamorphosis of the auricular surface of the ilium: a new method for the determination of adult skeletal age, *Amer. J. Phys. Anthrop.* 68: 15-28.

Lovejoy, C. O., Meindl, R. S., Mensforth, R. P. & Barton, T. J. (1985a), Multifactorial determination of skeletal age at death: a method and blind tests of its accuracy, *Amer. J. Phys. Anthrop.*, 68(1): 1-14.

Lovell, N. C. (1989), Test of Phenice's technique for determining sex from the os pubis, *Amer. J. Phys. Anthrop.*, 79: 117-20.

Lucy, D. (1993), *Teeth, Age at Death and Archaeology: the Application of Tooth Histology as a Means of Determining Age at Death for Human Remains*, Unpublished final year dissertation, Department of Archaeological Sciences, University of Bradford.

Lundy, J. K. (1985), The mathematical versus the anatomical method of stature estimation from long bones, *Amer. J. Forensic Medicine and Pathology*, 6 (1): 73-6.

MacLaughlin, S. M. & Bruce, M. F. (1986), Population variation in sexual dimorphism in the human innominate, *Human Evolution*, 1 (3): 221-31.

Mann, R. W. (1993), A method for siding and sequencing human ribs, *J. Forensic Sci.*, 38 (1):151-5.

Maples, W. R. (1989), The practical application of age-estimation techniques, in M. Y. Iscan, (ed), *Age Markers in the Human Skeleton*, Springfield, Illinois:319-24.

Maresh, M. M. (1943), Growth of major long bones in healthy children, *Amer. J. Dis. Children*, 66 (3): 227-54.

Maresh, M. M. (1955), Linear growth of long bones of extremeties from infancy through adolescence, *Amer. J. Dis. Children*, 89 (3): 725-43.

Masset, C. (1989), Age estimation on the basis of cranial sutures, in M. Y. Iscan, (ed) *Age Markers in the Human Skeleton*, Sprimgfield, Illinois: 71-103.

Masters, P. (1986a), Age determination of living mammals using aspartic acid racemisation in structural proteins, in M. Zimmerman & J. L Angel, (eds), *Dating and Age Determination of Biological Material*, London: 270-83.

Masters, P. (1986b), Age at death determination of autopsied remains based on aspartic acid racemisation in tooth dentine: importance of post-mortem conditions, *Forensic Sci. Int.*, 32: 179-84.

McKern, T. W. & Stewart, T. D. (1957), *Skeletal Age Changes in Young American Males Analysed from the Standpoint of Identification*, Environmental Protection Research Division (Headquarters of the Quartermaster Research and Development Center), Technical Report EP-45. U.S. Army, Natwick, Massachusetts.

McKinley, J. (1989), Cremations: expectations, methodologies and realities, in C. A. Roberts, F. Lee & J. L. Bintliff, (eds), *Burial Archaeology: Current Research, Methods and Developments*, British Archaeological Reports British Series 211, Oxford: 65-76.

McKinley, J. I. & Roberts, C.A. (1993), *Excavation and Post-Excavation Treatment of Cremated and Inhumed Human Remains*. Institute of Field Archaeologists Technical Paper No 13, Birmingham.

Meindl, R. S. & Lovejoy, C. O. (1985). Ectocranial suture closure: a revised method for the determination of skeletal age at death based on lateral-anterior sutures, *Amer. J. Phys. Anthrop.*, 68: 57-66.

Meindl, R. S. and Lovejoy, C. O. (1989), Age changes in the pelvis: implications for paleodemography, in M. Y. Iscan, (ed), *Age Markers in the Human Skeleton*, Springfield, Illinois: 137-68.

Meindl, R. S., Lovejoy, C. O., Mensforth, R. P. & Don Carlos, L. (1985), Accuracy and direction of error in the sexing of the skeleton: implications for paleodemography, *Amer. J. Phys. Anthrop.*, 68: 79-85.

Miller, C., Dove, S. & Cottone, J. (1988), Failure of use of cemental annulations in teeth to determinate the age of humans, *J. Forensic Sci.,* 33 (1): 137-43.

Molleson, T. & Cox, M. (1993), *The Spitalfields Project Volume 2. The anthropology. The Middling Sort*, Council for British Archaeology Research Report 86, York.

Moorees, C. F. A., Fanning, E. A. & Hunt, E. E. (1963a), Formation and resorption of three deciduous teeth in children, *Amer. J. Phys. Anthrop.*, 21: 205-13.

Moorees, C. F. A., Fanning, E. A. & Hunt, E. E. (1963b). Age variation of formation for 10 permanent teeth, *J. Dental Research*, 42: 1490-1501.

Murray, K. A. & Murray, T. (1991), A test of the auricular surface aging technique, *J. Forensic Sci.*, 36 (4): 1162-69.

Musgrave, J. H. & Harneja, N. K. (1978), The estimation of adult stature from metcarpal bone length, *Amer. J. Phys. Anthrop.*, 48: 113-120.

Nageshkumar, G., Nirmala, N., Pai, M. & Kotiau, M. (1989), Mandibular canine index - a clue for establishing sex identification, *Forensic Science International*, 42: 249-54.

Naito, E., Dewa, K., Yamanouchi, H. & Kominami, R. (1994), Sex typing of forensic DNA samples using male and female specific probes, *J. Forensic Sci.*, 39 (4): 1009-1017.

Nickens, P. (1976), Stature reduction as an adaptive response to food production in Mesoamerica, *J. Arch. Sci.*, 3: 31-41.

Nielsen, H. & Ravn, J. (1976), A radiographic study of mineralisation of permanent teeth in a group of children aged 3-7 years, *Scand. J. Dental Research*, 84: 109-118.

Owings Webb, P. & Suchey, J. M. (1985), Epiphyseal union of the anterior iliac crest and medial clavicle in a modern multiracial sample of American males and females, *Amer. J. Phys. Anthrop.*, 68: 457-66.

Owsley, D. W. (1994), Identification of the fragmentary burned remains of two US journalists, *J. Forensic Sci.*, 38 (6): 1372-1382.

Owsley, D. W. & Mann, R. W. (1990), Medico-legal case involving a bear paw, *J. Amer. Podiatric Assoc.*, 80 (11): 623-5.

Owsley, D.W., Mires, A. & Keith, M. (1985), Case involving differentiation of deer and human bone fragments, *J. Forensic Sci.*, 30 (2): 572-8.

Pan, N. (1924), Length of long bones and their proportion to body height in Hindus, *J. Anatomy*, 58:. 374-8.

Phenice, T.W. (1967), Newly developed visual method of sexing the os pubis, *Amer. J. Phys. Anthrop.*, 30: 297-302.

Reichs, K. J. (1992), Forensic anthropology in the 1990's, *Amer.J.Forensic Medicine and Pathology*, 13 (2): 146-53.

Roberts, C. A. (1984), Analysis of some human femora from a Medieval charnel house at Rothwell Parish Church, Northamptonshire, *Ossa*, 9-11: 119-134.

Roberts, C. A., Manchester, K. & Storey, A. (1992), Margaret Clitherow: skeletal identification of an historical figure, *Forensic Sci. Int.*, 57: 63-71.

Saunders, S. R., Fitzgerald, C., Rogers, T., Dudar, C. & McKillop, H. (1992), A test of several methods of skeletal age estimation using a documented archaeological sample, *Canadian Forensic Sci. J.*, 25 (2): 97-117.

Scheuer, L., Musgrave, J. H. & Evans, S. P. (1980), Estimation of late fetal and perinatal age from limb bone length by linear logarithmic regression, *Annals of Human Biology*, 7 (3): 257-65.

Schour, I. & Massler, M. (1944), *Development of the human dentition*, Chicago.

Schulter-Ellis, F. & Hayek, L. (1984), Predicting race and sex with an acetabulum/pubis index, *Collegium Antropologicum*, 8: 155-62.

Snow, C. C. & Williams, J. (1971), Variation in premortem statural measurements compared to statural estimation of skeletal remains, *J. Forensic Sci.*, 16 (4): 455-64.

Sorg, M. H., Andrews, R. P. & Iscan, M. Y. (1989), Radiographic ageing of the adult, in M. Y. Iscan, (ed), *Age Markers in the Human Skeleton*, Springfield, Illinois: 169-193.

Stead, I. M., Bourke, J. B. & Brothwell, D. (1986), *Lindow Man. The Body in the Bog*, London.

Steele, D. G. (1970), Estimation of stature from fragments of limb bones, in T. D. Stewart, (ed,), *Personal Identification in Mass Disasters*, Washington DC: 85-97.

Stewart, T.D. (1979), *Essentials of Forensic Anthropology*, Springfield, Illinois.

St Hoyme, L. E. & Iscan, M. Y. (1989), Determination of sex and race: accuracy and assumptions, in M. Y. Iscan & K. A. R. Kennedy, (eds), *Reconstruction of Life from the Skeleton*, New York: 53-93.

Stirland, A. (1984), *A possible correlation between os acromiale and occupation in the burials from the Mary Rose*, Proceedings of the 5th European Meeting of the Paleopathology Association, Siena: 327-334.

Stirland, A. (1990), The late Sir Thomas Reynes: a medieval identification, *J. Forensic Sci. Soc.*, 30: 39-43.

Stott, G., Sis, R. & Levy, B. (1982), Cemental annulation and age determination in forensic dentistry, *J. Dental Research,* 61 (6): 814-17.

Stout, S. D. (1986), The use of bone histomorphometry in skeletal identification: the case of Francisco Pizarro, *J. Forensic Sci.,* 31 (1): 296-300.

Stout, S. D. (1992), Methods of determining age at death using bone microstructure, in S. R. Saunders & A. Katzenberg, (eds), *Skeletal Biology of Past Peoples: Research Methods,* New York: 21-35.

Suchey, J. M. (1979), Problems in the aging of females using the os pubis, *Amer. J. Phys. Anthrop.,* 51: 467-70.

Suchey, J. M., Wiseley, D. V. & Katz, D. (1986), Evaluation of the Todd and McKern-Stewart methods of aging the male os pubis, in K. J. Reichs, (ed), *Forensic Osteology. Advances in the Identification of Human Remains,* Springfield, Illinois: 33-67.

Sundick, R. I. (1978), Human skeletal growth and age determination, *Homo,* 29: 228-49.

Sutherland, L. D. & Suchey, J. M. (1991), Use of the ventral arc in pubic sex determination, *J. Forensic Sci.,* 36 (2): 501-11.

Telkka, A. (1950), On the prediction of human stature from the long bones, *Acta Anat.,* 9: 103-117.

Todd, T. W. (1920), Age changes in the pubic bone I. The male white pubis, *Amer. J. Phys. Anthrop.,* 3: 285-334.

Todd, T. W. (1921), Age changes in the pubic bone II. The pubis of the male negro-white hybrid. III. The pubis of the white female. IV. The pubis of the female negro-white hybrid, *Amer. J. Phys. Anthrop.,* 4: 1-70.

Todd, T. W. & Lyon, D. W. (1924), Endocranial suture closure, its progress and relationship. Part I Adult males of white stock, *Amer. J. Phys. Anthrop.,* 7: 325-84.

Todd, T. W. & Lyon, D. W. (1925a), Cranial suture closure Part II. Ectocranial suture closure in adult males of white stock, *Amer. J. Phys. Anthrop.,* 8: 23-43.

Todd, T. W. & Lyon, D. W. (1925b), Cranial suture closure. Part III. Endocranial suture closure in adult males of negro stock, *Amer. J. Phys. Anthrop.,* 8: 44-71.

Todd, T. W. & Lyon, D. W. (1925c), Suture closure. Part IV. Ectocranial suture closure in adult males of negro stock, *Amer. J. Phys. Anthrop.,* 8: 149-68.

Todd, T. W. (1929), Entrenched negro physical features, *Human Biology,* 1: 57-69.

Trotter, M. (1970), Estimation of stature from intact long limb bones, in T. D. Stewart, (ed), *Personal Identification in Mass Distasters,* Washington DC: 71-83.

Trotter, M. & Gleser, G. C. (1952), Estimation of stature from long bones of American whites and negroes, *Amer. J. Phys. Anthrop.,* 10: 463-514.

Trotter, M. & Gleser, G. C. (1958), A re-evaluation of estimation of stature during life and of long bones after death, *Amer. J. Phys. Anthrop.,* 16: 79-123.

Trotter, M. & Gleser, G. C. (1977), Corrigenda to 'Estimation of stature for limb bones of American whites and negroes', *Amer. J. Phys. Anthrop.,* 47: 355-56.

Ubelaker, D. H. (1987), Estimating age at death from immature human skeletons: an overview, *J. Forensic Sci.,* 32 (5): 1254-63.

Walker, R. A. & Lovejoy, C. O. (1985), Radiographic changes in the clavicle and proximal femur and their use in the determination of skeletal age, *Amer. J. Phys. Anthrop.,* 68: 67-78.

Washburn, S. L. (1948), Sex differences in the pubic bone, *Amer. J. Phys. Anthrop.,* 6: 199-208.

Wells, C. (1978), Medieval burial of a pregnant woman, *The Practitioner* 221: 442-4.

Whittaker, D. & Rawle, L. (1987), The effect of conditions of putrefaction on species determination in human and animal teeth, *Forensic Sci. Int.,* 35: 209-12.

Wolf, D. J. (1986), Forensic anthropology scene investigations, in K. J. Reichs, (ed), *Forensic Osteology. Advances in the Identification of Human Remains,* Springfield, Illinois: 3-23.

Workshop for European Anthropologists. (1980), Recommendations for age and sex diagnosis of skeletons, *J. Human Evolution,* 9: 517-49.

Xiaohu, X., Philipsen, H. P., Jablonski, N. G., Pang, K. M. & Jiazhen, Z. (1992), Age estimation from the structure of adult human teeth: review of the literature, *Forensic Sci. Int.,* 54: 23-8.

Zivanovic, S. (1983), A note on the effect of asymmetry in suture closure in mature human skulls, *Amer. J. Phys. Anthrop.,* 60: 431-5.

Chapter seven

Forensic anthropology 2: Positive identification of the individual; cause and manner of death

C. A. Roberts

7.1 Identification of the individual

Determination of age, sex, stature and racial characteristics is the pre-requisite for a positive identification of an individual in any forensic context. However, these factors may provide only a general impression of the person's appearance - there might, for example, be scores of missing females aged 35-40 years with negroid features and a height of 5 feet 6 inches. In nearly every case, even when numerous individuals on the missing persons list can be eliminated according to a set of defining characteristics such as these, more detailed criteria are still needed in order that the skeleton can be identified to a particular named person. There is also a legal requirement that this should be achieved before the death of that individual can be certified, and before processes of inheritance, succession and insurance claims can be set in motion. Identifying a named person is especially important for surviving relatives who, in themselves, need to be certain of the identity so that they can gain 'peace of mind' that their kin has been discovered and that their body can be laid to 'proper' rest. In archaeology, positive identification is not possible unless there are detailed historical records which may describe or illustrate the person's physical appearance. Interpretation of biological anthropological data from archaeological sites creates visions of the age, sex and height of the individual and limited information on their lifestyle, but it is not possible to be more precise.

Many clinical features are now utilized in making a positive named identification of this nature; these include the state of the dentition, radiographic features of the skeleton, pathological lesions which may indicate specific disease processes (active and healed), and general bone anomalies. In more extreme cases, where these methods have proved unsuccessful or require further support, other techniques have been developed, for example the use of biochemical methods (notably DNA) which may detect factors unique to the individual in question, or facial reconstruction which has the potential to reproduce the *appearance* of the individual. The potential is common to both forensic and archaeological contexts, but in the latter there are no data available for comparison and the anthropologist is obliged to resort to general hypothesis and speculation about the appearance, lifestyle and status of the individual.

Items buried with the body, often as clothing or jewellery, may be equally useful in forensic cases. For example, the skeleton of Stephen Jennings, found in West Yorkshire in 1988 (see Chapter 3; also Hunter 1990), included the leather sandals he was wearing at the time of his death, subsequently identified by his mother. In other forensic cases, notable identifying features have included a gold chain (Rudnick, 1984), a casio watch (Costello and Zugibe, 1994), and a pacemaker (Huxley, 1994). Furthermore, if tissue other than bone is associated with the skeleton, identifying features such as vaccination and birth marks, hair colour etc. will also aid in final identification. In some instances, however, extreme mutilation of a body to remove identifying features may be an inhibiting factor (Glaister and Brash, 1937). In the so-called Ruxton case, the ears, eyes, nose, lips, terminal parts of the fingers and skin were removed from the bodies and some of

Plate 7.1 A dentition with a carious lesion

the teeth had been extracted - in this instance the accused had a formal medical training and an awareness of how bodies were identified in a forensic situation. As a general rule, forensic pathologists are most frequently faced with bodies with substantial soft tissue association, while forensic anthropologists are normally called upon to provide the identification of skeletal remains - an area which they are uniquely suited to occupy in view of their accumulated experience in dealing with dry bone.

Dentition

Perhaps the most commonly used feature for identification within forensic contexts is the dentition, based on its comparison, as found, with dental records of dental treatment and anomalies existing for that individual. Teeth survive well for recovery and the forensic odontologist is commonly involved with identification. Sometimes, however, teeth may not be available and the forensic anthropologist has to look for other clues to identification (eg, see Jensen, 1991) but, often, only teeth are available and may be the major clue to identification (plate 7.1). For example, identification of individuals who were victims of the fire at Kings Cross Underground station, London, relied on dental records for comparison with the dentitions of people who died in the fire. In the Lockerbie air disaster odontology was the principle means of identifying over 200 of the 270 victims (Moody and Busuttil 1994). In archaeological situations, however, individuals had limited access to dental care (but see Moller-Christensen, 1969; Bennike, 1985a; Zias, 1987; Molleson and Cox, 1993), and in any

event records were not kept. However, inferences can still be made about individuals in terms of their diet, dental care, disease suffered and, perhaps, cultural behaviour affecting teeth. For example, habits such as pipe smoking, using the teeth for functions such as holding pins in dressmaking or cleaning the teeth with a toothpick may alter the dental structure. Obviously, some of these habits may be general to the population or more specific to the individual. Merbs (1983) observed a unique pattern of loss of the anterior teeth of Inuit (Eskimo) dentitions. This was linked to the practice of using the teeth for stretching and softening animal skins for clothing. Comparing medical records with dental records may also aid in the identification process. For example, discolouration of the teeth may be specific to ingestion of a drug, or the individual may have been exposed to a polluting environment (for example lead) which has caused characteristic changes in the tooth structure. In modern times, with regular dental visits and associated records, dental identification takes on an important role. The macroscopic and radiographic comparison of the dentition of the victim with pre-existing dental records of missing individuals (based on other evidence of identification) is common in the process of identification in forensic cases, and often teeth may be the only surviving evidence. In the case of mass disasters, knowing the names of people, for example travelling on a plane, will narrow down the numbers of dental records necessary for comparison. Whittaker and Macdonald (1989) summarize the information which teeth provide and which can be usefully compared with dental records. Factors such as the arrangement of the teeth in the jaws, abnormalities in morphology or development, malocclusion, unusual wear, trauma, dental disease, extraction, fillings, crowns, inlays, dentures and other prostheses may help identify the individual and also offer age, sex and racial data (see chapter 6 above).

The quality of dental records determines the extent to which accurate comparison can be made. It is possible that a victim had visited a dentist up to 5 years before death and then changed dentists, with the new records being less detailed than the old. Many individuals do not even visit a dentist and this may be determined by their financial situation, for example. However, sometimes the dental report may be the factor which clinches identification. For example, in a case from Illinois, identification of a victim was based on X-rays of tooth restorative work (Rudnick, 1984). However, even if dental records do not exist for the suspected victim, some researchers in the field have developed complex methods which can help in identification. For example, episodes of stress identified on the teeth can be linked to events in the individual's life causing the stress, resulting in the possible identification of the individual (for example, see Skinner and Anderson, 1991, who used brown striae of Retzius in the enamel of the dentition of a native American Indian child's skull and correlated them with anecdotal reports and medical records describing specific episodes of stress). Although the authors emphasized the need for further research in this area, the method has potential for future use in problematic forensic cases.

Radiography

Radiography was first used in a forensic context in 1896 in locating metallic objects in a body in Nelson, Lancashire, England, only one year following the discovery of X-rays by Roentgen (Evans, Knight and Whittaker, 1981). In addition to examining the dentition to give information on dental disease, treatment and also age, this technique can help in other ways to identify a specific individual. Anomalies of the skeleton, pathological lesions and the patterning of the frontal sinuses of the skull, which could all be unique to an individual, contribute to the multidisciplinary approach to identification. In archaeology radiography is a regularly used tool particularly for the investigation of disease and trauma (for example, see Roberts 1988), although it is often the case that burial for long periods may affect the true radiological picture - a factor less applicable in recent forensic cases. Of course, it is a necessary pre-requisite

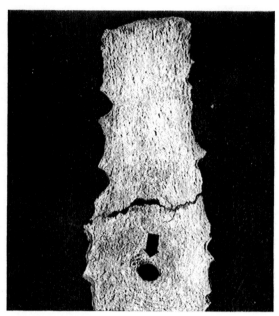

Plate 7.2 Sternal foramen

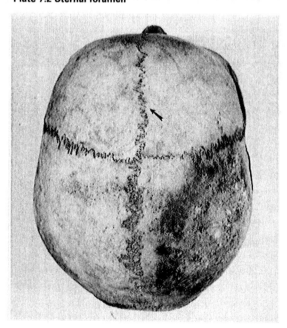

Plate 7.3 Retention of metopic suture

to have access to radiographs of the individual taken in the same views and preferably of relatively contemporary date, with associated medical records, to enable direct comparisons to be made. For example, if the skeleton has bone evidence of rheumatoid arthritis then do the medical records and radiographs support this finding? Furthermore, X-rays may reveal aspects of cause and manner of death, for example the presence and distribution of bullets and shotgun pellets, and the presence of recent antemortem injury to the skeleton. It may, however, be the case that the victim had not recently visited the doctor and their extant medical records may not include all the details of the individual's medical history.

Frontal sinus patterns have been used for many years for the identification of individuals, and many classification systems have been developed (for example, Ubelaker, 1984; Yoshino *et al.*, 1987); sinus patterns are different in every individual and appear as extensions to the nasal cavity in the second year of life in 95% of people (Krogman and Iscan, 1986, p. 466). The structure is permanent but may be altered by disease or old age and can be seen on an X-ray of the face, although X-rays of dry skulls produce a clearer picture than those in the living due to the interposition of soft tissue in the latter. Other features of skull radiographs used for identification include the sella turcica, visible on a lateral X-ray and holding the pituitary gland in life, the mastoid process and the ectocranial suture pattern of the skull (Sekharan, 1985).

The radiography of the structure of the human skeleton, the morphology of the individual bones and variations in these features may also help in identification of an individual. For example, Ubelaker (1990) describes a case of identification of an American Indian skeleton by looking at the unique shape of the lateral border of the scapula, while another individual was identified on the basis of the radiographic appearance of costal cartilage calcification in antemortem and postmortem X-rays (Martel, Wicks and Hendrix, 1977). In biological anthropology non-metric features of the skeleton, believed by some to be inherited, may also aid in specific identification. For example, the presence of the sternal foramen (a hole in the breast bone, plate 7.2), and the retention of the metopic suture (or frontal suture of the skull, plate 7.3) which normally disappears within the first few years of life, may still be visible on the adult radiograph. These traits are identifiable and easily compared with medical X-rays of the unidentified individual. There are numerous other reports of useful identifying features in the skeleton (for example, Klepinger, 1978 on bed sores and bone change; Frayer and Bridgens, 1985 on vertebral anomalies; Owsley and Mann, 1989), including skeletal features which may indicate occupation, activity or stress factors. For example, Wienker and Wood (1988) report on a skeleton found in Florida with unusual osteological features consistent with the actions necessary for fruit picking.

There are, however, problems in interpreting occupationally related changes and these include the lack of extensive studies on modern population activities and their associated skeletal changes. Activities in ancient populations are even more difficult to interpret because biological anthropologists are not always aware of the nature and type of activity associated with these societies even though some writers describe occupations of certain sectors of populations in particular periods eg. Louis (1990). Changes in the shape of bones (for example, Buxton, 1938-9; Townsley, 1946) and development of bony exostoses at sites of tendon and ligament insertions can be assessed, in terms of their distribution, to suggest a possible association between the skeleton, its suspected identity and occupation or activity of that individual (for example, Kennedy, 1983). Biological anthropologists have also attempted to determine occupation from the patterning of osteoarthritis of the joints (for example, Merbs 1983; Molleson, 1989) but there are problems which need attention. For example, Glassman and Bass (1986) indicated in their study of measurements of the long arm bones and the jugular foramen in 182 males and females from the Terry Collection that there was no statistically significant association between asymmetry and handedness. If a person used one arm for one occupation, and no other, it may be possible to link the occupation to the person but the number of different activities a person may do within their lifetime could be many, and the changes to the skeletal structure may be so varied and non-specific that identifying them is impossible. The nature of occupations of specific individuals from archaeological cemeteries is not known; at least in a forensic setting occupations of the suspected victim will probably be known and it may then be possible to infer the relationship of skeletal changes to that occupation. In a forensic setting identification of occupation would be useful for identification and in an archaeological context it would be interesting to infer occupation in past societies.

Pathological lesions

The presence of pathological lesions identified macroscopically, microscopically or radiographically can also aid the forensic anthropologist in a positive identification (for example, see Maples, 1984). In biological anthropology, the study of pathological lesions in individuals from archaeological sites (palaeopathology) provides information on the history of disease through long periods of time, with the data being interpreted

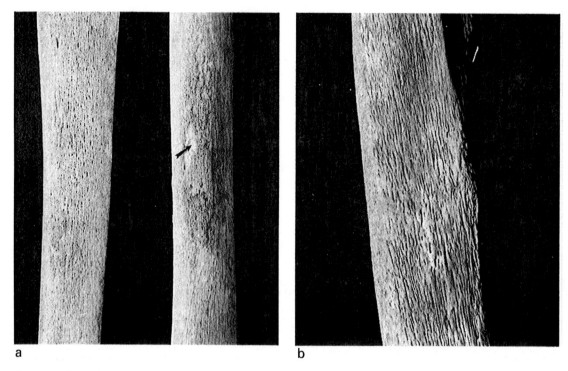

a
b

Plate 7.4 Active and remodelled bone: (a) porous, disorganized woven new bone formation; (b) older, remodelled lamellar bone

within the context of the archaeological site from which the skeletal remains were excavated. The changes in health patterns with changes in economy (for example, Cohen and Armelagos, 1984), or the differences between mortality rates in urban and rural societies, are just two of the many questions which can be tackled with the study of palaeopathology. Biological anthropologists are limited in their assessment of palaeopathology and these limitations are as follows:

1. **Soft tissue disease** - evidence is usually absent unless the whole body is being studied; some diseases only affect the soft tissues
2. **Fragmentary skeletons** - these cannot be assessed for their pathological distribution pattern and specific disease diagnosis
3. **Subadult skeletons** - there is little evidence for pathological change in subadult skeletons probably because of mortality from acute disease (see below)
4. **Acute disease** - this usually kills the person before bone change can occur unless the person's immune system can overcome the pathogen
5. **Fragile pathological bones** - these can degenerate in the ground and not be excavated
6. **Appearance of disease** - this may have changed through time

7. **Absent diseases** - some diseases in the past may not be present today and some diseases today may not be recorded in past populations

The study of disease in archaeology is multidisciplinary (documentation, art, ethnography etc.) but the only *direct* evidence is from skeletal remains. In this respect two of the main reasons for its study are the examination of pathological processes without the intervention of modern therapy, and the observation of disease through long periods of time. The forensic anthropologist, usually dealing with the dry bone skeleton, is limited in contributing to the assessment of disease; only diseases which affect bone will be potentially detectable, assuming that the individual did not die from the affliction when there would be no evidence of bony reaction. The forensic anthropologist will also be aware of the potential differences in manifestation of disease in bone between ancient and modern populations when the latter's disease may be affected by chemotherapy.

Bone is a dynamic tissue and its cells react to foreign invasion by forming bone (osteoblasts) and destroying bone (osteoclasts). An imbalance between the two presents abnormality in the bone. A more detailed discussion on structure and bone chemistry is

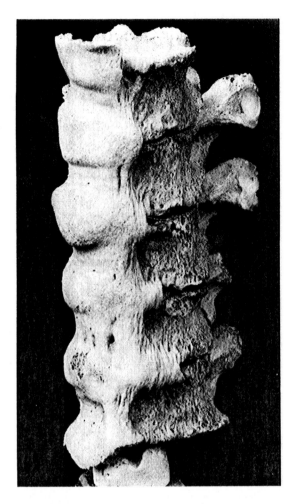

Plate 7.5 Part of spine showing 'flowing' new bone indicative of diffuse idiopathic skeletal hyperostosis

they died in the acute stages of the disease or from a disease only affecting the soft tissues? The forensic anthropologist should also be aware of the problems in distinguishing whether a lesion is antemortem, perimortem or the result of burial in the ground and the action of fauna and flora on the bone surface (Wells, 1967).

In a forensic context the study of pathological lesions of bone by comparing antemortem medical records and radiographs with postmortem observations and radiographs helps to make a positive identification. A recent case study illustrates this point; Varga and Takacs (1991) identified a victim by a congenital abnormality of the hip which was compared with a radiograph from a registry of persons with congenital dislocation of the hip. Evidence for trauma in the form of unhealed fractures may give information on cause and manner of death whilst it may be possible to match healed traumatic lesions to medical or radiographic records. For example, Evans, Knight and Whittaker (1981) reported on a body, washed up on the shores of the Bristol Channel, England, which was identified by the frontal sinus pattern and a healed lesion on the frontal bone, the latter the result of a road traffic accident seven years before. A mixture of both healed and unhealed traumatic lesions may indicate, for example, a young individual's suffering, as in 'battered child syndrome' where multiple trauma at metaphyses and epiphyses (areas of the long bones) in varying states of healing may be identified. This may suggest a series of traumatic episodes over several months or years; knowledge of the rate of healing of the various bones of the body may produce an interpretation of the sequence of the individual's injuries.

There are many categories of disease which could potentially be recognized in skeletal remains (for example congenital, infectious, metabolic, endocrine, joint and neoplastic disease); some are rarer than others but the availability of medical records or radiographs are seen as pre-requisite to the use of pathological lesions for identifying an individual. Pathological lesions may, in addition, help in elucidating the race, geographic origin, sex, age and even occupation of the individual, especially if the remains are fragmentary or if features are not unambiguous. Some diseases only occur in populations in certain parts of the world. For example, thalassaemia and sickle cell anaemia are most commonly seen today in Mediterranean and African countries and thalassaemia is not seen in North and Central Europe, whilst diseases transmitted from animal

contained in chapter 8 (appendix). When disease affects the skeleton woven or fibre bone is produced initially; this is immature and disorganized in structure. If the person died at this stage the bone change would indicate that the disease had been active at the time of death. However, with time the initial bone is remodelled and replaced with more mature, smoother, organized lamellar bone (plate 7.4). The presence of these types of bone can therefore help assess, in general terms, the stage the bone disease had reached when the person died, although determining the duration of the disease is extremely difficult. If, however, the individual suffered from a disease which only affects the soft tissues of the body, evidence on the skeleton would be absent. This is the case assumed for subadults from archaeological sites where little evidence for disease is encountered on the skeleton and dentition. Perhaps to human (zoonoses) may suggest occupational factors.

Some diseases affect specific age and sex categories more often than others. Ankylosing spondylitis, an inflammatory disease producing progressive fusion of the spine commencing in the sacroiliac joints and also affecting the peripheral joints, is seen today in a 9:1 ratio of males to females, manifesting itself in young adulthood. Diffuse idiopathic skeletal hyperostosis (plate 7.5) also involves fusion of the spine but has a different appearance to ankylosing spondylitis. It also includes the production of new bone at sites of tendon insertions widespread throughout the body. It is a disease which affects males in older age categories. Osteoporosis is a disease with a multifactorial aetiology but most commonly affecting older individuals, especially postmenopausal females and it is diagnosed as a loss of bone quantity predisposing to fractures. Older females are most at risk from this disease due to post-menopausal changes in circulating hormones leading to an imbalance between osteoblast and osteoclast action. The value of forensic anthropology in recording pathological lesions in individuals is undoubtable in forensic contexts as any disease which affects bone is potentially recognizable. However, it has to be assumed that the comparative medical records are up-to- date; it is also possible that a victim may have developed a disease which had not yet appeared in the medical records.

Biochemical methods

Positive identification may also be aided by biochemical methods such as blood typing from bone samples and DNA identification (fuller implications of DNA are explored in chapter 9). Iscan (1988) comments on both techniques and suggests that the prospects for establishing a blood group for an individual by analysing a bone sample are unpromising. The analysis of blood groups for modern populations is relatively straightforward and involves using a blood sample from the individual. In archaeological contexts the sample may be from a body with associated soft tissue or a skeletonized individual, and in these cases some work has been undertaken on blood analysis of ancient human remains (for example, Candela, 1937; Connolly, 1969; Lengyel, 1984; Gruspier, 1985; Smith and Wilson, 1990); Gruspier (1985) provides a good summary of the method's history for ancient material. In mummified bodies the techniques for blood grouping are well-known but not universally accepted; blood grouping of bone is also a problem with non-specific absorption,

contamination and possible technical error quoted as major specific difficulties (Heglar, 1972, p. 362). If blood grouping of bone which has been buried in the ground is possible, then genetic information may be extracted which could lead to a positive identification. Of note is an interesting study by Maat (1991) who found actual blood cells surviving in bone samples from skeletons dating to 330-150 years BC in the Persian Gulf. Some of these cells were identified as sickle cells which correlated with bone changes consistent with sickle cell anaemia. Clearly, this find has relevance for genetics as sickle cell anaemia is congenital and primarily occurs in Mediterranean countries today. This type of discovery may also aid in suggesting the ethnic origin of a victim.

With respect to DNA extraction, this method can also potentially provide positive identifications assuming that antemortem records of the DNA of the victim or his/her relatives are available for comparison. The method, however, is contentious although an increasing number of papers are appearing in the forensic literature (for example, Holland, et al., 1993). Again, it is easier to extract DNA from soft tissue than it is from bone and it is straightforward to analyse the DNA from a living (or even recently dead) person. In archaeological human remains it becomes more difficult after the body has been buried for a long period of time. Contamination of the remains (whether skeletonized or mummified) with DNA from extrinsic sources such as plants, animals and humans in the grave is a serious problem which is being addressed by many researchers (for example, Brown and Brown, 1992). How can one be sure that the DNA extracted from the bone belonged to that person and not to its excavator? The other main problem is that human DNA in archaeological material is very fragmented, although with the development of the polymerase chain reaction technique for amplifying trace amounts of DNA into amounts which can be quantified, the technique has developed greatly. The potential information which DNA might offer archaeology is extensive, notably the study of those disease processes which do not affect bone and population genetics (for example, Richards et al., 1993). In forensic science, the successful extraction of DNA from soft tissue or bone and its analysis is determined by the body's treatment and eventual resting place once dead, but there has, nevertheless, been some promising work on DNA of bone from forensic cases (for example, Hagelberg, Gray and Jeffries, 1991; Holland et al, 1993). Further work is essential if this method of identification is to be used and accepted routinely in forensic anthropology and in forensic science generally (Thompson and Ford, 1991).

Facial reconstruction

The final area for consideration in the identification of an individual is the reconstruction of the appearance of the person. The reader is referred to Caldwell (1986) and Iscan and Helmer (1993) for a summary of methods used and their usefulness. As Krogman and Iscan state (1986, p. 413), the skull is 'the bony core of the fleshy head and face in life' and methods are directed to relating the face to the underlying bone by one of three methods: comparing the skull to a portrait of the deceased; comparing the skull with a photograph of the presumed deceased; and restoring the head and facial features from the skull in three dimensions. This last method is the most popular but depends on the availability of appropriate data on facial soft tissue thicknesses and consideration of the effect of variables such as age, sex, race, weight and build on thickness. Although cost is not as much of an issue in forensic cases, photographic superimposition (see Glaister and Brash, 1937) is a cheaper method but depends on the correct orientation of the photograph and skull. Recent work using this method has been aided by modern technology (for example, Ubelaker, Brubniak and O'Donnell, 1992). Least accurate of the methods is that of comparing the skull to a portrait by contour cranial drawings based on metrical analysis and then fitting the contours on to a known portrait. Although all the methods currently used have their problems they can be useful in the final identification of a person. It is, however, likely that if the skull survives then there will probably be identifying features such as the dentition which will help to identify the person without the need to use more expensive time-consuming techniques. In archaeology the use of facial reconstruction has been limited, mainly due to cost, but has been used to reconstruct faces either from skulls of known individuals or to gain a picture of, say, a typical individual from a specific period of time (Neave, 1986; Neave and Quinn, 1986); most often this is for a museum display.

7.2 Cause and manner of death

It is not the aim of this section to cover in depth all the potential areas of investigation into cause and manner of death, rather, it is to highlight the most common areas of enquiry which a forensic anthropologist may be called upon to provide information and expertise.

Apart from the positive identification of a body, whether skeletonized or complete, a determination of both the cause and manner of death is desirable. In the United Kingdom and the United States this is undertaken by the forensic pathologist or medical examiner respectively who, with the vast array of techniques at their disposal, are able to examine various parts of the body - the 'post-mortem'. The forensic anthropologist can aid in the determination of cause and manner of death by providing information on injuries apparent on the skeleton.

In a forensic setting it is the violent, sudden or suspicious deaths which are in the domain of these investigators. Forensic pathology is the branch of medicine that applies the principles and knowledge of the medical sciences to a legal context (Mimaio and Dimaio, 1989).

Cause of death can be defined as any disease or injury that produces physiological derangement in the body. The mechanism which leads to the individual's death causes the physical derangement. The manner of death is how the death occurred; was it from natural causes with no suspicious circumstances (for example a heart attack or malignant disease), or due to homicide, suicide or an accident (Mimaio and Dimaio, 1989)? For example, the cause of death might be a head injury causing fatal brain damage due to an assailant hitting the victim with a hammer, the hammer being the mechanism behind the injury and death (manner of death).

In biological anthropology, determining the cause of death of an individual from an archaeological cemetery is usually impossible since most actual causes of death are only recorded in the soft tissues. There are, however, exceptions in archaeological contexts, for example, the now famous body dated to the Iron Age discovered in Cheshire, England and named Lindow Man, quite clearly showed evidence for his death in the form of a ligature around the neck (Stead, Bourke and Brothwell, 1986), a feature commonly found in many of the 'bog burials' of this period (plate 7.6). Without the soft tissue evidence and survival of the ligature, a skeletonized body may not have revealed its fate. Another possible scenario is evidence of an unhealed injury, especially to the cranium (for example, Manchester and Elmhirst, 1980; King 1992) or a projectile embedded in the skeleton (for example, Bennike, 1985b, pp. 210-211). Of course, it can only be surmised that these injuries actually caused or contributed to the death of the individual; the person in question may have died, for example, from haemorrhage from an additional soft tissue injury severing a major blood vessel. However, the forensic anthropologist is in a position to provide very

Plate 7.6 Ligature around the neck of Lindow man. By courtesy of the British Museum

detailed records of injuries to bone and is often able to distinguish unhealed antemortem injuries from postmortem damage. Detailed knowledge of osteology may also help to clarify the extent and distribution of bone and soft tissue damage resulting from a wound inflicted on the victim (see Mann, 1993). In this respect the forensic anthropologist is invaluable for the interpreta-

tion of skeletonized remains in forensic contexts when all the soft tissue has disappeared, but is more likely to be able to help in determining the manner rather than the cause of death.

Trauma to the head

The cause and manner of death in suspiciously

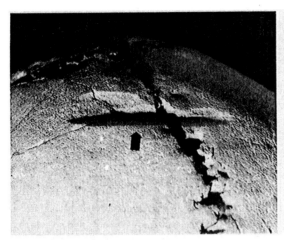

Plate 7.7 Unhealed blade wound

Plate 7.8 Depressed fracture

deceased victims will, in most cases, be traumatic in nature and usually consist of, for forensic anthropological purposes, fractures caused by physical violence. In archaeological contexts injuries to bone are one of the commonest abnormalities found in cemetery populations following dental disease and arthritis. Likewise, trauma in the form of head and neck injuries provides most of the work in forensic anthropology or pathology; Knight suggests three reasons for this (1991, p. 156):

1. The head is commonly the target of choice
2. A victim, in falling to the ground, often receives a blow to the head
3. The brain and skull are vulnerable areas

By examining the skull and assessing the skull fractures present it is possible in many cases to determine the type and direction of impact and the weapon used, not forgetting that the results of injuries to the head may not be revealed immediately. It is the accompanying brain damage which usually leads to the person's death. Nearly all people suffering head injuries have some evidence of increased intracranial pressure and many have an intracranial haematoma (collection of blood inside the skull).

Most fractures of the skull are caused by blunt trauma and these fractures often occur in the weaker areas of the cranial structure, for example the base of the skull where many foramina (or holes) lie, and quite commonly at a distance from the impact. There are many different types of skull fractures which may be caused by direct or indirect injury. The types of fractures which can potentially be seen in both archaeological and forensic settings are:

1. Linear - straight or curved lines radiating out from a depressed fracture or arising at a distance from the impact; also included in this group are Fissure or Radiating fractures (Polson, Gee and Knight, 1985) which are linear fractures radiating from a stellate/comminuted fracture (see below).
2. Depressed - when the bone is depressed below its adjacent surface; included here are Pond fractures which are shallow depressed fractures where a fissure circumscribes the affected area giving a circular form (Merbs, 1989), and the Stellate fracture which is a depressed fracture with radiating fractures.
3. Comminuted - these fractures are described as such when there are more than two fragments which compose the fracture; if they are depressed fractures they may be called a Mosaic/Spider's Web fracture (Knight, 1991).
4. Expressed - when the fragments are displaced out of the normal calvarium curvature (Leestma and Kirkpatrick, 1988).
5. Diastatic - separation of one or more sutures of the skull especially in the crania of children (Leestma and Kirkpatrick, 1988).
6. Gutter - when, for example, a gunshot grazes the bone of the skull and leaves a furrow in the outer table.

(King, 1992)

Linear and depressed fractures can result from blows to the head by blunt or sharp instruments; when the weapon has cut into the bone (plate 7.7), a penetrating injury may be the result. Depressed fractures (plate 7.8) usually occur when the bone fails at or around the point of impact and a linear fracture occurs when the bone rebounds after a blow. At the point of impact the skull flattens to conform with the shape of the surface against which it impacts. A fracture will also occur at the point of outbending. As the inbent area attempts to return to its normal configuration, the fracture line extends from this point to the area of impact and in the opposite direction (Gordon, Shapiro and Berson, 1988).

The resulting fracture is dependent on the area injured, velocity of the object causing the injury, its size and shape, energy expended and time taken to inflict the injury (Gurdjian, Webster and Lissner, 1950) plus physical characteristics of the skull, hair, scalp and elasticity of the skull (Gordon, Shapiro and Berson, 1988). Skull fractures and brain damage are usually caused by acceleration and deceleration injuries - when the head is struck by or strikes an object, or when there is a sudden movement of the head following injury (*ibid.*). Many 'stresscoat' experiments on skulls (where a strain sensitive lacquer is applied to the inside and outside of the skull) have revealed the pattern of fracture following certain directed blows (Gurdjian, Webster and Lissner, 1950). For example, a blow to the mid part of the back of the skull leads to a fracture in the base of the skull. The area at the point of impact bends inwards whilst the neighbouring parts bend outwards. 'Chance' characteristics of the skull such as a large diploic space (between the two tables of the skull), abnormal venous channels and the age of the person may influence the production of the fracture line (*ibid.*).

In most cases brain tissue is not preserved for the forensic anthropologist to examine. It is, however, important to note that brain damage can occur directly underneath an injury to the skull (with an injury to a fixed head) or at a distance away from the original impact, or contrecoup injury, (with an injury to a moving head). The movement of the brain over a sharp fracture line and corresponding increased cranial pressure can also lead to brain damage. It is usually the effects of a head injury on the skull's contents which cause the problems and not the injury to the skull itself. Obviously any head injury which may have led to the person's death will not have any evidence of healing. In archaeological contexts healing of bone lesions, including fractures, is usually recognized by rounding off or remodelling of the edges of the break, with evi-

dence of new bone formation. However, distinguishing unhealed antemortem or perimortem (around death) injuries from postmortem damage is often difficult and requires experience and skill with the application of more sophisticated techniques such as scanning electron microscopy of wound edges to see evidence of remodelling (see Wenham, 1987 for an example in archaeology). The forensic anthropologist should be aware that, for example, trepanation holes (deliberate surgical intervention), thinning of the parietal bones of the skull and secondary cancer lesions could be antemortem features which could imitate head injury. Likewise, erosion, holes produced by animals in the grave or during excavation by humans, and soil pressure, could be postmortem effects producing what may appear to be a skull fracture.

In a forensic context this is also very difficult to interpret and relies on experience; if soft tissue is associated with the bone lesion it is more likely that antemortem and postmortem damage will be distinguished. This is heavily dependent on the period of time the body has lain undiscovered. As bone dries out, the structure becomes harder and more brittle and therefore its character changes. The presence of greenstick fractures and concentric, radiating and stellate fractures in skulls all indicate that the fracture occurred when the bone was fresh (Maples, 1986).

Neck Injuries

Perhaps the next most common area of the body to suffer violence in a forensic setting is that of the neck and, as with the skull, much as been written. In the neck, the structures which may suffer damage and fracture are the hyoid bone and the calcified thyroid and cricoid cartilages, although argument still continues about the actual frequency of hyoid and neck cartilage fractures (see Paparo and Siegel, 1984). Manual and ligature strangulation, suffocation, a direct blow to the neck and hanging can all contribute to injuries to the neck structures. According to Ubelaker (1992), fractures of the hyoid bone are rare and thyroid cartilage fractures are more common (plate 7.9). The cartilages of the neck need to be calcified to be susceptible to fracture so they are more commonly seen in older people. In archaeological settings, the hyoid bone and cartilages of the neck are (sadly) rarely retrieved on excavation (probably because archaeologists are unaware that they exist) and are therefore not available for examination. In a forensic setting the neck is often examined but there are problems in interpretation of fractures of these

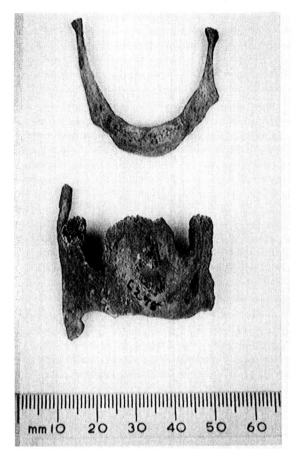

Plate 7.9 Hyoid bone and ossified thyroid cartilage

structures if they have occurred antemortem and just prior to death. It is difficult to distinguish them from postmortem breaks, but presence of haemorrhage at the site is often helpful. Hanging can also affect the cervical vertebrae in the form of fractures especially the odontoid process of the second cervical vertebra, the so-called Hangman's Fracture (James and Nasmyth-Jones, 1992). Obviously, the interpretation of this type of injury can be used to suggest cause and manner of death, and in archaeological contexts the survival of these structures may give more information on cause of death which is otherwise difficult to identify.

Trauma to other parts of the body
The rest of the postcranial skeleton is also subject to trauma which may help in both determining the cause and manner of death - unhealed fractures to the ribs, scapulae, sternum, and bones of the arm and hand give clues to manner of death. Fractures to the ribs, scapulae and sternum may suggest direct blows to the body and fractures to the upper limb may indicate a person's

attempt to prevent injury by protecting him or herself ('defence wounds'). A fracture to the clavicle and distal part of the radius is often produced when a person falls on the outstretched hand; in a forensic situation this may indicate a person's attempt to escape the attacker and a fall whilst doing so. Many fractures in other parts of the body indicate falls and these may also be used to interpret the events surrounding the death of the person. In any case, fractures to any part of the body may indicate violence resulting in the death of the person.

Certain fractures may give clues to the events surrounding the death of the individual. For example, a parry fracture to the forearm is accepted as an indication of a person trying to prevent a blow to the head by protecting that area of the body with the arm (see Vyhnanek, Stloukal and Kolar, 1965; plate 7.10). If an unhealed antemortem parry fracture is located on a body this will help considerably in the forensic investigation as this probably indicates defence. In addition, a fracture to the base of the metacarpals (knuckles) of the hand is often sustained in boxing incidents (Crawford-Adams, 1983), and in a forensic context, may illustrate a fight against an attacker.

Multiple antemortem healed and unhealed fractures in children and babies could be clues to child abuse. In addition, the periosteum or membrane covering the bones of the skeleton, being loosely attached, can separate from the bone as a consequence of trauma. Evidence for new bone formation and inflammation of the periosteum on X-ray, as a result of this process, particularly on the long bones, indicates that trauma may have played a part in the child's life. With the addition of fractures, healed and unhealed, a case of child abuse may be implicated. Rib fractures are especially common in this type of incident and were found by the forensic pathologist on the rib cage of Stephen Jennings, the murdered child found in 1988 in Britain. Multiple and unusual fractures at different stages of healing in individuals four years of age or less should signal possible child abuse. A child over four years may have the ability to escape this extensive type of trauma (Resnick and Niwayama, 1988). It must, however, be recalled that many disease processes can produce the same types of bone change; for example, infantile cortical hyperostosis is a disease which precipitates new bone formation especially on the long bones; this type of change could be confused with the new bone formation in child abuse cases. Patterning and character of the abnormalities is the key to interpretation.

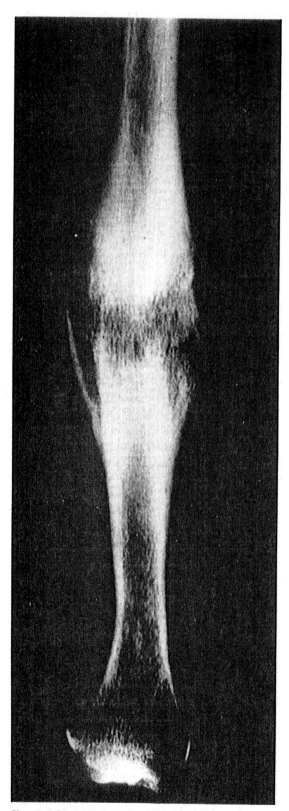

Plate 7.10 Parry fracture radiograph of the ulna

Weapons and injuries

By using simple and more complex methods of analysis it is also possible, by looking at the impressions of tool or implement marks, to suggest the weapon used to cause the injury. In forensic settings this is extremely important; forensic scientists specifically work on identification of tool impressions (for example, see Andahl, 1978; Bonte, 1975) and have catalogues of tools available for purchase by potential assailants for reference; they are therefore aware of the range of tools and 'weapons' available. Experts in this specialist field also maintain that characteristic wear patternings, for example on the blades of kitchen knives or axes, may leave equally characteristic impressions on the bone. Axes, clubs, spears, daggers, arrows and swords all produce different appearances on the bone. For example, blunt instruments often produce larger areas of damage while weapons such as swords produce narrow wounds. Wenham (1987), with scanning electron microscopy, was able to suggest the type of weapon used in the production of blade wounds to skulls from an Anglo-Saxon cemetery. Furthermore, and more recently (Stevens and Wakely, 1993), work using the same method revealed the existence of marks on a skull suggesting that mollusc shell was used as an implement to create a trepanation (surgical hole in a skull). Using this type of approach, matching a particular wound to a weapon, the potential to link the weapon to the assailant presents itself.

Injuries due to bullets or shotgun pellets are more common in a modern setting than an archaeological context; in England they may be investigated by forensic scientists from a specialist laboratory in Huntington. However, recently, the excavation of the nave of Glasgow Cathedral, Scotland (King, pers. comm.) revealed the skull of a young adult male dating from the nineteenth century with both fatal skull wounds and associated lead shot (plate 7.11). The forensic anthropologist may be called upon to examine evidence for gunshot wounds in bone and perhaps suggest, for example, the direction and velocity of the shot into the skull by examining bevelling of the edges of the wound (for example, see Smith, Berryman and Larhen, 1987). Firearm injury to the rest of the body usually creates comminuted fractures (consisting of many pieces of bone). Radiography is very helpful in this type of case since fragments of bullets or pellets may not be visible macroscopically. The type of weapon used may be determined by examining the bullet as the barrel of a gun marks it uniquely (Evans, Knight and

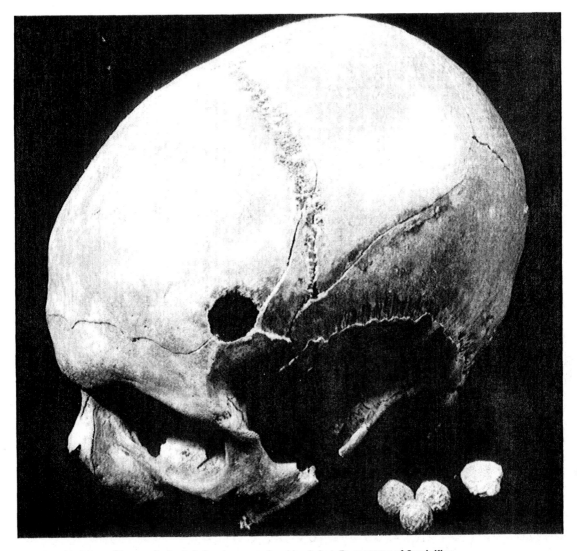

Plate 7.11 Skull from Glasgow Cathedral showing wound and lead shot. By courtesy of Sarah King.

Whittaker, 1981). The spread of the pellets in the body may also help, in the case of a shotgun, to reconstruct the course of the shot and its direction (Mann and Owsley, 1992). In addition, the presence of metallic fragments at the bullet hole site could help to identify whether the hole is actually antemortem and unhealed, and thereby seen to have contributed to the death, rather than postmortem damage from a rodent or other external agent.

7.3 Conclusion

The aim of this chapter was to consider how the forensic anthropologist can use the data generated from the skeletal remains to suggest a positive identification.

The establishment of the identity of a victim of crime relies on the comparison of features of the body with existing records of the person. In most United Kingdom forensic cases at least, the remains usually consist of fleshed bodies where positive identification is easier. Forensic anthropologists are better placed to establish the identity of skeletonized remains because their specialized expertise permits them to point out a skeleton's deviation from normal appearance and the presence of pathological lesions. Some of the methods used, for example radiography and pathological identification, are more familiar than others such as DNA analysis and facial reconstruction, neither of which are used very often in archaeological contexts because of lack of expertise and finance. The assessment of cause and manner of death is difficult without the soft tissues and a complex set of techniques is available to the forensic pathologist or medical examiner; they are better placed to deal with fleshed bodies. However, in cases where the remains consist of a skeleton, the forensic anthropologist's expertise in this area lies in the ability to recognize detailed features of traumatic lesions, determine how they were caused and assess whether healing has occurred.

References

Andahl, R. O. (1978), The examination of saw marks, *J. Forensic Sci.*, 18: 31-46.

Bennike, P. (1985a), Dental treatment in the stone age, *Bulletin History of Dentistry*, 34: 81-7

Bennike, P. (1985b), *Palaeopathology of Danish skeletons. A Comparative Study of Demography, Disease and Injury*, Copenhagen.

Bonte, W. (1975), Tool marks in bone and cartilage, *J. Forensic Sci.*, 20 (2): 315-25.

Brown, T. A. & Brown, K. A. (1992), Ancient DNA and the archaeologist, *Antiquity*, 66: 10-23.

Buxton, L. H. D. (1938-9), Platymeria and platycnemia, *J. Anatomy*, 73: 31-6.

Caldwell, P. C. (1986), New questions (and some answers) on the facial reproduction techniques, in K. Reichs, (ed), *Forensic Osteology. Advances in the Identification of Human Remains*, Springfield, Illinois: 229-245.

Candela, P. B. (1937), Blood group determination upon Sota and New York skeletal material, *Amer. J. Phys. Anthrop.*, 23: 71-8.

Cohen, M. & Armelagos, G. (eds) (1984), *Paleopathology at the Origins of Agriculture*, London.

Connolly, R. C. (1969), Kinship of Smenkhkare and Tutankhamen affirmed by serological micromethod, *Nature*, 224: 325.

Costello, J. & Zugibe, F. T. (1994), Identification of a homicide victim by a Casio data-bank watch, *J. Forensic Sci.*, 39 (4): 1117-1119.

Crawford-Adams, J. (1983), *Outline of Fractures,* 8th Edition, Edinburgh.

Evans, K., Knight, B. & Whittaker, D. (1981), *Forensic Radiology*, Oxford.

Frayer, D. W. & Bridgens, J. G. (1985), Stab wounds and personal identification from skeletal remains: a case from Kansas, *J. Forensic Sci.*, 30 (1): 232-38.

Glaister, J. & Brash, J. C. (1937), *Medico-legal Aspects of the Ruxton Case*, Edinburgh.

Glassman, D. M. & Bass, W. M. (1986), Bilateral asymmetry of long arm bones and jugular foramen: implications for handedness, *J. Forensic Sci.*, 31 (2): 589-95.

Gordon, I., Shapiro, H. & Berson, S. (1988), *Forensic Medicine: a Guide to Principles*, Edinburgh.

Gruspier, K. (1985), *Paleoserology: History and New Application to the Casal San Vincenzo Skeletal Material*, Unpublished M.A. Thesis, University of Sheffield.

Gurdjian, E. S., Webster, J. E. & Lissner, H. R. (1950), The mechanism of skull fracture, *J. Neurosurgery*, 7: 106-114.

Hagelberg, E., Gray, I. & Jeffries, A. (1991), Identification of the skeletal remains of a murder victim by DNA analysis, *Nature*, 352: 427-9.

Heglar, R. (1972), Paleoserology techniques applied to skeletal identification, *J. Forensic Sci*. 358-63.

Holland, M. M., Fisher, D. L., Mitchell, L. G., Rodriquez, W. C., Canik, J. J., Merril, C. R. & Weedn, V. W. (1993), Mitochondrial DNA sequence analysis of human skeletal remains: identification of remains from the Vietnam War, *J. Forensic Sci.*, 38 (3): 542-53.

Hunter, W. (1990), Digging for victory, *Police Review*, 23: 2306-2307.

Huxley, A. K. (1994), Analysis of ceramic substrate in cremations, *J. Forensic Sci.*, 39 (1): 287-8.

Iscan, M. Y. (1988), Rise of forensic anthropology, *Yearbook Phys. Anthrop.*, 31: 203-230.

Iscan, M. Y. & Helmer, R. P. (1993), *Forensic Analysis of the Skull*. New York.

James, R. & Nasmyth-Jones, R. (1992), The occurrence of cervical fractures in victims of judicial hanging, *Forensic Sci. Int.*, 54:81-91.

Jensen, S. (1991), Identification of human remains lacking skull and teeth - a case report with methodological considerations, *Amer. J. Forensic Med and Path.*, 12 (2): 93-97.

Kennedy, K. A. R. (1983), Morphological variations in ulnar supinator crests and fossae as identifying markers of occupational stress, *J. Forensic Sci.*, 28: 871-76.

King, S. (1992), *Violence and Death During the Fall of the Roman Empire. Interpretations of a Late 4th Century/Early 5th Century Charnel House Deposit from Arras, France.* Unpublished MSc Dissertation, University of Bradford.

Klepinger, L. L. (1978), The effect of bedsores on bone and its forensic implications, *J. Forensic Sci.*, 23: 754-57.

Knight, B. (1991), *Forensic Pathology*, London.

Krogman, W. M. & Iscan W. Y. (1986), *The Human Skeleton in Forensic Medicine*, Springfield, Illinois.

Leestma, J. E. & Kirkpatrick, J. B. (1988). *Forensic Neuropathology*, New York.

Lengyel, I. (1984), ABO blood typing of human skeletal remains in Hungary, *Amer. J. Phys. Anthrop.*, 63: 283-90.

Louis, D. S. (1990), Ramazzini and occupational diseases, *J. Hand Surgery*, 15: 663-4.

Maat, G. J. R. (1991), Ultrastructure of normal and pathological fossilised red blood cells compared with pseudopathological biological structures, *Int. J. Osteoarchaeology*, 1: 209-214.

Manchester, K. & Elmhirst, O. E. C. (1980), Forensic aspects of an Anglo-Saxon injury, *Ossa*, 7: 179-88.

Mann, R. W. (1993), A method for siding and sequencing human ribs, *J. Forensic Sci.*, 38(1): 151-5.

Mann, R. W. and Owsley, D. (1992), Human osteology: key to the sequence of events in a postmortem shooting, *J. Forensic Sci*, 37 (5): 1386-139

Maples, W. R. (1984), The identifying pathology, in T. Rathbun & J. E. Buikstra, (eds), *Human Identification. Case Studies in Forensic Anthropology*, Springfield, Illinois: 363-70.

Maples, W. R. (1986), Trauma analysis by the forensic anthropologist, in K. Reichs, (ed), *Forensic Osteology. Advances in the Identification of Human Remains,* Springfield, Illinois: 218-228

Martel, W., Wicks, J. D. & Hendrix, R. C. (1977), The accuracy of radiographic identification of humans using skeletal landmarks: a contribution to forensic pathology, *Radiology*, 124: 681-84.

Merbs, C. (1983), *Patterns of Activity Induced Pathology in an Inuit Population*, National Museums of Canada. Archaeological Survey of Canada Paper No. 119, Ottawa.

Merbs, C. (1989), Trauma, in M. Y. Iscan & K. A. R. Kennedy, (eds), *Reconstruction of Life from the Skeleton*, New York: 161-189.

Mimaio, D. & Dimaio, V. (1989), *Forensic Pathology*, New York..

Moller-Christensen, V. (1969), *A Rosary Bead used as Tooth Filling Material in a Human Mandibular Canine Tooth. A Unique Case from the Danish Middle Ages*, Proceedings of the 21st International Congress of the History of Medicine, Siena.

Molleson, T. (1989), Seed preparation in the Mesolithic: the osteological evidence, *Antiquity*, 63: 356-362

Molleson, T. & Cox, M. (1993), *The Spitalfields Project. Volume 2 - The Anthropology. The Middling Sort,* Council for British Archaeology Research Report 86. Council for British Archaeology, York.

Moody, G. H. & Busuttil, A. (1994), Identification in the Lockerbie air disaster, *Amer. J. Forensic Medicine and Pathology*, 15 (1): 63-69.

Neave, R. A. H. (1986), The reconstruction of skulls for facial reconstruction using radiographic techniques, in A. R. David, (ed), *Science in Egyptology*, Manchester: 329-333.

Neave, R. A. H. & Quinn, R. (1986), Reconstruction of the skull and soft tissues of the head and face of Lindow Man, in I. M. Stead, J. B. Bourke & D. Brothwell, (eds), *Lindow Man. The Body in the Bog*, London: 42-44.

Owsley, D. W. & Mann, R. W. (1989), Positive identification

based on a radiographic examination of the leg and foot, *J. Amer. Podiatric Association*, 79 (10): 511-13.

Paparo, G. P. & Siegel, H. (1984), Neck markings and fractures in suicidal hangings, *Forensic Sci. Int.*, 24: 27-35.

Polson, C. J., Gee, D. J. & Knight, B. (1985), *Essentials of Forensic Medicine*, Oxford.

Resnick, D. & Niwayama, G. (1988), *Diagnosis of Bone and Joint Disorders*, 2nd Edition, London.

Richards, M., Smalley, K., Sykes, B. & Hedges, R. (1993), Archaeology and genetics. Analysing DNA from skeletal remains, *World Arch.*, 25 (1): 18-28.

Roberts, C. A. (1988), Trauma and treatment in British antiquity: a radiographic study, in E. A. Slater & J. O. Tate, (eds), *Science and Archaeology Glasgow 1987*, British Archaeological Reports British Series 196, Oxford: 339-59.

Rudnick, S. A. (1984), The identification of a murder victim using a comparison of the postmortem and antemortem dental records, *J. Forensic Sci.*, 29 (1): 349-54.

Sekharan, P. (1985), Identification of a skull from its suture pattern, *Forensic Sci. Int.*, 27: 205-14.

Skinner, M. & Anderson, G. S. (1991), Individualisation and enamel histology: a case report in forensic anthropology, *J. Forensic Sci.*, 36 (3): 939-48.

Smith, O'B. C., Berryman, H. E. & Larhen, C. H. (1987), Cranial fracture patterns and estimate of direction from low velocity gunshot wounds, *J. Forensic Sci.*, 32 (5): 1416-21.

Smith, P. & Wilson, M. (1990), Detection of haemoglobin in human skeletal remains by ELISA, *J. Arch. Sci.*, 17: 255-68.

Stead, I. M., Bourke, J. B. & Brothwell, D. (1986), *Lindow Man. The Body in the Bog*, London.

Stevens, G. C. & Wakely, J. (1993), Diagnostic criteria for identification of seashell as a trephination instrument, *Int. J. Osteoarch.*, 3: 167-176.

Thompson, W. C. & Ford, S. (1991), Forensic DNA technology, in M. A. Farley, & J. J. Harrington, (eds), *Forensic DNA Technology*, Michigan: 93-152.

Townsley, W. (1946), Platymeria, *J. Path. Bact.*, 58: 85-8.

Ubelaker, D. H. (1984), Positive identification from the radiographic comparison of frontal sinus patterns, in T. Rathbun & J. E. Buikstra, (eds) *Human Identification. Case Studies in Forensic Anthropology*, Springfield, Illinois: 399-411.

Ubelaker, D. H. (1990), Positive identification of American Indian skeletal remains from radiographic comparison, *J. Forensic Sci.*, 35 (2): 466-72.

Ubelaker, D. (1992), Hyoid fracture and strangulation, *J. Forensic Sci.*, 37 (5): 1216-1222.

Ubelaker, D. H., Brubniak, E. & O'Donnell, G. (1992), Computer assisted photographic superimposition, *J. Forensic Sci.*, 37 (3): 750-62.

Varga, M. & Takacs, P. (1991), Radiographic personal identification with characteristic features in the hip-joint, *Amer. J. Forensic Med. and Path.*, 12 (4): 328-331.

Vyhnanek, L., Stloukal, M. & Kolar, J. (1965), Transverse isolated fractures of the ulnae in the ancient Slavonic skeletons, *Rivista di Antropologia*, 52: 185-188.

Wells, C. (1967), Pseudopathology, in D. Brothwell & A.T. Sandison, (eds) *Diseases in Antiquity*, Springfield, Illinois: 5-19.

Wenham, S. (1987), *Anatomical and Microscopical Interpretations of Ancient Weapon Injuries*, Unpublished thesis submitted to the University of Leicester for the degree of BSc Medical Sciences.

Whittaker, D. & Macdonald, D. (1989), *A Colour Atlas of Forensic Dentistry*, London.

Wienker, C. W. & Wood, J. E. (1988) Osteological individuality indicative of migrant citrus laboring, *J. Forensic Sci.*, 33 (2): 562-7.

Yoshino, M, Miyasaka, S., Sato, H. & Seta, S. (1987), Classification system of frontal sinus patterns by radiography. Its application to identification of unknown skeletal remains, *Forensic Sci. Int.*, 34: 289-99.

Zias, J. (1987), Operative dentistry in the 2nd century BC. *J. American Dental Assoc.* 114: 665-6.

Fulton, B. A., Meloan, C. E. & Finnegan, M. (1986), Reassembling scattered and mixed human bones by trace element ratios, *J. Forensic Sci.*, 31: 1455-62.

Giles, J. J. (1987), The analysis of waxes and greases using high resolution gas chromatography, *J. Forensic Sci. Soc.*, 27 (4): 231-39.

Hagelberg, E., Sykes, B. & Hedges, R. E. M. (1989), Ancient bone DNA amplified, *Nature*, 342: 485.

Hagelberg, E., Gray, I. C. & Jeffreys, A. J. (1991), Identification of the skeletal remains of a murder victim by DNA analysis, *Nature*, 352: 427-429.

Hagelberg, E., Bell, L. S., Allen, T., Boyde, A., Jones, S. J. & Clegg, J. B. (1991), Analysis of ancient bone DNA: techniques and applications, in G. Eglinton & G.B. Curry (eds) *Molecules Through Time: Fossil Molecules and Biochemical Systematics*, London: 399-407.

Haigh, T. & Flaherty, T.A. (1992), Blood grouping, in A. R. David & E. Tapp (eds) *The Mummy's Tale: The Scientific and Medical Investigation of Natsef-Amun, Priest in the Temple at Karnak*, London: 154-161.

Hedges, R. E. M. & Sykes, B. C. (1992), Biomolecular archaeology: past, present and future, in A.M. Pollard (ed) *New Developments in Archaeological Science, A Joint Symposium of the Royal Society and the British Academy*, February 1991, Proceedings of the British Academy 77, Oxford: 267-283.

Heron, C., Evershed, R. P. & Goad, L. J. (1991), Effects of migration of soil lipids on organic residues associated with buried potsherds, *J. Arch. Sci.*, 18: 641-59.

Heron, C. and Evershed, R. P. (1993), The analysis of organic residues and the study of pottery function, in M. B. Schiffer (ed) *Archaeological Method and Theory V*, Arizona: 247-286.

Hocart, C. H., Fankhauser, B. & Buckle, D. W. (1993), Chemical archaeology of kava, a potent brew, *Rapid Communications in Mass Spectrometry*, 7: 219-24.

Hodder, I. (1992), *Theory and Practice in Archaeology*, London.

Hodder, I. (1993), Changing configurations: The relationship between theory and practice, in J.R. Hunter & I. Ralston (eds) *Archaeological Resource Management in the UK: An Introduction*, Stroud: 11-18.

Hunter, J. R. (1994). Forensic archaeology in Britain, *Antiquity*, 68, pp. 758-769.

Hurst, J., Martin, R., Tarka, S. & Hall, G. (1989), Authentication of cocoa in Maya vessels using high performance liquid chromatographic techniques, *J. Chromatography*, 466: 279-89.

Hyland, D. C., Tersak, J. M., Adovasio, J. M. & Siegel, M. I. (1990), Identification of the species of origin of residual blood on lithic material, *Amer. Antiquity*, 55 (1): 104-12.

Iscan, M. Y. (1988), Rise of forensic anthropology, *Yearbook of Phys. Anthrop.*, 31: 203-230.

Katsunama, R. & Katsunama, S. (1929), On the bone marrow cells of man and animal in the Stone age of Japan, *Proc. Imperial Academy of Japan*, 5: 388-89.

Keiller, A., Piggott, S. & Wallis, F. (1941), First report of the sub-committee of the south-western group of museums and art galleries on the petrological identification of stone axes, *Proc. Prehist. Soc.*, 7: 50-72.

Kind, S. S. (1987), *The Scientific Investigation of Crime*, Harrogate.

Kobilinsky, L. (1992), Recovery and stability of DNA of forensic significance, *Forensic Sci. Review*, 4: 67-87.

Kooyman, B, Newman, M. E. & Ceri, H. (1992), Verifying the reliability of blood residue analysis on archaeological tools, *J. Arch. Sci.*, 19: 265-69.

Kubo, S. (1989), Changes in the specificity of blood groups induced by enzymes from soil fungi, *J. Forensic Sci.*, 34 (1): 96-104.

Levine, B. (1993), Forensic toxicology, *Analytical Chem.*, 65 (5): 272A-276A.

Locard, E. (1928), Dust and its analysis: An aid to criminal investigation, *Police J.*, 1: 177-92.

Lowenstein, J. M. & Scheuenstuhl, G. (1991), Immunological methods in molecular palaeontology, in G. Eglinton & G. B. Curry, (eds), *Molecules through Time: Fossil Molecules and Biological Systematics*, London: 375-380.

Loy, T. H. (1983), Prehistoric blood residues: detection on tool surfaces and identification of species of origin, *Science*, 220: 1269-71.

Lucas, A. (1926), *Ancient Egyptian Materials and Industries*, London.

Lynch, B. D. & Lynch, T. F. (1968), The beginnings of a scientific approach to prehistoric archaeology in 17th and 18th century Britain, *Southwestern J. Anthrop.*, 24: 33-65.

McKerrell, H., Mejdahl, V., Francois, H & Portal, G. (1974), Thermoluminescence and Glozel, *Antiquity*, 48: 265-272.

Martin, A. (1991), *The Application of Archaeological Methods and Techniques to the Location, Recovery and Analysis of Buried Human Remains from Forensic Contexts*, Unpublished MA dissertation, University of Bradford.

Morse, D., Duncan, J. & Stoutamire, J. (eds), (1983), *Handbook of Forensic Archaeology and Anthropology*, Tallahassee, Florida.

Neff, H. (ed). (1992), *Chemical Characterization of Ceramic Pastes in Archaeology*, Monographs in World Archaeology No. 7, Wisconsin.

Newton, R. G. & Renfrew, A. C. (1970), British faience beads reconsidered, *Antiquity*, 44: 199-206.

Pääbo, S. (1985), Preservation of DNA in ancient Egyptian mummies, *J. Arch. Sci.*, 12: 411-17.

Price, T. D., (ed), (1989), *The Chemistry of Prehistoric Human Bone*, Cambridge.

Renfrew, C. (1973), *Before Civilisation: The Radiocarbon Revolution and Prehistoric Europe*, London.

Renfrew, C. (1975), Glozel and the Two Cultures, *Antiquity*, 49: 219-222.

Renfrew, C. (1992), Archaeology, genetics and linguistic diversity, *Man*, 27: 445-478.

Renfrew, C., & Aspin all, A. (1990), *Aegean obsidian and Franchthi Cave*, in Perles, C., *(ed) Les Industries lithiques tailleés (Argolide, Grèce)*, Vol2: 257-259.

Renfrew,C., Dixon, J.E. & Cann, J.R. (1966), Obsidian and early cultural contact in the Near East, *Proc. Prehist. Soc.*, 32: 30-72.

Renfrew, C., Dixon, J. E. & Cann, J. R. (1968), Further analysis of Near Eastern Obsidians, *Proc. Prehist. Soc.*, 34: 319-31.

Rowe, W. F. (1986), The ABO grouping of human remains: A review, in S. Barry, D. R. Houghton, G. C. Llewellyn & C. E. O'Rear (eds), *Biodeterioration VI, Proceedings of the International Biodeterioration Symposium 1984*, Washington D.C: 134-142.

Ryland, S. G. (1986), Sheet or container? Forensic glass comparisons with an emphasis on source classification, *J. Forensic Sci.*, 31 (4): 1314-29.

Saferstein, R. (ed), (1982), *Forensic Science Handbook*, New Jersey.

Sandford, M. K. (ed), (1993). *Investigations of Ancient Human Tissue: Chemical Analyses in Anthropology*, Philadelphia.

Sandford, M. K. & Kissling, G. E. (1993), Chemical analyses of human hair: anthropological applications, in M. K. Sandford, (ed) *Investigations of Ancient Human Tissue: Chemical Analyses in Anthropology*, Philadelphia: 131-166.

Sensabaugh, G. F. (1986), Forensic science research: Who does it and where is it going? in G. Davies, (ed) *Forensic Science*, (second edition), Washington, D.C: 129-140.

Smith, P. R. & Wilson, M. T. (1990), Detection of haemoglobin in human skeletal remains by ELISA, *J. Arch. Sci.*, 17 (3): 255-68.

Smith, P. R. & Wilson, M. T. (1992), Blood residues on ancient tool surfaces: A cautionary note, *J. Arch. Sci.*, 19 (3): 237-41.

Stead, I. M., Bourke, J. B. & Brothwell, D. (eds), (1986), *Lindow Man: The Body in the Bog*, London.

Stone, J. F. S. & Thomas, L. C. (1956), The use and distribution of faience in the ancient East and prehistoric Europe, *Proc. Prehist. Soc.*, 22: 37-84.

Tebbett, I. R. (1991), Chromatographic analysis of inks for forensic science applications, *Forensic Sci. Review*, 3 (2): 71-82.

Thomas, J. (1991), Science versus anti-science? *Archaeological Review from Cambridge*, 10 (1): 27-36.

Thomas, K. D. (1993), Molecular biology and archaeology: a prospectus for interdisciplinary research, *World Arch.*, 25 (1): 1-17.

Thorpe, E. (1912), *A Dictionary of Applied Chemistry*, London (revised and enlarged edition).

Tite, M. S. (1991), Archaeological science - past achievements and future prospects, *Archaeometry*, 33 (2): 139-51.

Trigger, B. G. (1988), Archaeology's relations with the physical and biological sciences: a historical review, in R. Farquhar, R. G. V. Hancock & L. Pavlish (eds), *Proceedings of the 26th International Archaeometry Symposium*, Toronto: 1-9.

Trigger, B. G. (1989), *A History of Archaeological Thought*, Cambridge.

U.S.National Research Council (1992), *DNA Technology in Forensic Science*, Committee on DNA Technology in Forensic Science, Washington, D.C.

van Zelst, L. (1991), Archaeometry: the perspective of an administratrator, in R. L. Bishop & F. W. Lange, (eds), *The Ceramic Legacy of Anna O. Shepard*, Colorado: 345-357.

Vayson de Pradenne, V. (1930), The Glozel forgeries, *Antiquity*, 4: 201-222.

von Stokar, W. (1938), Prehistoric organic remains, *Antiquity*, 12: 82-86.

Warren, S. E. (1975), A second 'Affaire Glozel'?, *Antiquity*, 49: 222-223.

Williams, J. (1991), *The Modern Sherlock Holmes, An Introduction to Forensic Science Today*, London.

Wilson, C. (1989), *Written in Blood, A History of Forensic Detection,* Wellingborough.

Yoffee, N. & Sherratt, A. (1993). Introduction: The sources of archaeological theory. In N. Yoffee & A. Sherratt (eds), *Archaeological Theory: Who Sets the Agenda?* Cambridge: 1-9.

Zias, J., Stark, H., Seligman, J., Levy, R., Werker, E., Breuer, A. & Mechoulam, R. (1993), Early medical use of cannabis, *Nature*, 363: 215.

Index